Theatres of War

Theatres of War

Contemporary Perspectives

Edited by Lauri Scheyer

methuen | drama

LONDON • NEW YORK • OXFORD • NEW DELHI • SYDNEY

METHUEN DRAMA
Bloomsbury Publishing Plc
50 Bedford Square, London, WC1B 3DP, UK
1385 Broadway, New York, NY 10018, USA
29 Earlsfort Terrace, Dublin 2, Ireland

BLOOMSBURY, METHUEN DRAMA and the Methuen Drama logo
are trademarks of Bloomsbury Publishing Plc

First published in Great Britain 2022
This paperback edition published 2023

Copyright © Lauri Scheyer and contributors, 2022

Lauri Scheyer and contributors have asserted their right under the Copyright,
Designs and Patents Act, 1988, to be identified as authors of this work.

For legal purposes the Acknowledgments on p. viii constitute an
extension of this copyright page.

Cover design by Ben Anslow
Cover image: Banksy Basquiat, Barbican Centre, London,
September 2017 (© Robert Alexander / Getty Images)

All rights reserved. No part of this publication may be reproduced or
transmitted in any form or by any means, electronic or mechanical,
including photocopying, recording, or any information storage or retrieval system,
without prior permission in writing from the publishers.

Bloomsbury Publishing Plc does not have any control over, or responsibility for,
any third-party websites referred to or in this book. All internet addresses given
in this book were correct at the time of going to press. The author and publisher
regret any inconvenience caused if addresses have changed or sites have
ceased to exist, but can accept no responsibility for any such changes.

A catalogue record for this book is available from the British Library.

A catalog record for this book is available from the Library of Congress.

ISBN: HB: 978-1-3501-3292-4
PB: 978-1-3502-6483-0
ePDF: 978-1-3501-3294-8
eBook: 978-1-3501-3295-5

Typeset by Integra Software Services Pvt. Ltd.

To find out more about our authors and books visit www.bloomsbury.com
and sign up for our newsletters.

Contents

Acknowledgments — viii

Introduction: Theatres of War: Contemporary Perspectives — 1
Lauri Scheyer

Section One   British, Irish, and American Perspectives on Theatres of War

1. "Carry on to the Place of Pain": Embodiment and Aversion in Sean O'Casey's *The Silver Tassie* — 9
Robert Brazeau

2. "I Do Want to Take a Man's Part in this Show": The Early War Diary as Rehearsal Stage for the Creation and Navigation of the Newly Militarized Masculine Self — 16
Nancy Martin

3. Mothers and Lovers Mourning Fallen Soldiers: Tracing the Shift from Victorian to Interwar Period Mourning in Noël Coward's *Post-Mortem* — 24
Anna Rindfleisch

4. The Romans at War: Shakespeare's *Julius Caesar* and *Antony and Cleopatra* on the Nazi Stage — 31
Alessandra Bassey

5. *Eros* and Terror in Ernest Hemingway's *The Fifth Column*—A Play on the Spanish Civil War — 38
Jon Woodson

6. The Early African American Theatre of Joshua McCarter Simpson during the Civil War — 46
Lauri Scheyer

7. Performing Trauma: Narratives of Rupture in Caryl Churchill's *Seven Jewish Children* — 54
Mamata Sengupta

8. Two Truths and a Lie: Theatrical Form, Plays about Terrorism, and the Search for Understanding — 61
Lindsey Mantoan

Section Two Global Perspectives on Theatres of War

1. Unremaking the War: Theatrical Historiography in Alfian Sa'at's *Tiger of Malaya* — 71
   Kevin Riordan
2. Ferenc Molnár's *The White Cloud* and the First World War — 79
   Márta Pellérdi
3. Presenting *Picasso Presents*: Exploring the Process of Crafting and Staging Historical Docudrama — 86
   Annika C. Speer and Begoña Echeverria
4. War, Tyranny, and Political Sacrifice in Luis Vélez de Guevara's *Más pesar el rey que la sangre y blasón de los Guzmanes* — 94
   Alani Hicks-Bartlett
5. Women and War: Seeing Trauma with Theatre — 102
   Oana Popescu-Sandu
6. Wartime Gender Advocacy and Revival of Theatre in Afghanistan — 110
   Bahar Jalali

Section Three Perspectives on *Black Watch*

1. Unities, Communities, and Disunities in Gregory Burke's *Black Watch* — 121
   Kate McLoughlin
2. Better Break It: A Case Study of *Black Watch* — 129
   Christopher Merrill
3. Gallant Forty Twa: The National Theatre of Scotland's *Black Watch* as Exemplary and Unintentional Political Theatre — 135
   Shawn Renee Lent
4. *Black Watch:* Revising Scotland's Militarized Identity — 143
   Lynn Ramert
5. Bringing War Home: Staging the Stories of Soldiers and Refugees — 150
   Eva Aldea

Section Four Perspectives on *The Great Game: Afghanistan*

1. "My Country Has Been Imagined Enough": *The Great Game*, Neo-Imperialism, and Gender — 159
   Emer O'Toole and Daniel O'Gorman
2. The Geography of Identity — 167
   Reza Aslan
3. The Legacy of an Empire — 169
   Farid Younos

4	Imagining the Great Game *Christopher Merrill*	177
5	*The Great Game* as Diplomacy: From London to the Pentagon *Nicholas J. Cull*	180
6	The Freedom of Boredom *Shane Belvin*	189
7	Narrating Peace and Healing in Multinational Theatres of War: From Ancient Greece to Afghanistan to DARPA *Tyler D. Reeb*	193

Contributor Biographies   201

Acknowledgments

My deepest gratitude is expressed to each of the contributors. This book is the result of their expert knowledge, belief in the value of this project, and patient attention to every detail. It has been my privilege and pleasure to collaborate with such collegial and brilliant writers.

Thank you to the British Council for their role in engendering international dialogue and understanding through such major cultural events as *Black Watch* and *The Great Game: Afghanistan*. Programming related to these productions first brought together many of the contributors to this book. My special thanks to Molly Michal, Alison Reid, and Jacqui Bassett, and especially to Sarah Frankland, whose quiet vision has sparked inspiration in countless audiences and collaborators.

Bloomsbury has believed in this book and nurtured its development through every stage. My sincere appreciation to the anonymous reviewer whose transformative advice expanded the book's scope immeasurably. No one could hope for more support, professionalism, and faith than were provided by Senior Publisher Anna Brewer. Editorial Assistant Samuel Nicholls and his predecessor Meredith Benson were encouraging at each step of the process. Thank you to Senior Production Editors Amy Jordan and Ian Buck and Project Manager Suriya Rajasekar for turning our vision into a beautiful book that we hope brings insight and enlightenment.

This book is dedicated to families—the families in all times and places that have been impacted by wars, the families of all contributors to this book, and to my own family whose love and support have never wavered. May they all be remembered and blessed.

Introduction
Theatres of War: Contemporary Perspectives

Lauri Scheyer

When this book was first conceived in 2010, my concern and hope—propelled by naive optimism—were that "theatres of war" might become an atavistic topic and the book's moment of utility would have passed into history. Before that date, amidst countless worldwide battles, conflagrations, and tensions, the concept of war was most likely, at least initially, to be interpreted as having a specific and literal military referent. In the last decade, the world is transformed. We find references to war becoming increasingly indexical and iconographic. The war on the pandemic, the war on systemic racism, and the war on ethnic, social, religious, and sexual discrimination have become normative diction in international news and cultural dialogue. The contemporary period is replete with metaphorical uses of "the war on" phrases, including crime, terror, women, disease, gangs, culture, freedom, ignorance, drugs, poverty, hunger, democracy, prejudice, and fascism. Some usages are more hyperbolic than others, some are tinged with irony, yet they tend to focus on the gravest issues of crisis and devastation that confront humanity and world civilization. This evolution returns us to the literal core meaning: war as political agendas, surreally unimaginable yet horrifically real, transformed into acts of physical violence by human beings on human beings.

Theatre has functioned throughout history as a unique medium to address such key issues as spectatorship and participation, power and disenfranchisement, direct involvement and safe distancing from peril, and the precarious balance of life and death. In various ways, the chapters in this book encompass and reveal the lived experience of war and its impact to the extent that it can be represented and encountered in a performative space. The authors aim to show theatre's efforts to convey the admittedly incommensurate nature of war as a means of illuminating its fundamentally inhumane decimation. The book's scope is sweeping, with twenty-six international and interdisciplinary chapters covering a wide array of topics, periods, nationalities, and theories discussing more than thirty theatrical scripts and productions.

From a decorated combat veteran to a specialist in political jargon, the authors offer a wealth of revealing insights on why playwrights and audiences across time and space turn to theatre to make sense of war. Some examples are drawn from canonical Anglo-American literary figures, including Shakespeare, Noël Coward, Sean O'Casey,

Ernest Hemingway, and Caryl Churchill. Others provide a broadened global scope to enrich the knowledge of readers and suggest exciting new opportunities for teaching, research, and study in the fields of literature, ethnicity, trauma, postcolonialism, theatre, performance, history, communication, political science, diaspora, gender, public policy, transnationalism, globalization, heritage, and culture. This book respectfully acknowledges its place within the burgeoning field of interdisciplinary studies where performance and theatre scholars have made some of the major contributions to the interrelated themes of war, trauma, violence, memory, and history. Recent notable publications include *Watching War on the Twenty-First Century Stage: Spectacles of Conflict* by Claire Finburgh, *Terror and Performance* by Rustom Bharucha, *Performance in a Time of Terror: Critical Mimesis and the Age of Uncertainty* by Jenny Hughes, and *Performance, Space, Utopia: Cities of War, Cities of Exile* by Silvija Jestrovic. Influential critical theorists on these topics must also be mentioned, and these include Judith Butler and Jenny Edkins, among others cited in the chapters.

Historically, theatre has played an essential role in encompassing and preserving significant human experiences. Plays about global issues including terrorism and war have long been—and remain—the urgent focus of playwrights, scholars, critics, and audiences. The last century has displayed increased, and even passionate, interest in the role played by theatre in political events. Ironically, the book's moment of completion is one of shuttered and dark physical theatres, but we also experience the traditional resiliency of theatre in navigating and surmounting times of challenge, a thematic thread in many of the chapters. Audiences who can choose to be "safer at home" discover numerous great performances being shared on the internet. New productions have been created where individuals isolated in their homes are technologically enabled to work together to perform as an ensemble. This moment amplifies what history has proven: theatre and performance, as modes of creating community and empathy, play a special and ineradicable role in human history to overcome obstacles.

Why have so many writers and audiences turned to theatre to try to resolve overwhelming topics of pain and suffering? In this up-to-date and sophisticated yet accessible collection of new writings, diverse and scintillating contributors explain theatre's special ability to generate dialogue and promote healing when dealing with human tragedy. This book is divided into four sections designed to offer exceptional breadth and resonance on international productions from varied chronological periods set in or against a backdrop of war. Using numerous critical approaches, the authors imaginatively reconsider theatre's capacity to mediate war's impacts and experiences. Section One addresses Contemporary Perspectives on British, Irish, and American Theatres of War. Section Two addresses International Perspectives on Theatres of War. The nationally, culturally, ideologically, and chronologically varied perspectives in the first two sections are followed by two sections of closely focused contemporary case studies. Sections Three and Four, respectively, illuminate two twenty-first-century plays that garnered rave reviews and powerful emotional responses from audiences around the world. Section Three presents chapters on *Black Watch* by Gregory Burke, National Theatre of Scotland's formally and historically significant inaugural production, centering on the deployment of the Black Watch regiment to Iraq and aftermath of their readjustment when returning home. The fourth and concluding section focuses on *The Great Game: Afghanistan*, twelve plays by British and American playwrights tracing the 150-year history of foreign involvement in Afghanistan.

All four sections present readers with a chorus of theatrical and critical voices from around the world contemplating the inexpressibility and incommensurability of war. Another continuing thread is to problematize notions of a unitary representational authorship and the possibility of a single artistic or cultural perspective when dealing with the subject of war, especially in its international and intercultural dimensions. Class, gender, and race are global topics of immense contemporary relevance that form additional themes of shared focus. The contributors provide myriad academic and affective perspectives that place these plays, and theatres of war in general, in dynamic and illuminating frameworks. Their shared objective is to offer numerous critical methods to help us understand and appreciate examples of theatres of war in all nations and time periods, and constructively apply these insights to the worlds of today and the future. As teachers, cultural critics, scholars, and politically engaged thinkers, the contributors share a sense of humane responsibility and constructive sociocultural orientation.

Section One contains eight essays about contemporary perspectives on British, Irish, and American theatres of war, ranging from Shakespeare to twenty-first-century productions. Robert Brazeau discusses Sean O'Casey's symbolic use of the war-damaged body in *The Silver Tassie* to reveal society's fundamental ambivalence over the violence of which it is capable and the difficulty of accepting the consequences. Nancy Martin presents First World War diaries as stages for male social scripts to be built and rehearsed in the transformation of young men into soldiers. Anna Rindfleisch also writes about the transition from the Victorian to the modern era by tracing the types and evolutions of women's mourning rituals in Noël Coward's *Post-Mortem*. Alessandra Bassey moves to the Second World War to historically analyze the productions, and speculate on the ideological messages, of two Shakespeare plays in Nazi Germany, *Antony and Cleopatra* and *Julius Caesar*. In a little-known and enigmatic play by Ernest Hemingway, *The Fifth Column*, Jon Woodson reveals Hemingway's use of experimental mythical modes to create a classical allusion between the Spanish Civil War and the Trojan War. Lauri Scheyer discusses the scripts of Joshua McCarter Simpson, who created early African American theatrical forms during the Civil War as abolitionist performances of resistance and communal protest. Caryl Churchill's *Seven Jewish Children* is the subject of Mamata Sengupta, who applies theories of inherited trauma to illustrate the national and generational impact of individual suffering in the Second World War. Lindsey Mantoan interrogates the definitions, understandings, uses, and limitations of the concept of verbatim theatre in three examples: Gillian Slovo's *Another World: Losing Our Children to the Islamic State*, Omar El-Khairy's *Homegrown*, and Robin Soans's *Talking to Terrorists*.

Section Two expands the Anglo-American angle of vision by presenting global perspectives on theatres of war, demonstrating the national, geographical, chronological, and cultural universality of this tragic phenomenon. Kevin Riordan opens with an essay on Alfian Sa'at's *Tiger of Malaya*, a contemporary reconstruction and reaction to the 1943 Japanese film by the same name, which scrutinizes how performance can upset and reopen accepted historical narratives. Márta Pellérdi discusses Hungarian playwright Ferenc Molnár's *The White Cloud* to reveal how fantasy becomes a vehicle to represent the reality of war for families who are pawns and victims of political machinations. The impact of war on family units and tearing asunder of parents and children, with reverberations for future generations, is a theme of several chapters. Annika C. Speer and Begoña Echeverria discuss their partnership in staging *Picasso Presents*, a fictionalized historical play by Echeverria based on Hitler's bombing of Gernika and the tragedy's lasting ramifications for civilians. Alani Hicks-Bartlett raises questions of responsible leadership in nationhood and politics in Luis Vélez de Guevara's *Más pesar el rey que la sangre y blasón de los Guzmanes*, and how character is especially tested during times of war. With other authors in this book, Oana Popescu-Sandu focuses on war's impact on women, using Matei Vișniec's *The Body of a Woman as a Battlefield* set in the Bosnian War to address the lingering effects on wartime victims of sexual and ethnic abuse. Bahar Jalali continues the concern with women by showing the crucial role of theatre and international outreach to restore and preserve women's rights and roles in public space in Afghanistan during the first two decades of the twenty-first century. The chapters in this section illuminate another theme woven throughout this book: how and whether it is possible to recreate a sense of whole and functional identity after experiencing war's traumas, whether one is an active military participant or civilian casualty.

Section Three presents case studies on Burke's *Black Watch*. Kate McLoughlin positions the character of "The Writer" against the cohesive "insider" group of soldiers and questions whether the experience of war can be accurately represented by a reporter outside the shared experience of active participants. Christopher Merrill also focuses on the dimension of reportage in war by addressing the philosophical issues raised by *Black Watch* about how a nation is perceived both internally and externally as represented by its institutions, artists, and individuals. Shawn Renee Lent credits this play's success as political theatre to three elements: the characters' likeability, the production's liveliness, and the function of the ensemble in generating group empathy for the audience. Lynn Ramert analyzes the way *Black Watch* reveals complex correlations in Scottish history and culture between masculine and military identity, national pride and colonial entanglement, and how past lessons can be beneficially applied in the present. Eva Aldea also questions the representational capacity of theatre by comparing the differing rhetorical and physical postures of *Black Watch* and *The Jungle* by Joe Murphy and Joe Robertson as vehicles for audience members to awaken to their own inevitable emotional and physical positions as spectators to the personal impacts of war.

The book's final section contains views on *The Great Game: Afghanistan*, an acclaimed cycle of plays by multiple playwrights commissioned by London's Tricycle Theatre. Emer O'Toole and Daniel O'Gorman credit the diversity of the multiplay format with the capacity to represent issues of gender, neo-imperialism, and women's rights with more depth and nuanced cultural critique than a single-authored script. Reza Aslan elucidates why the centralized model of government and Afghan identity that Western powers tried to enforce in Afghanistan was destined to fail because it is unsuited to this nation's history and culture. Farid Younos offers a historical assessment of a pivotal play in this production, "Durand's Line" by Ron Hutchinson, illuminating the past and present significance of this artificial geographical border. Christopher Merrill claims that theatre's special capacity to present disparate world views makes it an ideal medium to forge empathetic connections and perform cultural diplomacy, exemplified by the communal audience experience of *The Great Game: Afghanistan*. Nicholas J. Cull also analyzes the crucial topic of theatre as diplomacy, explaining that the effectiveness of this production rests on its success in fulfilling four approaches: The Prestige Gift, Cultural Information, Dialogue, and Capacity Building. Shane Belvin brings to bear his experience as a decorated combat veteran in presenting the reality of a soldier's life alternating between adrenaline and boredom in arguing that theatre, despite its limitations, can still effectively represent the emotional weight of war for audiences. Tyler D. Reeb's essay closes this section and the book by emphasizing the importance of narratives in theatre to perform acts of empathy and healing by tracing a lineage for telling stories about war from ancient Greek tragedy to *The Great Game: Afghanistan*.

This book's inspiring and individualistic voices display how vastly differing nations and historical periods have used theatre to convey the encounters and outcomes of war. A wide array of themes, cultures, periods, and theories invites deepened appreciation of the universality of theatre in its ability to present and mediate the experiences of war. The chapters interrogate theatre's capacity to alternately immerse or distance audience members in the reality of the subject while acknowledging that a play can approximate but never fully reproduce war's actuality. The renowned authors convey their contemporary views in chapters that are equally impassioned and rigorous to reach a wide readership and explain how theatre can help us understand and potentially even avoid war. The aim, above all, is to engender productive dialogue on theatrical productions that have raised issues of universal importance in order to generate compassion and connection across barriers of time and space, and hopefully lead to new understandings, positive actions, and healing.

Section One

British, Irish, and American Perspectives on Theatres of War

1

"Carry on to the Place of Pain": Embodiment and Aversion in Sean O'Casey's *The Silver Tassie*

Robert Brazeau

Sean O'Casey's play *The Silver Tassie* offers a thorough critique of the ideology of war, focusing largely on the mass psychological inability of society to reconcile its own investment in war with the effects that war registers on the bodies of dead and surviving soldiers. O'Casey also critiques social discourses around masculinity that forge the pervasive expectation that soldiers should be unscathed by their traumatic experiences in battle, and overcome, on their own and silently, whatever physical and psychological problems they bring back from the war. In his compelling examination of the processes that structure the return of the wounded soldier to the home society, O'Casey focalizes attention on how the mass disavowal of the wounded soldier is part of a larger problem around the meaning of war for any society, even when ideology or propaganda does the work of convincing a nation that the war was, in the first instance, a just one. *The Silver Tassie* turns its critical gaze away from war itself and back onto the audience to ask fundamental questions about how wars are simultaneously acknowledged and disavowed by societies that wage them, and how this dynamic influences the reception of the soldier who returns wounded and scarred by battle.

The Silver Tassie opens in the Dublin apartment of the Heegan family. Harry Heegan is home on a short leave from the war and has been instrumental in winning the coveted Silver Tassie for his home football club. His girlfriend, Jessie, is physical in her affections and hints at marriage between the two upon Heegan's return from the front. Act 2 shifts to the trenches of France and is dominated by dark shadows and foreboding archetypal symbols and imagery, and also asserts, in its mostly incantatory dialogue, the uncanny and monstrous aspects of war. Act 3 shifts back to Dublin and is set in the hospital ward where Heegan is recovering from battle injuries, but where, it is also clear, he will be permanently paralyzed. Jessie now refuses to see her former boyfriend, signaling her intention to leave Heegan for another soldier who returned uninjured from the war. The break between Harry and Jessie is confirmed in Act 4, set in the dance hall of the football club; Jessie makes clear her amorous desires for Heegan's former friend and fellow soldier, Barney. Angry and dismayed about the future, Heegan smashes the cup that he had been instrumental in winning.

The Silver Tassie occupies a central place in O'Casey's biography as the play that severed the relationship between the playwright and the Abbey Theatre, which produced O'Casey's previous work to much acclaim. Critics and biographers have been unstinting in their support for O'Casey against The Abbey's decision not to produce the play in 1928, and most critics now agree that W.B. Yeats's view that the play strayed too far from specifically Irish cultural and historical matters is not credible, since many Irish soldiers enlisted in the British Army to fight in the First World War. What is more likely is that the play served as a reminder, to Yeats and others, of how fraught the issue of Irish service in the British Army during the First World War had been, and O'Casey's play threatened to stir up this divisive controversy. As Irish war historians like John S. Ellis have noted, the emergence of the First World War was politically fraught in Ireland because it exposed deep political and social fissures within the nation, especially around recruitment. *The Silver Tassie* takes up this debate, and while O'Casey would not have identified himself with the nationalist position in Ireland, his play offers something near to a dismantling of the Unionist and constitutionalist view of the war, which the Abbey directorate, especially Yeats and Lady Gregory, supported. As Ellis asserts, "constitutionalists widely believed that the blood of nationalist and unionist soldiers would provide the cement that would seal the national divisions of Ireland" (2001: 20).

Recruitment, in Ireland as elsewhere, relied on exploiting pervasively held social investments in masculinity, especially around perceptions of strength, bravery, aggressivity, and self-sacrifice. There is, in Act 1 of *The Silver Tassie*, a somewhat exaggerated and irrationally giddy celebration of youth, vitality, and aggressivity because these are traits that men, according to O'Casey, learn in peacetime and use in war. For example, shortly after Harry appears on stage hoisting the Silver Tassie, he narrates the moment where he scores the winning goal:

> HARRY. Slipping by the back rushing at me like a mad bull, steadying a moment for a drive, seeing in a flash the goalie's hands sent with a shock to his chest by the force of the shot, his half-stunned motion to clear, and then carrying him, the ball and all with a rush into the centre of the net.
> BARNEY. [enthusiastically] Be-God, I did get a thrill when I seen you puttin' him sittin' on his arse in the middle of the net! (1965: 40–1)

The imagery and diction here is expressly militaristic: the domination of space and attacking strategy implied in the phrase "slipping by the back" gives way to the evasive gesture required when the enemy rushes at you headlong "like a mad bull." A soldier would "[steady] a moment" before shooting and might also see the enemy take the bullet in the chest in a "half-stunned" way. Barney completes the picture: not only has the enemy been shot and stunned, but has also been knocked to the ground, in a virtual or proxy death that points to how sport allows competitors to engage in vicarious life and death scenarios.

Furthermore, in Act 1, Harry is, largely because of his prowess in the realm of sport, also the object of sexual attention from both Jessie and Susie Monican. Jessie's flirtations with Harry are overt, while Susie sublimates her seemingly unrequited desire for Harry through overt religiosity. She chides Barney's attempts to flirt with her, but encourages Harry's flirtation, despite the fact that Harry is informally betrothed to Jessie.

> SUSIE. [*slipping her arm around Harry's neck, and looking defiantly at Barney*]. I don't mind what Harry does; I know he means no harm, not like other people. Harry's different. (1965: 42)

Harry is different because he is revealed, in Act 1, to be something like the apotheosis of heteronormative masculine agency: he is sexually forward, athletic and vital, and also carefree and adventure-seeking. He does not dwell on the consequences of his actions or choices, recede from any challenge, and he boldly embraces the moment for whatever pleasure it gives him.

The overdetermination of agential, even aggressive masculinity in Act 1 is undercut in the surreal battle scene of Act 2, where the men are depicted as static and helpless in the face of the technologies of war. The bleak and archetypal images of sacrificial death describe a world that is so unrecognizable as to be rendered fundamentally incompatible with the world of Act 1. O'Casey's highly expressionist mode in Act 2 is meant to stress the irreconcilability of the world of war and the world of relative peace, and portend the unlikeliness of a return to normalcy for the men who serve. This sense of rupture is communicated in a number of ways in the scene, but most strikingly in mesmeric, almost incantatory passages like the following:

> CORPORAL. Dreams of line, of colour, and of form;
> Dreams of music dead for ever now;
> Dreams in bronze and dreams in stone have gone
> To make thee delicate and strong to kill. (1965: 64–5)

Act 2 is meant to communicate the conditions of battle less through denotation than visceral affect, with the corollary proposition that war is not something the soldier understands, or even necessarily does, but is something that happens to him or her viscerally, deepening, as James Moran observes, its symbolic meaning "through song, rhythmical movements and repetitive chant" (2013: 78). In important ways, this description of war confirms an argument advanced by Elaine Scarry in her landmark work, *The Body in Pain*. War, Scarry says, exposes the body to pain that "remains inarticulate or else the moment it first becomes articulate it silences all else: the moment language bodies forth the reality of pain, it makes all further statements and interpretations seem ludicrous and inappropriate, as hollow as the world content that disappears in the head of the person suffering" (1985: 60). O'Casey centralizes this aspect of pain and injury in Acts 3 and 4, where Heegan is progressively alienated from others and the social world, in contrast to Act 1, where he is literally and figuratively centralized in the world of the play. O'Casey's blocking of Act 1 has Heegan occupy the center of the stage with the other characters gathered around him, intimating he is the center of this social world. Heegan dominates the space of the stage physically, lifting up the women and exuberantly pushing and shoving the men. This will all be starkly contrasted in Acts 3 and 4, where the scene blocking has Heegan in the center of the stage far less, and where he does not physically dominate the space in the same expressive ways that he does in Act 1.

Harry's displacement from the center of society to the margins is confirmed at the beginning of Act 4:

> JESSIE. [*hot, excited, and uneasy, as with a rapid glance back she sees the curtains parted by Harry*]. Here he comes prowling after us again! His watching of us is pulling all the enjoyment out of the night. It makes me shiver to feel him wheeling after us.
> BARNEY. We'll watch for a chance to shake him off, an' if he starts again we'll make him take his tangled body somewhere else. [*As Harry moves forward from the curtained entrance*] Shush, he's comin' after us. (1965: 88)

Harry has become something of a spectral presence, reminding the social world of its recent wartime past. That Jessie is looking backward at Harry suggests that it is the recent past that is chasing after her. In terms that we might borrow from Scarry, Harry embodies a past that continues to haunt a present that seeks to disqualify and disown that past formation. Barney's response to Jessie, that they simply go somewhere else, confirms O'Casey's (and Scarry's) view that it is easier for a society to attempt to evade this kind of self-understanding than face it. Through these three characters, O'Casey allegorizes the ways in which the returning soldier is socially decentered and becomes the site of intense feelings of aversion and avoidance.

The character of Jessie has proven most vexing for even O'Casey's more perceptive critics. Bernard Benstock condemns what he calls "Jessie's treachery in choosing the healthy Barney in preference to the crippled Harry Heegan" (1976: 158) adding that "Jessie is incapable throughout of feeling anything for anyone but herself, and is unable to hide her discomfort in the presence of the cripple who had been her lover" (1976: 158). Heinz Kosok notes that "without reflection, she simply and instinctively admires the strongest and most impressive" (1985: 97) male characters: in Act 1, this is Harry, while in Acts 3 and 4, this is Barney. The problem with both readings, which is endemic to much of the criticism of the play, is that Benstock and Kosok are reading the character of Jessie on the level of psychological and social realism after the play has made a decisive turn toward allegory. Jessie is not acting out human instincts (Kosok) or self-serving choices (Benstock) but is emblematic of the wider social reception that the wounded, returning soldier can expect to receive.

What O'Casey focalizes for the audience through the character of Jessie, then, is the mass disavowal the postwar society performs around the figure of the dead and wounded soldier. As Scarry contends, a society must transform itself into a war society in order to succeed in war, but it will, as a rule, have no interest in continuing to see itself as a murder and maiming society after the war is over. The disavowal of that disturbing, prior sense of self is transacted through the disavowal of the war dead and the returning, injured soldier. As Scarry notes in her reading of the mass psychosis around war and aversion:

> The only thing more overwhelming than that a human community should have a use for death, the extreme "use for" that is signaled by the shift from "it is needed" to "it is required" (and soldiers understand that it is *this use* to which have been summoned, *this* to which they have consented: that they are going either "to die for one's country" or "to kill for one's country") the only thing more overwhelming than that fact that it will have this use for death is that the community will then disown that use and designate those deaths "useless." (1985: 73)

It is not just Jessie and Barney who want Heegan removed from society; they are simply the most overt voices advocating for this. It is all of the characters who believe that Harry should be removed from social space for the collective benefit. For example, the otherwise oblivious figure of Simon notes, in Act 4, "To carry life and colour to where there's nothing but the sick and helpless is right; but to carry the sick and helpless to where there's nothing but life and colour is wrong" (1965: 90). Harry's father, Sylvester Heegan, remarks that "When we got the invitation from the Committay to come, wearin' his decorations, me an' the old woman tried to persuade him that, seein' his condition, it was better to stop at home, an' let me represent him, but [with a gesture] no use!" (1965: 91). Simon and Sylvester might believe that absenting him from society would spare Harry what Ron Ayling, in discussing an earlier O'Casey play, terms "the spiritual anguish" (1980: 30) that his characters frequently embody, but both advocate that Harry be removed from social space so others do not have to face the effects of the war on its injured victims. In fact, late in the play, Susie Monican, who seems genuinely sympathetic toward Harry in Act 3, observes, "Teddy Foran [who has also been injured in the war] and Harry Heegan have gone to live their own way in another world. Neither I nor you can lift them out of it. No longer can they do the things we do" (1965: 105).

The "we" that Susie utters here is meant to include not just the characters on stage, but, importantly for O'Casey, the audience as well. As *The Silver Tassie* concludes, the audience itself becomes increasingly the object of O'Casey's critical attention. This is made evident in a number of subtle and explicit ways in the play, but among the more interesting and important involves a protracted exchange between Simon and Sylvester Heegan around their aversion to the ringing telephone at the dance hall. What quickly emerges is that neither feels sufficiently confident in handling the new technology of the telephone to accept the call:

> SYLVESTER. [*nervously*] I never handled a telephone in my life.
> SIMON. I chanced it once and got so hot and quivery that I couldn't hear a word, and didn't know what I was saying myself. (1965: 91)

Two things are accomplished in this scene. The first is that O'Casey is able to extend the view, central to the play, that we are frightened by things that are unfamiliar to us, that force us to change our abiding perception of the world. The men certainly fare poorly in the task, taking so long to answer the telephone that the caller hangs up. In this respect, they resemble some of the "failed masculine subjects" (2006: 42) that are central, as Cathy Airth reminds us, to O'Casey's earlier plays. But more than this,

this scene is, like all of Act 4, meant to engage with the ethics of spectatorship. Here, O'Casey presents us with a comic scene that invites the audience to laugh at the spectacle of incapacity and uncertainty that plagues both male characters. Significantly, the audience is laughing at two people who cannot perform a behavior that many, even at the time, would have seen as automatic, effortless, and not fraught to the point of panicked insecurity. Immediately following this jocular scene, we are confronted with the depths of Harry's anger over his plight, which, similarly, derives from his inability, in his current state, to perform acts that we might take for granted. Now, though, the members of the audience have to ask themselves what it was that made them laugh at Sylvester and Simon. What is it that we find funny in people who cannot do things that we think are easy? What does it say about society that laughter could resonate through a crowded theatre where nobody would pause long enough to see that they and their fellow audience members were chuckling at scared, helpless people who were finding their new reality overwhelming?

The Silver Tassie offers us a keen example of what Robert Meister, in *After Evil*, terms "social melodrama." It is a highly fraught genre conditioned by subtle operations of spectatorship and distanciation, of judgment, aversion and, perhaps sympathy or empathy. According to Meister,

> Social melodrama is not in the voice of a victim crying out against the oppressor and is not generally addressed to the victims of the suffering portrayed. Instead, it is meant to be read by people who may *want* to feel bad about the conditions described but who would be made highly uncomfortable if the victim were portrayed as blaming them. (2011: 63–4)

Meister contrasts social melodrama with the "literature of social reconstruction, which would exhort the bystander to confront his beneficiary position and ask why the victimary position should be allowed to exist" (2011: 64). In social melodrama, the victim's presence is a challenge because it continuously asks the question of the ways in which society simultaneously benefits from the sacrifice made by the victim while also desiring not to have to acknowledge that sacrifice.

What Meister describes here, then, is a process that has also been examined by Wendy Brown in her landmark work *Regulating Aversion*. Brown is interested in the ways in which Western cultures fail to measure up to their own self-satisfied accounts of their liberalism (2006: 37). While these societies claim to make space for others, they often fall far short of actual recognition and subscribe to political and ethical values located in the somewhat more amorphous zone of the tolerance/aversion dichotomy. As Brown cogently argues:

> Despite its pacific demeanor, tolerance is an internally unharmonious term, blending together goodness, capaciousness, and conciliation with discomfort, judgment, and aversion. Like patience, tolerance is necessitated by something one would prefer did not exist. It involves managing the presence of the undesirable, the tasteless, the faulty—even the revolting, repugnant, or vile. (2006: 25)

The Silver Tassie offers a complex treatment of the fraught dynamics that accompany the return of the wounded soldier to postwar society. While publicly asserting the heroism and sacrifice of this figure, society practices overt and covert strategies of marginalization and aversion as it fails to reconcile the dual sense of itself as a society that spurns murder and yet has had to use it to keep itself together. O'Casey explores the various and numerous dimensions of this process in the play, with characters embodying and condoning society's aversion to the wounded soldier and the tangled, dark history of war that this figure brings into the social spaces of the present. The war lingers with him, in him. Heegan becomes a ghostly, uncanny character operating at the fringes of society. Moreover, he comes to embody that society's essence as a war society. O'Casey turns his critical gaze toward the audience itself, who is confronted with its own complicity in the various strategies of alienation and disavowal that emerge out of its aversion to the wounded and damaged body and mind of the soldier. O'Casey offers no answers to these compelling and difficult questions, nor does he forecast any moment of reconciliation in the play. Rather, he lays bare the knot of issues that surround war, peace, and violence which are borne by the pained and injured body of the soldier.

Works Cited

Airth, C. (2006), "Making the Least of Masculinity: Sean O'Casey's 'Paycock' and 'Plough and the Stars,'" *Canadian Journal of Irish Studies*, Vol. 32, No. 2, pp. 42–7.

Ayling, R. (1980), "Seeds for Future Harvest: Propaganda and Art in O'Casey's Earliest Plays," *Irish University Review*, Vol. 10, pp. 25–40.

Benstock, B. (1976), *Paycocks and Others: Sean O'Casey's World*, Dublin: Gill and MacMillan.

Brown, W. (2006), *Regulating Aversion: Tolerance in the Age of Identity and Empire*, Princeton: Princeton University Press.

Ellis, J. S. (2001), "The Degenerate and the Martyr," *Éire-Ireland*, Vol. 35, Nos. 3–4, pp. 7–33.

Kosok, H. (1985), *O'Casey the Dramatist*, Gerrards Cross: Colin Smyth.

Meister, R. (2011), *After Evil: A Politics of Human Rights*, New York: Columbia University Press.

Moran, J. (2013), *The Theatre of Sean O'Casey*, London: Bloomsbury.

O'Casey, S. (1965), *The Silver Tassie*, in *Three More Plays by Sean O'Casey*, London: MacMillan, pp. 17–114.

Scarry, E. (1985), *The Body in Pain: The Making and Unmaking of the World*, Oxford: Oxford University Press.

2

"I Do Want to Take a Man's Part in this Show":[1]
The Early War Diary as Rehearsal Stage for the Creation and Navigation of the Newly Militarized Masculine Self

Nancy Martin

After completing his training in August 1916, Coningsby Dawson, a budding writer and eldest son to a wealthy and pious family, eagerly awaits his departure for France. While the decimated western front has seen two years of constant battle, this date marks the beginning of Dawson's war; his identity as soldier remains untested. As he awaits orders to cross the Channel from Shorncliffe, he writes an anxious and highly contemplative letter to his family—his father, mother, and younger sister. In it, he draws on multiple public scripts as he attempts to both navigate and secure his newly militarized masculine identity:

My Dearests,

[…] I read Father's letter yesterday. You are very brave—you never thought that you would be the father of a soldier and sailors; […] Confess—aren't you more honestly happy to be our father as we are now than as we were? I know quite well you are, in spite of the loneliness and heartache. We've all been forced into heroism of which we did not think ourselves capable. We've been carried up to the Calvary of the world where it is expedient that a few men should suffer that all generations to come may be better.

[…] For me, I can go forward steadily because of the greatness of the glory. I never thought to have the chance to suffer in my body for other men. The insufficiency of merely setting nobilities down on paper is finished. How unreal I seem to myself! […]. I think the multitude of my changes has blunted my perceptions. […]

Good-bye for the present. Be brave.

Yours, Con (Dawson 1917: 31–3)

While the pride and excitement in this letter is palpable, it would be inadequate to simply read it as an example of one young man's blind "war enthusiasm" or "patriotic fever." This letter is, in fact, an early example of what will be an ongoing, and highly self-conscious, personal navigation of Dawson's role as soldier, a role he here attempts to both create and secure through declaration, performance, and, upon receipt of a letter in return, recognition. The latter he hopes to receive from his father in particular, his primary model for moral manhood—"Confess—aren't you more honestly happy to be our father as we are now than as we were?" The scripts of Dawson's performance of identity are thus multiple and overlapping. The references to "bravery" and "heroism," along with the elevated language of phrases like "Calvary of the world" and "greatness of the glory" are literary in nature, drawn from the selective syllabi of the public schoolroom, and co-opted by propaganda. Other scripts—or narrative threads—are arguably more personal in nature. The son of a minister, and once student of religious doctrine himself, Dawson also cites the war as an opportunity for him to "suffer in [his] body for other men." This is the language of Christian sacrifice, of purge and redemption, a language that offers Dawson the role of Christ figure, willing to sacrifice himself so that others might live better. The letter, in short, offers a venue for the simultaneous creation, navigation, and performance of the newly militarized identity, an identity for which he seeks confirmation and validation from his recipients, or audience. As he writes in a later letter, "Whatever happens, I know you will be glad to remember that at a great crisis I tried to *play the man*" (Dawson 1917: 33). As Dawson seeks connection to his, as yet, untested identity, he thus uses the written page as a kind of rehearsal space, trying out various public scripts as he seeks shape and definition for this new role.

This chapter will examine the early life-writing of a selection of middle-class combatant men written during the First World War, focusing in particular on the letters of Coningsby Dawson as a case study. Drawing on script theory, it will consider how men used the private written page to help create, navigate, bolster, and solidify their new wartime identities—this in a social context of crude dichotomies and extreme shifts regarding conceptions of, and attitudes toward, male behavior. "Let the country be served by free men, and let them deal with the coward or the sluggard who flinches," fiercely wrote Arthur Conan Doyle in 1914 (Doyle 1914: 13). As the war's early months brought rapid change, redefining, and ultimately creating a new hierarchy for acceptable forms of masculinity, men—whether enlisted or not—were left to navigate their identities *as men* in this new context of war. "Life here is very sweet," writes E.W. Hewish in his diary, "but I do want to take a man's part in this show" (Hewish 1914: 13). "Nothing would please me better than to die fighting for my country," writes B.W.S. Seymour Baily in a pleading letter to his father, "[d]o please say I can do this or I shall never respect myself again" (Baily 1914). In this context, life-writing held heightened significance for many men. The blank page provided a safe venue where newly militarized social scripts could be tried out and rehearsed; they were also, in turn, sites for the navigation of early fears, tensions, and anxieties. Drawing together the fields of cognitive psychology, war representation, and life-writing, this chapter will illuminate the ever-changing form and function of these early war "performances of self."

Identity, in its multiple facets and fragments, is here conceptualized as an ongoing social reality, one derived from what cognitive psychologists call the "defining community" (Crossley 2000: 40). It is from "the recognitions and observations by others," argues Eric Leed, that we "create[ ] categories of persona, simplifications, rigidities, masks, and veils which constitute the essence and reality of social being" (Leed 1991: 264). In this poststructuralist conception, behavior, and thus identity, is socially determined. What behavioral psychologists call "social scripts" provide the "blueprints for behaviour and […] guide both our actions and our understandings of events," asserts Joan Atwood (Atwood 1996: 13). They "provide us with a general idea of how we are supposed to behave and what is supposed to happen" (Atwood 1996: xvi). The individual is thus positioned in the role of actor, performing on a social stage. Our successful performance of the society's scripts elicits the recognitions and observations of others; we are, in turn, rewarded for acting in accordance with dominant scripts. We are also, conversely, limited, and, in some cases, harmed by the rigidities and simplifications of these scripts. Scripts relating to masculinity in wartime, for example, promote control, competitiveness, and stoicism, traits which, in practice, could bring bodily harm and which in turn demanded the stifling of other behaviors—the expression of fear and emotion.

Public Scripts and the Performance of the Newly Militarized Masculine Self on the Pages of Diaries and Letters

The most visible and highly valued behavioral script in war belonged to that of the soldier. Representing the highest form of manhood in the war's early months, he was generally represented as moral, stoic, cheerful, self-sacrificing, and, above all, brave. He is a hero of "wonderful coolness and daring" (*The Telegraph* August 1914) and an honorable and fearless protector of the nation's "homes from distress" (Lloyd George 1914). That bravery was a crucial element in his construction had been established by long-standing cultural, social, and educational influences. The public schools, for example, often celebrated the steadfast soldier who fearlessly performed his imperial duties, while popular boys' literature presented its masculine heroes as physically dominant athletes, full of pluck and prowess. Indeed, the public-schooled recruit was undoubtedly well-educated in the language of duty, sacrifice, and bravery. He took for granted the honor and greatness of his country. His school syllabus celebrated past wars and military heroes, while his favorite writers presented danger and combat as sanctified opportunities for displays of courage and valor. In the words of one beloved George Alfred Henty character: "Our duty is clear. God has sent us here to their aid, and whatever be the risk, we must run it" (Henty 1893: 7). Drawing on this highly romanticized language, the war's dominant rhetoric constructed the soldier as the epitome of not only masculinity but male morality and civility. As public discourse increasingly drew on stories of German atrocities inflicted on Belgian women and children, soldiering meant more than defending the nation; it meant defending one's *own* home and family from similar barbarity. Positioned against unrestrained German brutality then, the British soldier was chivalrous and controlled. This script was undoubtedly highly appealing to the public-school man in particular. Indeed, for Charles Carrington, when war was declared, "[T]here was no doubt what we ought to do." To the seventeen-year-old, contemplating his Oxford scholarship exam, the war happily entwined "inclination, actual necessity and the highest principles of conduct" (Carrington 2006: 46, 259).

The Diary and the Private Performance of the Newly Militarized Role

Speaking of the diary, Felicity Nussbaum writes that it "becomes necessary at the point when the subject begins to believe that it cannot be intelligible to itself without written articulation and representation" (Nussbaum 1988: 135). As the war's early months positioned the fighting soldier as the epitome of masculine prowess, the identity of countless men across the country undoubtedly required such new "articulation and representation." This can be seen, in particular, in the stories of enlistment that are recounted on the pages of many diaries and letters, as men draw the initial parameters of their newly militarized role. Men are able to try out and rehearse the various social scripts of the heroic soldier, as they seek to authenticate this new facet of their identity. For some, generally younger, middle- and upper-class men, the day of enlistment is framed by reference to a romanticized past. It is the day they become "players in history," joining the proud procession of knights that came before. For C.W. Beaumont, for example, war enlistment meant "taking part in the old French wars, the days of knighthood and cavalry when lance met lance and sword met sword" (Fletcher 2013: 46). For A.D. Gillespie it was a "great privilege to save the traditions of all the centuries behind us" (Laffin 1973: 12). Writing from South Africa, Julian Grenfell imagined that, "It must be wonderful to be in England now [...] It reinforces one's failing belief in the Old Flag and the Mother Country [...] which gets rather shadowy in peace time, don't you think?" (Mosley 1976: 230). These men, raw from school or new employment, thus turned to constructions of the soldier that were familiar, drawing on martial metaphors and alluding to ancient mythologies in order to rhetorically authenticate the newly militarized masculine identity.

The unpublished diary of one young recruit, W.T. Colyer, captures the experiences of many men in the early months of the war. An ex-public schoolboy from Merchant Taylors, he had rushed from his London office to Duke Street, Euston, where he joined the Artists' Rifles on August 5, 1914. His diary recalls his initial thoughts the morning after war was declared: "Would they invade us, I wondered. By George! [...]. And then the impulse came, sending the blood tingling over all my body: why not join the Army now? A great and glorious suggestion. It might not be too late" (Colyer n.d.: 314–15). The pride and excitement of this passage is palpable. Colyer's use of emotionally-charged language—"a great and glorious suggestion"—highlights his internalization of the period's heroic script.

Indeed "Glory" was a staple of the high tradition, a staple that would be famously mocked by Wilfred Owen later in the war. Conditioned by various public scripts to view war as the greatest "game" he could partake in, it is not surprising that his writing depicts what he describes as a new and revitalized "sense of self" after "the great deed was done" (Colyer n.d.: 315). Colyer's romantic illusions of war here reveal a fundamental assumption held by many—an assumption rooted in the soldier's idealized behavioral script: the war would provide countless opportunities for individual displays of courage and bravery. Indeed, his image is of *active* combat, of exciting battles with clear and swift victories. The heroic knight wields a sword, the cavalry charges the foe. This image of war would of course soon change for Colyer, as he would soon experience the realities of the trenches. But at this moment, viewing the war as a test of manhood, his writing reflects a desire to rhetorically authenticate the newly militarized, masculine identity, an identity he begins to draw the contours of and perform on the pages of his war diary. I will turn now to an examination of the letter and its function as a site of performance of a different kind. Indeed, while both the diary and letter are sites of rehearsal for the newly militarized masculine self, the letter, with its known audience, at times invites the writer to temporarily "step off the stage," when the performance of public scripts is difficult, if not impossible.

The Letter and the Expectations of the Audience

In *Memory, Narrative and the Great War*, David Taylor rightly argues that in primarily emphasizing bravery, strength, and prowess, dominant public scripts had "made it very difficult to tell stories that centered on fear" (Taylor 2013: 58). Indeed, while the words "duty," "honour," and "the right" are near-ubiquitous on the early diary pages of the public-schooled recruit, so too is the absence of fear's words—"afraid," "scared," "doubt," for example, rarely appear. Furthermore, while young men imagine taking part in victorious charges and abstract displays of strength and valor, the same subjective connection is withheld from war's other potential outcomes: death or maiming. This, of course, is not surprising; avoidance and selective omission are vital components in the composition of what Dan McAdams calls our "personal myths" (McAdams 1993: 12). This, however, makes consideration of the silences and subtleties in men's early war writings ever more important; we must read "between the lines" as it were. Indeed, men had subtly committed fears of death to the written page long before they had seen the trenches. Before leaving Southampton, Lionel Sotheby hastily wrote a last will, quickly listing his few valued possessions for the family solicitor (Richer 1997: xx). Lieutenant Colonel Herman enclosed a farewell poem in a letter to his wife as he left for the front "in case of accidents" (Nason 2008: 6). These fears for one's personal safety, as well as for those left behind, are often conveyed subtly in letters. In these moments, it seems that what the writer most desires is the comfort and confirmation of a familiar audience. While the diary is, as Thomas Mallon notes, "a very pliable priest," its "absolution" is only as kind as the anxious writer permits (Mallon 1985: 204). The letter, in contrast, allows the troubled mind to seek a direct response, specifically from those who are most likely to provide comfort, counsel, and consolidation. It offers, in other words, a receptive audience to the wearied performer. Writing on July 23, 1916, Coningsby Dawson composes an additional anxious letter to his family as he prepares to depart for the front:

My Dear Ones,

[…] You are thinking of me this quiet Sunday morning at the ranch, and I of you. And I am wishing—As I wish, I stop and ask myself, "Would I be there if I could have my choice?" And I remember those lines of Emerson's which you quoted:

> "Though love repine and reason chafe,
> There comes a voice without reply,
> 'Twere man's perdition to be safe,
> When for the Truth he ought to die."

I wouldn't turn back if I could, but my heart cries out against "the voice which speaks without reply."

Things are growing deeper with me in all sorts of ways. Family affections stand out so desirably and vivid, like meadows green after rain. And religion means more. […]. I hope I come back again—I very much hope I come back again; there are so many finer things that I could do with the rest of my days—bigger things. But, if by any chance I should cross the seas to stay, you'll know that that also will be right and as big as anything that I could do with life, and something that you'll be able to be just as proud about as if I had lived […]

God bless and keep you.
Con (Dawson 1917: 26)

In this highly self-conscious letter, Dawson's multiple identities are brought into conflict. As son and brother, he seeks reassurance from his family as he confronts the possibility, and fear, of death; "my heart cries out against 'the voice which speaks without reply'"—this, an eloquent poetic rendering of fear, which functions in distancing Dawson from the grim realities of the thing itself. At the same time, as newly minted soldier and protector, he seeks simultaneously to *provide* reassurance. This tension between his desires as son and his perceived duty as soldier is found symbolized in the first paragraph's strategically placed dash: "And I am wishing—As I wish, I stop and ask myself." Herein lies an equally significant function of the letter in the war's early months. While offering a safe place for the subtle confession of fear, its epistolary form also demands performance from the writer. In writing a letter, one is ever conscious of the expectations of the reader; the identity, or self, performed is dependent on the writer's relationship to the addressee. The letter, in short, offers Dawson a safe venue for the navigation of fear, as well as an opportunity to continue to seek a narrative frame for his wartime identity as soldier. For Dawson, the scripts of this frame, which provide meaning and coherence amid rapid change, are three-fold, consisting of family, religion, and nation.

Conclusions

In the war's early months, the diary and letter provided a safe space where public scripts could be tried out and rehearsed. The new recruit could find initial shape and definition for his newly militarized identity as heroic soldier. Serving both mnemonic and performative functions, "stories," argue Alan Stewart and Robert Neimeyer, "consolidat[e] a sense of who we are as the protagonists of our accounts, and scripting the ways we engage in our lives with others" (Stewart and Neimeyer 2001: 8). In wartime, such consolidating "stories of self" are rendered infinitely more significant. Indeed, as one's identity—as a citizen, a patriot, a man—is threatened, the desire for both clarity and control is made markedly more necessary. In the face of death, this desire, for many, is increased exponentially. Indeed, Dawson's desire for control and clarity within his "protagonist role" as soldier is undoubtedly made all the more pressing as he prepares to depart for the front. His rhetorical performance, in other words, must soon be embodied or enacted. The relative safety and freedom offered by the letter's "rehearsal stage" will transition into the real "theatre of war." It is telling, for example, that as he awaits his departure, he writes a total of seven letters, each rhetorically reasserting the scripted contours of his new identity—brave, honorable, stoic, self-sacrificing. The tension and anxiety present "between the lines" in each of these lengthy letters is palpable. No matter how skilled public discourse had become at obscuring many of the war's realities, men were generally well aware of the soldier script's potential end—he could die. This fact made self-declaration and self-performance more frequent and more pressing, and life-writing, through its offer of a sense of solidification and validation, more significant. Contemplating the precipice on which he stands, between imagination and fantasy and *lived* experience, Dawson writes: "Life has become so stern and so scarlet—and so brave. From my window I look out on the English Channel […] Over there beyond the curtain of mist lies France—and everything that awaits me. News has just come that I have to start. Will continue from France. Yours ever lovingly, Con" (Dawson 1917: 36).

Note

1   Captain E.W. Hewish, diary, May 6, 1917, IWM, Documents (02/43/1). The unpublished diaries referenced in this chapter, those of Captain E.W. Hewish, Captain B.W.S. Seymour Baily, and Captain W.T. Colyer, are housed in the Documents and Sound Section of the Imperial War Museum, London. My sincere thanks are given to the IWM for permission to quote from these papers.

Works Cited

Atwood, Joan D. (1996), "Social Construction Theory and Therapy Assumptions," in Joan D. Atwood, ed., *Family Scripts*, New York: Taylor and Francis.
Baily, Captain B. W. S. (1914), Seymour, Letters, IWM, Documents. 12642 (03/16/1).

Carrington, Charles (2006), *Soldier from the Wars Returning*, Barnsley: Pen & Sword.
Colyer, Captain W. Y. (n.d.), Diary/Memoir, IWM, Documents. 7256.
Crossley, Michele L. (2000), *Introducing Narrative Psychology: Self, Trauma, and the Construction of Meaning*, Buckingham: Open University Press.
Dawson, Coningsby (1917), *Khaki Courage: Letters in War-Time*, ed. W. J. Dawson, London: John Lane.
Doyle, Arthur Conan (1914), *To Arms!* London: Hodder and Stoughton.
Fletcher, Anthony (2013), *Life, Death and Growing Up on the Western Front*, New Haven: Yale University Press.
Henty, George Alfred (1893), *Tales from the Works of G. A. Henty*, London: Blackie & Son.
Hewish, Captain E. W. (1914), Diary, Imperial War Museum, Documents (02/43/1).
Laffin, John, ed. (1973), *Letters from the Front, 1914–1918*, London: J.M. Dent & Sons.
Leed, Eric (1991), *The Mind of the Traveler, From Gilgamesh to the Global Tourism*, New York: Basic Books.
Lloyd George, David (1914), "Through Terror to Triumph: An Appeal to the Nation, A Speech Delivered at the Queen's Hall," September, London: Parliamentary Recruiting Committee.
Mallon, Thomas (1985), *A Book of One's Own: People and Their Diaries*, London: Pan Books.
McAdams, Dan P. (1993), *The Stories We Live By: Personal Myths and the Making of the Self*, New York and London: The Guilford Press.
Mosley, Nicholas, ed. (1976), *Julian Grenfell: His Life and the Times of His Death, 1888–1915*, New York: Holt, Rinehart and Winston.
Nason, Anne, ed. (2008), *For Love and Courage: The Letters of Lieutenant Colonel E.W. Hermon from the Western Front 1914–1917,* London: Preface.
Nussbaum, Felicity, ed. (1988), "Toward Conceptualizing Diary," ed. James Olney, *Studies in Autobiography*, New York: Oxford University Press.
Richer, Donald C., ed. (1997), "Introduction," in *Lionel Sotheby's Great War: Diaries and Letters from the Western Front*, Athens: Ohio University Press.
Stewart, Alan E. and Robert A. Neimeyer (2001), "Emplotting the Traumatic Self: Narrative Revision and the Construction of Coherence," *The Humanistic Psychologist*, Vol. 29, pp. 8–39.
Taylor, David (2013), *Memory, Narrative and the Great War: Rifleman Patrick MacGill and the Construction of Wartime Experience*, Liverpool: Liverpool University Press.

3

Mothers and Lovers Mourning Fallen Soldiers: Tracing the Shift from Victorian to Interwar Period Mourning in Noël Coward's *Post-Mortem*

Anna Rindfleisch

The First World War is often positioned as a turning point in history, a moment where incomprehensible trauma rippled across the Western world. The massive number of civilians and men in uniform who died between 1914 and 1918, the brutal nature of industrialized warfare, anonymity of death, and absence of corpses created a universal grief that never before had been felt on such a large scale. In Britain, bereaved women responded to this unprecedented loss by altering Victorian and Edwardian mourning practices to accommodate for the absence of a loved one's postmortem body. Etiquette manuals published between 1900 and 1939 show the impact that absence had on female-conducted funerary rituals, namely the final goodbye. The final goodbye is a ritual where mourners see the body of the deceased and pay their last respects. It is the performative rite of passage in which the living take part to usher the spirits of their loved ones into the unknown land of the dead.

Etiquette manuals are created by women for women; they instruct women on the proper way to carry themselves within their society's culture. When Queen Victoria died in 1904 ushering the UK into the Edwardian Age, Victorian Age mourning practices such as funeral processions, formalized mourning etiquettes, the dawning of creperie, and beliefs in the eternity of the soul did not disappear. Mourning traditions, death rites, and acceptable modes through which one can express grief filter through the boundaries of historical eras. In an etiquette manual published in 1901, there are numerous subsections that deal with "dressing the body" (Randall 1901: 322) so the corpse appears "in that of a peaceful repose" (Randall 1901: 322). A section details the customs of "watching the dead" (Randall 1901: 322), preparing for "funeral services" (Randall 1901: 324), and a distinction for "military funerals" (Randall 1901: 325). It is only after funeral rites are completed that the manual shifts to how one can mourn afterwards. The ability to hold a funeral, take part in watching the dead, and dress the corpse become obsolete when mourning the dead of the First World War. In *Vanity Fair* in 1920, G.K. Chesterton notes a sharp change in funerary customs: "Our fathers were more festive at a funeral than we are at a wedding" (Chesterton 1920: 51). In viewing a row of tombstones created prior to the First World War, he remarks, "They are livelier dead than we are alive" (Chesterton 1920: 51). In an etiquette manual published just four years later, Lillian Watson writes that "a new simplicity has entered burial customs, and one watches the stilted, tradition-bound funeral pageant pass with relief" (Watson 1924: 223). There is no mention of dressing or seeing the corpse laid out. The structure of the funeral does not focus on the individual family but on the community, who takes part in the ritual, as she writes, "the church is a unit of social life" (Watson 1924: 229). A decade later, an etiquette manual by Emily Post says, "The general congregation no longer expects, nor wishes to go to the internment" (Post 1934: 481). By the 1930s, the shift in needing the corpse and having an elaborate funeral is no longer required to conduct a funerary rite. Post continues, "The solemn vigil through long nights by the side of the coffin is no longer essential as a mark of veneration or love for the departed" (Post 1934: 479).

Given the absence of bodies and massive number of deaths, rites involving the internment of an individual soldier's body were nearly impossible to conduct in the interwar period. Instead, as the etiquette manuals show, the bereaved made corporeal the memory of the deceased by staging the corpse's return in performative mediums like theatre, reenactments, dances, spectacles, poetry readings, and sculpting. Women mourning First World War dead built a set of amalgamated mourning practices around the image of a dead frontline soldier. The popularity of war memorials, in-home séances, bedroom shrines, public commemoration ceremonies, and multinational cemeteries imbued landscapes and spaces with spiritual significance. The transference of those settings into the performing arts transformed those performances into a mourning activity. Noël Coward's mourning play *Post-Mortem* stages an example of how the final goodbye altered the Victorian tradition of watching the dead to meet the needs of the universal grief and absent corpses.

Born in 1900, Coward was too young to serve at the start of the war, and when of age in 1918, he was found unfit for service due to an upper respiratory illness. As a civilian, Coward experienced the First World War in his home; his testimony then focused on the experience of waiting for news to come from the front lines. After playing Stanhope, a disillusioned frontline soldier, in a production of Robert Sherriff's 1928 play *The Journey's End,* Coward was inspired to write the tale of what would happen if the ghost of a soldier could return to his family. Written in 1930, *Post-Mortem* was Coward's "snarled out" testimony of the First World War (Hoare 1996: 219). The plot of the play, a one-act staged in eight scenes, is the story of the supernatural return of a dead frontline soldier, John Cavan, to his family and friends. In each scene, Cavan's apparition visits his loved ones on a search to find out if the sacrifices of the war created a better future. His ghost travels in time from 1917 to 1930, moving from the trenches to his mother, lover, father, best friend, comrades, to his mother again, and then back to the trenches where he dies. This chapter focuses on Scenes 2 and 3, where Cavan interacts with his mother, Lady Cavan, and Monica, the woman with whom he was in a relationship at the time of his death. They are contextualized within historical accounts of bereaved women in the 1930s parsing larger societal questions: to what extent can mourning women during the interwar period be understood as living memorials to the soldiers who died during the First World War; and how were British women expected to mourn given their age and relationship to a dead frontline soldier?

When a mourning play stages a landscape of grief, the setting becomes more than a display case containing the actions of the scene. It becomes imbued with an atmosphere of sorrow and the stage becomes a space for mourning, transforming the social unit of the theatrical house into a realm of sacredness. Mourning plays are theatre pieces that stage a part of the mourning process. It is where "the physiologies of mourning" are placed "into a cultural area which includes social interactions with the public sphere as well as an actor's interactions with their audience in the theatre" (Döring 2006: 147). In mourning plays, there are often female lamenters: figures whose outward manifestation of sorrow signals the start to a mourning rite. In *Post-Mortem*, Lady Cavan and Monica do not just refract memories of grief and violence to the audience; they signal the start of a mourning rite. Professional female lamenters are historically called upon to mourn war dead, as Tanja Luckins writes in *Gates of Memory*: "The death of a warrior required a woman to robe herself in specific dress to indicate loss and enact lamentations … A woman robed in black was telling the world that she had suffered loss, and was also representing the loss her family and friends experienced" (Luckins 2004: 56–7). The female mourner conducts the collective lamentation of the dead by performing the memory of the dead.

Lady Cavan appears on stage as somber, stoic, and lethargic. In the stage directions, Lady Cavan is silent with her only movement being to occasionally pause her card game and "look out at the distant lights coming to life along the coast" (Coward 1930: 15). Perpetually embodying the stuck-ness of grief, the death of her son and the absence of his body to bury dislodged Lady Cavan from the chronological flow of time. When Cavan returns, Lady Cavan takes special care not to disrupt the atmosphere of her bedroom, speaking in a whisper as she says, "I daren't speak loudly, or move, you might disappear" (Coward 1930: 15). Lady Cavan's primary concern is Cavan's feelings, information she can only get from him. She asks, "Oh darling! You weren't in very great pain were you, when—" (Coward 1930: 16). While a telegraph would have been posted to Lady Cavan by the British government upon Cavan's death, vague sentences were often repeated: "Died in combat shelling;" "Died on advance, bullet;" "Died in trench, gas attack." She continues, "They said you couldn't have been because it was all over so quickly, but I wasn't sure" (Coward 1930: 16). What the bereaved did not have that Lady Cavan demonstrates were the intimate details: what Cavan was feeling at the time of his death and if he is at peace now. Cavan's responses are the verbal confirmation that only he can give—yes, it had hurt. With Cavan's confirmation, Lady Cavan becomes unstuck as "she suddenly crumbles" (Coward 1930: 16). It is not the physical touch of Cavan that wakes his mother out of her haze but the details of his death. Her grief does not bring about tears, as Lady Cavan says she is incapable of crying: "I tried to [cry] because I thought it would be a relief, it was no use" (Coward 1930: 16). Instead, she describes her grief as "something inside, twisting horribly like it did years ago" (Coward 1930: 16). What she articulates is a rupture between the initial shock response to the war dead and the stagnant state of intrapersonal mourning of the 1930s.

Lady Cavan was seemingly unable to move past the shock of losing her son and into the phase of healing that "twisting" pain. According to Luckins, women linked "the person and the collective: women wore clothing to express loss, led collective lamentations for the dead and, in the long term, were usually the keepers of the family memories" (Luckins 2004: 16). As elders in their communities, mothers of fallen soldiers remained stoic living memorials to their sons; in so doing, they had authority to judge the way others mourned their sons. Indeed, how Monica mourned Cavan is the way Lady Cavan introduces her character in the play. When Cavan asks his mother how Monica responded to the news of his death, she says, "She wrote me a very sweet letter," and waited three years to marry another man (Coward 1930: 20). Cavan replies, "It's nice to think she waited a bit" (Coward 1930: 20). This shows that female identity in the interwar period was partially determined by a woman's expected display of public grief. That expectation was further mediated by a woman's age and relation to the dead soldier. Older widows and mothers were understood to never move on while younger betrotheds were understood to mourn for an allocated time period before marrying. Monica's character in *Post-Mortem* reveals a tension between younger women needing to marry for practical reasons like financial security, social respectability, and repopulation, and being criticized for dishonoring the memory of their fallen lover by moving on too quickly.

Before Monica even appears on stage, she is the girl who waited before marrying to mourn her lost love and the dutiful would-have-been daughter-in-law who wrote a nice letter to her betrothed's mother. She is not an individual whose first love died before she had time to grow up with him. It is this subtle distance between Monica as a collective representation of young female mourners and Monica as an aggrieved individual that creates her stuckness. Whereas Cavan's reappearance to his mother filled a void, John's reappearance to Monica only confuses her. This confusion is manifested in the play as an immaterial barrier between Monica's inability to process her loss or recall her initial experience of trauma. The result is a palpable mental anxiety that leaks into her speech, severing cohesion, as she stutters: "Don't speak … don't go" (Coward 1930: 20). The contrast between these two phrases produces an atmosphere of agonized disarray as Monica strains to remember her grief but cannot seem to grasp it as every moment of contemplation is cut short by external forces. Her butler brings drinks, her friend Kitty and stammering columnist Eggie bring party plans, her husband brings a reminder of societal obligations. With each intrusion, Monica the individual, whom Cavan knew and loved, slides away into the persona of a modern flapper.

Monica's character throughout her scene represents all the youthful women who grew up watching their first loves go off to war only to see them never return. Like the young soldiers who became known as the "lost generation," these young women can be seen as the "lost femmes." The Monica that Cavan knew is as dead as himself, which is why when Monica asks Cavan if he approves of her, Cavan replies, "I haven't seen you yet" (Coward 1930: 20). The girl that Cavan left in 1914 is not the woman Monica is in 1930. She has acquired a new language that Cavan cannot comprehend when he says, "We haven't said anything yet" (Coward 1930: 20). Cavan is the source of grief, not the mourner; as he looks at Monica, he sees the refracted image of a society that does not resemble the one he left behind. As Monica looks at Cavan, she sees a corporeal figure of the losses of the First World War and her failure to process that grief. It led her to exclaim in a panic, "This won't last, will it—this feeling I've got now? … I couldn't bear it if it didn't. I just couldn't bear it" (Coward 1930: 20).

The effect of the unprecedented nature of the First World War, the commonality of mass graves, and non-repatriation policies employed in the UK after the war severed Monica's access to her intrapersonal grief. Grief, so pervasive and universal, moved mourning out of the purview of individual families and placed it into a realm of largescale commemoration. As everyone had either known someone who died during the First World War or knew someone who had lost someone, it became a taboo to suggest that one's war grief was greater than another's. Instead of graveside funerals, personalized processions, and wakes, there were public spectacles held at the Tomb of the Unknown Soldier. Spiritualist séances, tourist pilgrimages to battlefield memorials, and Armistice Day commemorations addressed a universal audience. The unbearable sorrow Monica holds was inaccessible to her because it was suppressed by the community of mourning after the war. As Cavan begins to leave, he says, "I'm grateful to you for a lot of happiness. It was jolly planning a future, it passed the time" (Coward 1930: 20). Monica replies, "Yes, it passed the time all right– and that's all I've done since" (Coward 1930: 20). Just as Cavan told his mother in the previous scene that he had not had time to get over loving Monica, Monica had not had time—even with a near two-decade distance—to get over losing Cavan.

Both Lady Cavan and Monica are trapped in their shrine-rooms. Monica fills her space with a disorganized zeal for modern consumerism. She hops from chaise lounge to record player to bar then back to the lounge. She is incapable of staying still long enough to reflect on sorrow in the same way as Lady Cavan who appears incapable of moving or deviating from her meditations on the death of her son. While both women are unable to process their intrapersonal feelings of grief, they express their stuckness differently. The mother is portrayed as a calcified symbol of her son's valor, the grief of losing him being too great to recover from; the lover distracts herself from the pain of losing her first love by filling every available space in her life with music, alcohol, material things, and people. Lady Cavan and Monica are not just refracting the recycled image of female mourners back to the audience, they are acting out what in reality women could not: the final goodbye. As Cavan's apparition reappears in their lives, their mourning process is re-jumpstarted. The mother who lost her son can hold him once more and the lover, who lost the promise of a future with the man she loved, can kiss him one last time. By staging the final goodbye, Coward creates literary figures who transcend the theatre stage and represent the monumentality of female mourning during the interwar period. These on-stage women transform the theatre house as they become conductors of their own mourning rituals.

As civilians, the First World War took place in Lady Cavan and Monica's homes and villages. Much like the popularity of turning soldiers' childhood bedrooms into shrines, Lady Cavan and Monica keep shrines to their traumatic memories stored in the most intimate spaces: their bedrooms. Robert Graves's *Goodbye to All That* tells of a mother who frequently went into her dead son's bedroom to commune with him. This practice of using the objects of the departed as a conduit for the missing body was widely popular in the interwar period. The *Psychic News*, a London-based spiritualist magazine, speculated that an average of 100,000 in-home séances took place in 1932 alone (*Psychic News* 1932: 1). Lady Cavan and Monica's conversations with John can be viewed as an in-home séance. The notable difference in the play is that Lady Cavan and Monica do not need a professional medium to summon John; they conduct the ritual themselves.

Monica and Lady Cavan represent a large cavern that existed in mourning during this era. Elders faced a shift in identity as notions surrounding what it meant to be a wife and mother were reconstructed. The younger generation faced a lack of reference to look toward for understanding who they were without the war. Writing mourning into a play and making the resolution of the play be the reconciliation of John to his closest friends and family, complicates notions of the secular status of theatre-going during the interwar period. The performative aspects of mourning, displays of sorrow, production of mourning statuary, and resuscitating of the dead were all moments where female mourners had the authority to conduct a social and spiritual rite. The transference of a mourning rite onto the stage bridges the gap between public-collective mourning practices and individual-private expressions of loss. In choosing to stage the final goodbye, there is an attempt to reach catharsis on stage. Theatre is capable of not just staging a reflection of mourning in the interwar period but also of facilitating a mourning rite on stage. Mourning plays, when presented to an audience who would have gone through the same grief as being performed on stage, could provide what other collective mourning ceremonies of the era did not: the individual's participation in communing with a corporeal representation of the missing bodies and the final goodbye to their fallen soldiers.

Works Cited

Chesterton, G. K. (1920), "The New Renascence: Thoughts on the Structure of the Future," *Vanity Fair*, Vol. 13, United States: University Microfilms, p. 51.

Coward, Noël (1986), "Post-Mortem," in *Collected Plays: Two: Private Lives, Bitter-Sweet, The Marquis, Post-Mortem*, intro. Sheridan Morley, London: Methuen.

Döring, Tobias (2006), *Performances of Mourning in Shakespearean Theatre and Early Modern Culture*, London: Palgrave Macmillan.

Graves, Robert (1960), *Goodbye to All That*, Harmondsworth: Penguin Books.

Grogan, Suzie (2017), "'A Solace to a Tortured World....'—The Growing Interest in Spiritualism during and after WW1," World War I Centenary. Available online: http://www1centenary.oucs.ox.ac.uk/body-and-mind/a-solace-to-a-tortured-world-the-growing-interest-in-spiritualism-during-and-after-ww1/. Last accessed May 30, 2017.

Hoare, Philip (1996), *Noël Coward. A Biography*, New York: Simon & Schuster.

Lang, Fritz (1922), *Dr. Mabuse der Spieler*: Part 1.

Luckins, Tanja (2004), *The Gates of Memory: Australian People's Experiences and Memories of Loss and the Great War*, Freemantle: Curtin University Books.

Post, Emily (1934), *Etiquette: The Blue Book of Social Usage*, New York: Funk & Wagnalls Company.

Psychic News (1932), London: Psychic Press Ltd.

Stanley, Peter (2014), "Spiritualism in Australia and the Great War," World War I Centenary. Available online: http://ww1centenary.oucs.ox.ac.uk/body-and-mind/spiritualism-in-australia-and-the-great-war/. Last accessed May 30, 2017.

Watson, Lillian Eichler (1924), *The New Book of Etiquette*, New York: Garden City Publishing Company.
White, Annie Randall (1901), *Twentieth Century Etiquette: An Up-to-Date Book for Polite Society: Containing Rules for Conduct in Public, Social and Private Life, at Home and Abroad, Including Suggestions for Oriental Teas.… Also, Correct Dress for Weddings, Receptions, and All Other Occasions, Designed for Both Men and Women, Young and Old*, n.p.

4

The Romans at War: Shakespeare's *Julius Caesar* and *Antony and Cleopatra* on the Nazi Stage

Alessandra Bassey

Since the beginning of the war in 1939, rumors and discussions about the potentially unjustified, yet prominent position of Shakespeare's plays within the German theatres had grown louder and become more frequent. Before 1939, Shakespeare's popularity went largely uncontested (apart from Alfred Rosenberg's continued criticism of the Bard and his English origins), but with the beginning of the war, it became more and more complicated to celebrate a writer who was, regardless of the regime's efforts to prove otherwise, part of the enemy nation that German soldiers would soon have to face in battle. The continued presence of Shakespeare and his plays in the theatres needed revised justification after the beginning of the war, and his presence on stage was at odds with "the anti-English propaganda that began to rage in public" (Habicht 2012: 27). In 1940, for example, an entire edition of *Wille und Macht*, the organ for Hitler Youth leaders, was devoted to Shakespeare and his position within German culture. The edition took pains to justify the continued presence of the English playwright on the German stages and contained essays and thoughts on the issue by Rainer Schlösser, Hermann Burte, Herbert A. Frenzel, and even the popular director and actor Gustaf Gründgens (*Wille und Macht* 1940).

The discussion around Shakespeare's plays and their place within German theatre became so ubiquitous that, in 1941, the regime saw itself forced to make a decisive move. Scholars seem to disagree on the exact date or month of the official change in policy: Thomas Eicher argued that from March 1941, every potential Shakespeare production had to be sanctioned by Goebbels himself (Eicher 2000: 299), while Gerwin Strobl sets the date for the decision in November of the same year (Strobl 1997: 21). Eicher added that from April 1941, there was a provisional ban on Shakespeare's plays, but that there are no records that show when the ban was officially lifted and how strict it was. We do know for certain, however, that the ban was not total, since Jürgen Fehling mounted a production of *Julius Caesar* during this time (Eicher 2000: 300), and Heinz Hilpert produced *Antony and Cleopatra* as late as 1943, not long before the final closure of the theatres until after the war. Even though scholars may disagree on the exact events and timeframes, what becomes clear is that with the beginning of the Second World War, Shakespeare's presence within German theatres became more and more contested.

Julius Caesar: A Fascist Manifesto?

The Deputy Führer to Adolf Hitler, Rudolf Hess, admitted in private that *Julius Caesar* could be a "dangerous play if it fell into the wrong hands" (London 2000: 250). Hess is presumably referring to the fact that *Julius Caesar* is a play in which the dictator is overthrown and murdered. The opinion of the regime and the staging possibilities of the play in the Reich were, however, not as simply one-sided as Hess's view. Since *Julius Caesar* is at once a work by the revered playwright Shakespeare, and features a prominent Roman leader, it could not just be done away with easily. Initial attempts were, rather unsuccessfully, made to equate Julius Caesar to the Weimar Republic, and the conspirators to the "avenging angels of Nazism" (Symington 2005: 232). Indeed, the regime tried to interpret *Julius Caesar* as a "Führerdrama" (leader drama), which could be used for propagandistic purposes, and Caesar was meant to be seen as the ultimate apotheosis of the "Führer" (leader). Despite the fact that Caesar eventually died, history proved to have been on his side (Eicher 2000: 313). The more obvious, and at the same time, more dangerous parallel to Nazi Germany, however, became clearer as the Nazi period continued: Hitler himself could be equated to the tyrannical Caesar, and not in the positive, regime-friendly light that was envisaged by the Reich's leaders.

In 1937 in Bochum, during the Second German Shakespeare Week (organized by Saladin Schmitt), Werner Deetjen (the president of the German Shakespeare Society) wrote in the program accompanying their *Julius Caesar* production that "Caesar […] is the hero of this highly political drama, not Brutus, as they seem to think nowadays in France. To represent Caesar […] as a weak-willed old man is completely wrong" (Deetjen 1937: 6–10, in Höfele 2016: 195). This explanation, or rather clarification, by the president of the German Shakespeare Society shows that the regime was trying to make sure that the interpretations and understandings of *Julius Caesar* across the Reich were clear and free from potential criticism, or were perceived as encouragement toward rebellion.[1] When Leni Riefenstahl's film *Victory of Faith (Der Sieg des Glaubens)*, which focuses on the 1933 National Socialist rally in Nuremberg, premiered on December 3, 1933, the Berlin correspondent of the *Observer*, who was invited to the gala premiere, wrote an article about the film, titled "Hail Caesar." He described it as "one long apotheosis of the Caesar spirit in which Herr Hitler plays the role of Caesar and the troops play Roman slaves" ("Hail Caesar," *Observer*, in Boyd 2018: 163). This remark demonstrates how much likeness there was projected to be between Hitler and Caesar (intentionally or not) already in 1933. Regardless of the Nazis' or Riefenstahl's intentions, parallels between Hitler and Caesar would continue to be drawn and would become stronger as time went on. In this way, an analysis of Fehling's *Julius Caesar* production will give compelling insights into both the regime's and Fehling's views on the play.

Andrew J. Hartley argues that in this production, the controversial director Jürgen Fehling was largely uninterested in a specific political critique and that he had to be careful, as the play was already very politically charged (Hartley 2014: 168). It is, nonetheless, unlikely that nothing in the production stood in direct relation to the then-present-day Nazi Germany and that Fehling wanted to avoid clear political statements. Looking at the surviving pictures of the *Julius Caesar* production, held at the archive of the *Theaterwissenschaftliches Institut* of the *Freie Universität* in Berlin and the *Academy of Arts* in Berlin, for example, we can see a mise-en-scène that was reminiscent of Nazi Germany precisely in the predominant Roman or "classic" aesthetic and style. The organized marches and parades, and Hitler's larger vision for a revival of the Roman style, order, and architecture within Germany all seemed to chime with the Roman flair of the production. Ancient Rome was often shown as a great inspiration for a magnificent "Aryan future" in Germany, and mock-ups of future (and mostly unrealized)[2] buildings and sites such as those shown in the propaganda film *The World Made of Stone* (directed by Kurt Rupli) were used to inspire and encourage the following of Hitler's vision for a glorious future (Griffin 2018: 10–11). The Nazis used classicism as a blueprint for their vision of a new world, which was, at the same time, "historically rooted" in the ancient civilizations, thus creating the solution to their contemporary problem of a decaying Germany, whose culture and sociopolitical life and standard had, they argued, been degraded by democratic institutions, Jews, and foreign influences (Griffin 2018: 43).

Under Fehling's directorship, Werner Krauss played Caesar, and Bernhard Minetti starred as Brutus. The reviewer Paul Fechter stated that despite the then-ongoing debate as to whether Caesar or Brutus should be the main protagonist, Fehling did not let these problems dissuade him from mounting a successful production (Fechter 1933). In line with the fascist reading of the play, most newspaper articles agreed that Fehling's Caesar was the unsung hero of the production, the man of the future, and that his death was followed by an unimaginable era of darkness. Caesar's fall and murder appeared as a historical catastrophe of epic and mythic proportions. The aftermath was described in one of the reviews as "the downfall of the original order […] of Rome," which would, of course, play right into the Nazirhetoric (*Der Mittag* 1941).[3] Long minutes of "breathless silence cover[ed] the stage and the auditorium. The murderers are paralyzed. Any previous harmony […] is rescinded," states the review in *Der Mittag* (1941). Karl Heinz Ruppel described the "cold, chalky light that [filled] the huge hall [of the *Staatstheater*] with an evil, merciless brightness, where the victim lay mutilated and bleeding before the eyes of the murderers;" the icy terror of their deed "choke[d] their breaths"; they were lame, their thoughts escaped them, and their tongues fell silent; the moment after Caesar's murder was "the moment of extreme horror, the moment in which the world [broke] into pieces" (Ruppel 1962: 27).

The costumes worn by the actors were stock Roman togas and gowns, and classical lines dominated the mise-en-scène (Hartley 2014: 167). The Roman soldiers wore traditional uniforms with helmets, breastplates, and spears. Surviving photographs of the play show an imposing scenery; the stage design was dominated by symmetrical, clean, and ordered elements. Traugott Müller, the stage designer, recreated Rome's architectural elements and style. However, a reviewer mentioned how the soldiers wore black, shining uniforms, carrying the proud "eagle," the symbol of the Roman Empire, which was also the symbol of the Third Reich (*Der Mittag* 1941). The associations between details of this production and Nazi Germany might, therefore, have struck both the general audience and the regime officials in the auditorium. Since the regime applauded this production, we can assume that these associations proved popular. In addition, the fascists promised a return to the past, a better place and time, where traditional values and aesthetics were upheld. A traditional, "set in the past" *Julius Caesar*, which could have been intended to bypass a political reading of the play, may have ended up being in perfect keeping with the fascist aesthetic, whether that was Fehling's intention or not.

Even though Fehling's *Julius Caesar* was undoubtedly less overtly politically critical than previous productions, for example, it is noteworthy that his more subversive productions (such as *Richard III* in 1937 or *Richard II* in 1939) were mounted before or just at the cusp of the war, whereas *Julius Caesar* was staged two years into the conflict. While the pre-war years still left space for direct or indirect political engagement, it seems that, by 1941, the war had weakened the morale of Fehling, as reflected in his production. The initial shock of a Nazi-takeover seems to have subsided and the bleak reality of living in a country at war had settled in, thus relegating sharp and open criticism from the list of priorities. Nonetheless, it would be incorrect to claim, as some critics have done, that because Krauss was cast as Caesar,[4] having starred in the notorious film *Jud Süß*, the production was a purely fascist rendition of Shakespeare's play. Fehling's aim to create an apolitical production inevitably became a political statement, which in turn made it popular among Nazi officials and led some later critics to consider it a pro-fascist production. Despite the potential ambiguity that Fehling may have worked into this production, the context within which it was staged affected its interpretation and led to a problematic reading of Shakespeare's work. While the acknowledgment of the production's less openly critical stance should not be misconstrued as a way of excusing the director's choice to lessen his stance against the regime, it is important to acknowledge that the production was inevitably affected by the immediate historic context. In addition, it is also worth mentioning that, even though this may not have been the case for Fehling, by the 1940s many actors, directors, and artists would have become party members and national socialists—some through coercion, yes, but many others through their own convictions (or because of convenience).

Antony and Cleopatra in Berlin in 1943

Mounting a play like *Antony and Cleopatra* during the Nazi period posed fundamental problems as it went against both the Nazis' racial prejudice and their fascist patriotism (Strobl 1997: 21). Putting *Antony and Cleopatra* on in 1943, four years into the war and ten years into racially motivated persecution and extermination attempts, posed an entirely different level of issues and, I would suggest, should be seen as political statement in its own right.

On February 11, 1943, Heinz Hilpert's production of *Antony and Cleopatra* premiered at the Deutsches Theater, and it would be one of the last Shakespeare productions before the theatres closed in September 1944 (Hortmann 1998: 155). Similarly to Fehling's *Julius Caesar* production, Hilpert's production elicited the opposition and protest of chief ideologist Alfred Rosenberg (Habicht 2012: 30), who argued that a play like *Antony and Cleopatra* in which a warlord leaves the battlefield to run after his mistress must be judged as particularly negative (Drewniak 1983: 252), especially if his mistress is a non-Aryan queen and the enemy of the Roman Empire.

Karl Heinz Ruppel stated that Hilpert opened his production with an intense love scene between Antony and Cleopatra. Anna Dammann as Cleopatra and Paul Hoffmann as Antony were seen lying together on stage, embracing each other in a deep, erotic kiss. The Berlin audience was thus transported deep into a sensual and fantastic Egyptian world of love and lust, and Hilpert seemed to have made it no secret that the focus of his production would lie on the love story between Antony and Cleopatra, rather than the politics at play (Drewniak 1983: 252). Interestingly, and maybe purely coincidentally, the surviving photos of the production, which are held at the archive of the Theaterwissenschaftliches Institut at the Freie Universität in Berlin, do not show any intimate or intense moments between the two main characters. The closest we get to seeing Antony and Cleopatra touch each other in the photos is a moment when Dammann hugs Hoffman, wrapping her arms around his shoulders, while his arms are hanging down his sides, not reciprocating her embrace, looking away from her as if unmoved or unconcerned by her display of affection. Judging from their costumes and the backdrop of the scene, it appears that Antony and Cleopatra are in the Egyptian queen's chambers, with just two maids positioned on either side of them, away from public and prying eyes. As to why the moments Ruppel described as intense and intimate between the lovers were not captured in photographs, it could be that they simply disappeared, were destroyed over the years, or are held somewhere else, but it could also be that the photographer of the time did not dare or want to photograph such a bold and open love scene between an Aryan and a non-Aryan. After all, family ties in the Viennese productions of *The Merchant of Venice*, staged the same year as Hilpert's *Antony and Cleopatra*, had to be adjusted to the political climate and laws of the time, and direct mention and display of the interracial love between Desdemona and Othello also had to be avoided and downplayed in productions of the time, but Hilpert seemed to have plainly disregarded conventions and laws in this rendition of *Antony and Cleopatra*. In addition, the number of photographs and reviews of the production is much lower than for Fehling's *Julius Caesar* production, for example. This could, again, be purely coincidental, but it could also reflect the state of the theatres and the general atmosphere in 1943: the fast approach of the final stages of the war, heavy bombing, and severe destruction of cities like Berlin hindered the normal functioning of everyday life as well as the cultural life of the city. Mounting productions came with its own particular set of difficulties, and so did the publications of reviews in newspapers. Equipment of all kinds was scarce, and the theatre practitioners had to improvise, so it does not seem too far-fetched to assume that taking photographs of a production posed its own problems—even more so in 1943 than in 1941.

Later on, in 1944, Hilpert was asked why he chose to produce *Antony and Cleopatra* in 1943, and he explained that he was fascinated with this play and with the way in which Shakespeare managed to transcend the notion of a "worthy and unworthy" life, celebrating the power and importance of all lives. "Shakespeare," Hilpert (1944: 92–3) said, "does not open the door to worthy or unworthy—small or big—but to the whole of life" (Hilpert 1944: 92–3). This was a very courageous statement to make, because in

1943 and 1944, the official policy of extermination of "unworthy" or "non-Aryan" life was at its height, and in the middle of it all, Hilpert now decided to produce a play that celebrated all lives, or the whole of life (Hortmann 1998: 156). He explained that he chose the play explicitly because of its quality of celebrating the whole of life, because "only [or especially] in an age which is so close to death as our own" can a play such as *Antony and Cleopatra* sow a seed of such abundant life, and give hope for the future that was yet to come (Hilpert 1944: 93). In the context of "unworthy" versus "worthy" life, Cleopatra, as an Egyptian, would have fallen under the first category. Antony should technically have been considered as "worthy" of life, but his failure to withstand the allure of the African queen and to remain unquestioningly faithful to his fatherland could make him fall under the same category as Cleopatra in the eyes of the regime. Thus, the simple fact of producing a play such as *Antony and Cleopatra* can be interpreted as an act of defiance against the regime, maybe not in favor of political dissidence, but at least in favor of art itself, against the odds and against the oppressive regime.

Conclusion

Even though both the *Julius Caesar* and *Antony and Cleopatra* productions may not exactly be seen as examples for brave political criticism, and even though Fehling's production in particular could at times seem to have been very much in line with the regime's rhetoric, it is important to remember that Shakespeare's canon consists of thirty-six plays, and that out of all of them, Fehling chose to mount *Julius Caesar* and Heinz Hilpert chose *Antony and Cleopatra*, both of which are politically precarious and contentious plays, during politically even more precarious times. Their choices can be seen, if not as a way of protesting or criticizing, at least as a way of disregarding the regime's ideologies, even just temporarily; because, as Corey Stoll said in an interview about the 2017 *Julius Caesar* production in New York, in "our new world," or in a world such as Nazi Germany, "where art is willfully misinterpreted […] doing the work of an artist has become a political act" in its own right (Milman 2017).

Notes

1   The president's remarks also demonstrate the complicated relationship of the German Shakespeare Society with the National Socialist regime. Andreas Höfele briefly mentions and elaborates on it; see Höfele (2017: 195).
2   One example of a Roman-inspired building whose construction was eventually suspended is the "Colosseum-inspired Congress Hall" in Nuremberg (suspended in 1943), "designed by Franz and Ludwig Ruff"; see Griffin (2018: 44).
3   All the citations from German newspapers, reviews, books, etc. are translated from the original German. All translations are mine.
4   Later on, Gründgens played Caesar, but the reviews and the later critics focus mostly on Krauss.

Works Cited

Boyd, Julia, ed. (2018), *Travellers in the Third Reich. The Rise of Fascism Through the Eyes of Everyday People*, London: Elliott and Thompson Limited.
Der Mittag (1941), "Tragödie des Caesarischen Roms. Jürgen Fehlings neue Inszenierung des 'Julius Caesar.'"
Deetjen, Werner (1937), "Die Zweite Deutsche Shakespeare-Woche," in City of Bochum and the German Shakespeare Society, ed., *Festschrift zur Zweiten Deutschen Shakespeare-Woche*, Leipzig: Max Beck, pp. 6–10.
Drewniak, Bugoslaw (1983), *Das Theater im NS-Staat. Szenarium deutscher Zeitgeschichte 1933–1945*, Düsseldorf: Droste.
Eicher, Thomas (2000), "Spielplanstrukturen 1929–1944," in Henning Rischbieter, Thomas Eicher, and Barbara Panse, eds., *Theater im "Dritten Reich:" Theaterpolitik, Spielplanstruktur, NS-Dramatik*, Seelze/Velber: Kallmeyersche Verlagsbuchhandlung GmbH, pp. 279–488.
Fechter, Paul (1933), "Der erste Shakespeare. 'Julius Caesar' im Staatstheater," undocumented provenance.
Griffin, Roger (2018), "Building the Visible Immortality of the Nation: The Centrality of 'Rooted Modernism' to the Third Reich's Architectural New Order," *Fascism. Journal of Comparative Fascist Studies*, Vol. 7, pp. 9–44.
Habicht, Werner (2012), "German Shakespeare, the Third Reich, and the War," in Irena R. Makaryk and Marissa McHugh, eds., *Shakespeare and the Second World War*, Toronto: University of Toronto Press, pp. 22–34.
Hartley, Andrew James (2014), *Julius Caesar*, Manchester: Manchester University Press.
Hilpert, Heinz (1944), *Formen des Theaters. Reden und Aufsätze*, Vienna: Leipzig.
Höfele, Andreas (2016), *No Hamlets*, Oxford: Oxford University Press.
Hortmann, Wilhelm (1998), *Shakespeare on the German Stage: The Twentieth Century*, Cambridge: Cambridge University Press.
London, John (2000), "Non-German Drama in the Third Reich," in John London, ed., *Theatre under the Nazis*, London, Manchester: Manchester University Press, pp. 222–61.
Milman, Oliver (2017), "Actor Who Played Assassin of Trump-like Caesar Tells of Cast 'Exhaustion and Fear,'" *The Guardian*, June 24. Available online: https://www.theguardian.com/stage/2017/jun/24/corey-stoll-trump-julius-caesar-play-new-york. Last accessed July 17, 2020.
Ruppel, K. H. (1962), *Großes Berliner Theater*, Velber bei, Hannover: Erhard Friedrich Verlag.
Strobl, Gerwin (1997), "Shakespeare and the Nazis," *History Today*, Vol. 47, No. 5, pp. 16–21.
Symington, Rodney (2005), *The Nazi Appropriation of Shakespeare*, Lampeter, Ceredigion, Wales: The Edwin Mellen Press.
Wille und Macht (1940), "Inhalt," *Wille und Macht. Führerorgan der Nationalsozialistischen Jugend*.

5

Eros and Terror in Ernest Hemingway's *The Fifth Column*—A Play on the Spanish Civil War

Jon Woodson

There has been no agreement as to what Ernest Hemingway's play, *The Fifth Column*, is about. Critics dismiss the play as agitprop or melodrama (Vaill 2014: 330) and moral confusion (Valis 2008: 19). Reduced to its fundamentals, it is a drama set in a city under siege. The hero is a man with two identities. His first action is to forcibly take a woman from another man. These actions equate to the outline of the Trojan War. The Trojan War is the Ur-war of Western civilization. Thomas Putnam observes that "No American writer is more associated with writing about war in the early 20th century than Ernest Hemingway" (Putnam 2006: 1). Given his traditional education and deep interest in war, Hemingway would have the Trojan War in mind when writing about the Spanish Civil War. My argument is that Hemingway sought an experimental mode that would fuse the realization of meaning in the modern world with the embrace of primordial will. In *The Fifth Column,* Hemingway distilled a new mode of consciousness through which life was lived fully even when confronted by technological warfare.

James Joyce's *Ulysses* established an "intertextual dialogue with the *Iliad* as an archetypal key to the cultural memory of the roots of Western civilization" (Fuchs 2013: 11). *The Fifth Column* has the same mythical realism—the fusion of the topical and the archetypal (Fuchs 2013: 13)—practiced by T.S. Eliot and Joyce. Hemingway's play is structured by Eliot's mythic method: "Instead of narrative method, we may now use the mythic method. ... a step toward making the modern world possible for art" (Eliot 1975: 178). Hemingway's use of the mythic method derived from his closeness to Joyce, "the greatest writer in the world" (Jones 2015). Hemingway's borrowing of Joyce's synthetic handling of reality realigns the moral problems attributed to Hemingway's play.

Hemingway's life made the Trojan War a suitable model for his drama. Hemingway wrote *The Fifth Column* in 1937, when he was a correspondent in Madrid. The Siege of Madrid was a more than two-year barricade of the Spanish capital city during the Spanish Civil War of 1936 to 1939. Hemingway arrived in Madrid in March 1937, so the city had already been under siege for five months. The play is partly a recapitulation of the affair between Hemingway and journalist Martha Gellhorn.

The play revolves around the personal and political passions of Philip Rawlings (Hemingway), a counterespionage agent secretly working for the Loyalist cause and

Dorothy Bridges (Gellhorn). Had Hemingway adhered to the plot of the Trojan War, Rawlings and Gellhorn would have been consigned to the losing, Trojan, side of the war, since they were residents of the besieged city, Madrid/Troy. Rawlings has a split identity: a playboy and an assassin, so he is both Trojan Paris and Greek Achilles.

Rawlings is both inside the besieged city of Madrid/Troy and outside laying siege. This duplicity resolves if we look at Hemingway's characters through the lens of Joyce's innovations—mythical realism, superposition, and simultaneity. Hemingway applies Joyce's spatiotemporal experiments to the stage. Mythic realism stacks the Trojan War atop the Spanish Civil War. The reportedly beautiful Gellhorn is Helen of Troy/Dorothy Bridges; Gellhorn is also Briseis. Philip is both Paris and Achilles.

Names used by Hemingway in his texts resulted from careful attention (Flora 2004; Windham n.d.). In Dorothy Bridges we read Briseis, while Dorothy is an anagram for "H [*do*/of] Troy"—Helen of Troy. The characters' names make a substantial contribution to the drama's meaning. Had *The Fifth Column* been written as a novel the reader would have been able to work out the author's use of the mythic method. However, Hemingway's employment of mythic parallelism in his drama is largely invisible. Only twice is the double temporal structure of the play revealed—where the patriotic poster is described as seen "backwards from here" (Hemingway 2008: 17), and when Philip speaks of his "back name" (Hemingway 2008: 46).

Philip enters delivering a catalog of allusive names. In myth Paris was a bastard. Robert Preston is the man from whom Philip is soon to take Dorothy, so we see that bastard-Preston is Paris, supported by the imperfect anagram—Preston/Paris. Reading Robert as "robber" reduces Dorothy/Helen to an object: later in the play Philip calls her a commodity. Philip is poised between the war and love for Dorothy, yet the play's treatment of love is consistently satirical. This labeling is in keeping with the play's central problem, which is *eros*: "In tragedy, 'metaphorical *erôs*' applies in the vast majority of cases to annihilating and deadly drives …" (Thumiger 2013: 36).

Hemingway calls Dorothy/Helen "Comrade Boredom Bridges" because the play follows an alternative version of the *Iliad*'s narrative; Steichorus and Euripides disseminated the idea that the Helen who lived in Troy was a phantom, and Hemingway allows Philip long passages hinting at Dorothy/Helen's unreality: "She has the same background all American girls have that come to Europe with a certain amount of money. They're all the same" (Hemingway 2008: 78–9).

The mythic method aligns the electrician's name, Marconi, with Mercury, the Latin form of Hermes. In the *Iliad*'s only episode where Hermes plays an important part, he must conduct Priam to the tent of Achilles, so he can plead for the return of Hector's corpse. In an earlier scene Philip greets the manager as Comrade Stamp Collector; the presence of the electrician marks this as the meeting of Rawlings/Achilles and Comrade Stamp Collector/Priam. They discuss inferior stamps instead of Hector's mutilated corpse: Hemingway has demoted the tragic nature of life. Stamps are canceled to prevent their reuse. The implication is that corpses are likewise canceled, though theatrically, Hemingway has brought the personages of the *Iliad* back to life. Hemingway revisits the trope of reanimation with his parodic depiction of the death of Hector. Philip's execution of a captured German officer who refuses to walk back to Security is a parody of the killing (by Achilles and Athena) of Hector, who will not stop running. Philip reverses the mutilation of Hector, by propping up the German general and placing a cigarette in his mouth. The cigarette that will not stay lighted suggests the triumph of terror, since the officer's corpse was used to torture a fifth columnist, leading to the mass murder of the hundreds betrayed by the officer's confession.

Hemingway has layered his play with assorted devices and fragments from epic and tragic literature to examine the interplay of *eros* and terror. Philip's full name is never divulged within the dramatic action. Rawlings is pronounced four times in the play—once when he says, "My back name is Rawlings," as shown above. This emphatic handling of Philip's name directs the audience's attention toward the intertextuality at the play's heart. Phonetically "Philip Rawlings" divulges *raw feelings*, alluding to Achilles's assertion that he will eat Hector raw (Homer *Iliad* 22.337–54). Achilles is able to withdraw from his cosmic wrath because he "has already accepted his impending death and the emptiness of human action" (Boddice 2019: 32). Not only does Philip face the terrors of modern warfare, he plays out the backstories of Paris, Achilles, and Menelaus. Thus, in 1.3 Philip/Paris awakens after his duel with Preston/Menelaus. On awakening, Philip/Paris looks at the reverse side of a patriotic poster that hangs between the rooms and asks, "And what is that horrible thing?" (Hemingway 2008: 17). The Manager tells Philip it is a patriotic poster seen "backwards" (Hemingway 2008: 17), an allusion to the parallel realities of the two wars. We are to take Philip's use of "horrible" literally as a reaction to the reverse side of patriotism. The chronologically transparent poster conducts Philip beyond patriotism and directly to the terrors of the war.

Hemingway divulges his Greek sources when he has Philip say that the electrician Marconi/Hermes resembles a Greek chorus:

> ELECTRICAN. Camaradas, no hay luz! [He says this in a loud and almost prophetic voice, suddenly standing up and opening his arms wide]
> PHILIP. He says there isn't any light. You know the old boy is getting to be rather terrific. Like an electrical Greek chorus. Or a Greek electrical chorus.
> (Hemingway 2008: 13)

Philip's banter robs the electrician's speech of any appearance of authority. "Terrific" sounds like drollery but meaning fearful, it is an introduction of terror. The phrases "an electrical Greek chorus" (Hemingway 2008: 13) and "a Greek electrical chorus" (Hemingway 2008: 13) imitate the comedic chiasmus of the Marx Brothers in *The Cocoanuts* (1929): we are reminded of Karl Marx's comment that history repeats itself first as tragedy, then as farce (Marx 1852). Hemingway's play demonstrates many farcical aspects, and its screwball treatment of Wilkinson's murder undercuts the treatment of political ideology. Philip's electrician alludes to Electra, a murderous figure on the fringes of the Trojan War and the subject of tragedies by Aeschylus and Euripides. The darkness announced by the electrician is Hemingway's embrace of the conclusion that Euripides reaches in *Electra*: "In the irrecoverable dark world of *Electra*, blood death and defilement are the deepest truths, the ultimate realities" (Morwood 1981: 370). In 1.2 the Manager tells Preston that because of his constant drunkenness the electrician "resembles a catastrophe" (Hemingway 2008: 4), the denouement of a tragedy. Philip's use of "pity" (Hemingway 2008: 32) at the inevitable death of Wilkinson similarly suggests a character's self-consciousness about being in a tragic drama: "pity" alludes to Aristotle—"incidents arousing pity and fear" (*Poetics* VI.2). Here the electrician remains in character as Hermes, and he has refused the divine aid for which Electra has prayed.

The introduction of Electra implicates the other characters from her narrative. Electra's brother, Orestes, is distinguished by his facial disfigurement. Max, a counterespionage colleague of Philip's who was tortured and disfigured by the Gestapo, stands in as Orestes. Max's terrible face reverses *eros*, for in intercourse with Max, women are forced to look the other way (Hemingway 2008: 77). Erotically, Max is Philip's opposite, since in 2.4 Philip sleeps with Dorothy, while Max sleeps alone in Philip's bed. The name Max is cryptic: Orestes killed his mother, so his name resolves into "Ma-X"—where the X reads as "X out," to kill. Orestes is the agent who introduces terror into the drama. As Orestes, Philip is tormented by Furies who punish him for his countless atrocities. At times Max stands alone as Orestes, but when Philip confesses to Dorothy that he is plagued by psychological torments that drive him to the brink of despair ("Gives me the horrorous …. Sort of super horrors" [Hemingway 2008: 25]), Philip has incorporated the role of Orestes.

The Moorish Tart, called Anita in the play, also generates many difficulties. In the realist reading of the play, Anita is an erotic foil for Dorothy/Helen. In establishing why Anita should be opposed to Dorothy, we enter another dimension of Hemingway's complex drama. Hemingway's libraries (Brasch 1981) and reading (Reynolds 1981) show an abiding interest in Greek tragedy. The Greek tragedy that comes closest to modeling the Dorothy/Anita rivalry is Euripides's *Helen*. *Helen* provides two Helens: if Dorothy/Helen is the phantom Helen at Troy, then Anita (Anita-anti)/Helen is the *anti-Helen* who lived in Egypt and was the protagonist of Euripides's play. This influence is confirmed at the end of Hemingway's play; Philip/Menelaus breaks off his relationship with Dorothy/Helen and resumes his affair with Anita/Helen, recapitulating the main action of *Helen*. In Euripides's play Menelaus arranges and attends his own comedic funeral—the lynchpin of *Helen*. In another of Hemingway's ironic reversals of an ancient narrative, the proxy funeral is tragically parodied in Hemingway's play when Philip unwittingly stages his own death by proxy. Hemingway's play reverses many conventions of Greek tragedy, here bringing violence on stage and treating it preposterously. There are two choruses—both are kept off stage. The erotic chorus is reduced to recordings of Chopin's dreamy piano versions of the Mazurka, a lively Polish folk dance. The terror chorus (the Comrades) sings three political songs that are overheard in Dorothy's room, the last being the Comintern song, which is sung at funerals. Hemingway's concern with reversals parodies *Helen*, which is driven by several comic reversals—Helen's *doppelganger*, Menelaus's return, and Theoclymenus's loss of Helen. Despite the happy ending of *Helen*, Menelaus murders the crew of the ship in which the escape from Egypt is accomplished. Similarly, murders drive the action of Hemingway's drama.

Once Dorothy has replaced Anita, an unstable rivalry is established. Anita was aware of Dorothy at the play's commencement, when she demands to know the meaning of the sign on Dorothy's door: WORKING / DO NOT DISTURB

(Hemingway 2008: 2). Later, Anita tempers her animosity for Dorothy and Dorothy gives her the sign. Looking beneath the realistic surface, Anita evidences other personalities. Anita's exchanges with Philip combine the rapid-fire speech of screwball comedies and the stichomythia of Greek tragedies. These effects demonstrate that Hemingway is invested in the comic irony of Euripides (Pippin 1960: 153). The most telling speech comes in a purportedly comic exchange between Philip and Anita when Anita states: "That great big blonde. Tall like a tower. Big like a horse" (Hemingway 2008: 49). This passage's seriousness emerges when Anita's pairing of a tower and a horse is questioned. Troy was characterized by its high walls and well-built towers. The city's destruction happened through the trickery of the men hidden in the wooden horse. In Homer's *Iliad*, Cassandra succinctly joined these two structures when she warned that the horse would bring about the fall of the towers, thus, Dorothy/Helen's sign is Anita/Cassandra's prophetic revelation. The meaning of Anita/Cassandra's sign goes nowhere, just as Cassandra's warnings were not heeded by the Trojans. Anita is not the only eruption of Cassandra in *The Fifth Column*. The maid, Petra (rock, trap), recapitulates another episode of Cassandra's narrative when she attempts to warn Dorothy that Philip is a bad man.

Anita has bitten Mr. Roger Vernon five times demonstrating that *The Fifth Column* possesses a meta-discourse. Anita represents not only the doubling of Anita/Cassandra in the mythic method, she shows that the play also expresses an Apollonian-Dionysian duality. Christopher Kuhn shows that a case cannot be made for an influence from Nietzsche's ideas in Hemingway (Kuhn 1995: 236). Unlike the novels, the play demonstrates a heavily Nietzschean influence. The trope of Anita and biting presents Anita as a Dionysian maenad. The maenads became intoxicated, tore apart animals and humans, and ate them raw. Most famously, they are said to have torn and eaten Orpheus. Philip's behavior is profoundly Dionysian:

> PRESTON. He's much livelier, all right. You know what he was doing last night before they shut Chicote's? He had a cuspidor, and he was going around blessing people out of it. You know, sprinkling it on them. It was better than ten to one he'd get shot. (Hemingway 2008: 5–6)

Philip's spittoon alludes to the *krater*—a bowl that the ancient Greeks used to mix water and wine. Philip's ad hoc ritual recapitulates a crude Dionysian ritual by the Orphics: "In the Orphic rite of initiation … the candidates for initiation were purified and wiped clean with mud and pitch" (Willoughby 1929). The doubling throughout *The Fifth Column* suggests that the biting of Vernon by Anita is Hemingway's presentation of the killing of Orpheus by the maenads. Roger Vernon suggests "orgy" in Roger as well as vulgar slang meaning to have sexual intercourse, and "vernal" in Vernon suggests the Dionysian cult's spring orgies. In *The Birth of Tragedy* Nietzsche speaks in positive terms of "the meaning of the festivals of world redemption and days of transfiguration in the Dionysian orgies of the Greeks" (Nietzsche 1886: 11). Once again, we have been confronted with Hemingway's appropriation of Euripides: "This myth of Dionysiac ritual comes from the Athenian playwright Euripides's 'Bacchae'" (Koontz 2013: 1).

The Fifth Column is thoroughly invested in an Apollonian-Dionysian dichotomy, which is attributable to Hemingway's being under the influence of Nietzsche's *The Birth of Tragedy*. As an example of this split, the "Do Not Disturb" sign on Dorothy's door parodies the inscription from the temple of Apollo in Delphi, "Nothing in Excess." Dorothy spends all her time on stage trying to dissuade Philip from his Dionysian excesses.

The death of Wilkinson is a crucial instance of the Dionysian confusion of terror and *eros*. Philip planned to send Wilkinson on an assignment during which he was sure to be killed. When Wilkinson reports for duty, Philip says to himself that what will transpire is an "awful pity" (Hemingway 2008: 32). Later an assassin shoots Wilkinson instead of Philip. When Philip discovers that Wilkinson is dead, he is forced to look at his own proxy corpse in pity and terror. The name Wilkinson presents an explanatory anagram: "no skin," identifying Wilkinson as the flayed Marsyas. Marsyas establishes the centrality of the Nietzschean Dionysian-Apollonian context, since Marsyas (a Dionysian stand-in) was killed by the god Apollo. However, by having Wilkinson/Philip refuse to drink alcohol, Hemingway has assigned Wilkinson/Marsyas a reversed Apollonian cast. The "will" in Wilkinson alludes to the "Hellenic will" that culminates the metaphysics in *The Birth of Tragedy*. Hemingway provided a Dionysian counter-narrative to his insertion of the Marsyas episode, for in a later scene Philip decides that a fascist officer who will not cooperate with his interrogation should be killed, and Philip assassinates him in a wood. In this instance, Philip is a stand-in for the god Dionysus, and the murder of the fascist officer is a reversal of Pentheus's interrogation of Dionysus in Euripides's *Bacchae*. Through another of the many reversals in Hemingway's drama, it is Pentheus who succumbs to Dionysus/Philip's cruelty after being interrogated.

To resolve Hemingway's disparate pursuits, we must turn back to the killing of Wilkinson/Marsyas. Hemingway centered his play around one of Nietzsche's insights: "What if the Greeks in the very wealth of their youth had the will *to be* tragic and were pessimists?" (1886: 7). The name Wilkinson also contains the "the will to be tragic." Hemingway has grounded his drama in the will to be pessimistic: this pessimism has been explicitly defined by "Accepting the necessity of pain in a life of growth and change, *setting aside the goal of happiness as the ultimate aim of a human life* … detachment from whatever exists at present—something that will inevitably appear as callousness towards others: '*Dionysian wisdom*'" (Dienstag 2004: 92–3). This point—that Dionysian wisdom appears as callousness to others—is made throughout *The Fifth Column*: at the opening a soldier states "I'm not supposed to be nice" (Hemingway 2008: 3). Hemingway's use of the mythic method shifts his play away from agitprop, suggesting that it has been underrated. The assessment of the play as indifferent to moral dimensions (Raeburn 1998: 15) is thrown into doubt by Hemingway's demonstrably Nietzschean concerns. Additionally, it seems that the tone of the play has been misread. Since Philip Rawlings—a self-proclaimed "second-rate cop" (Hemingway 2008: 42)—speaks like Nick Charles in *The Thin Man* (1934), his delivery ought to be similarly "so droll and insinuating, so knowing and innocent at the same time, that it hardly matters what he is saying" (Ebert 2002)—not that of a politically hardboiled, Machiavellian gunman.

Works Cited

Aristotle (n.d.), *Poetics*, trans. Ingram Bywater. Dept. of English, CUNY, Available online: http://academic.brooklyn.cuny.edu/english/melani/cs6/poetics.html. Last accessed July 11, 2020.

Boddice, Rob (2019), *A History of Feelings*, London: Reaktion Books.

Brasch, James and Joseph Sigman (1981), *Hemingway's Library: A Composite Record*, New York: Garland Publishing, Inc.

Dienstag, Joshua Foa (2004), "Tragedy, Pessimism, Nietzsche," *New Literary History*, Vol. 35, No. 83–101. Available online: www.jstor.org/stable/20057822. Last accessed July 11, 2020.

Ebert, Roger (2002), "The Thin Man" [Great Movies]. Available online: https://www.rogerebert.com/reviews/great-movie-the-thin-man-1934. Last accessed July 11, 2020.

Eliot, T. S. (1975), "Ulysses, Order, and Myth," in Frank Kermode, ed., *Selected Prose of T. S. Eliot*, New York: Harcourt.

Flora, Joseph M. (2004), "Names and Naming in Hemingway's Short Stories," *South Atlantic Review*, Vol. 69, No. 1, Winter, pp. 1–8.

Fuchs, Dieter (2013), "James Joyce's Trojan Hobby-Horse: The *Iliad* and the Collective Unconscious Ulysses," *Annals of Philosophy, Social and Human Disciplines*. Available online: http://www.apshus.usv.ro/arhiva/2013II/001.%20pp.%2011-18.pdf. Last accessed July 11, 2020.

Hemingway, Ernest (2008), *The Fifth Column: And Four Stories of the Spanish Civil War*, Scribner: Kindle Edition.

Jones, Josh (2015), "Deal with Him, Hemingway," *Open Culture* [in *Literature*, November 3]. Available online: https://www.openculture.com/2015/11/james-joyce-picked-drunken-fights-then-hid-behind-ernest-hemingway.html.

Koontz, Alana (2013), "The Art and Artifacts Associated with the Cult of Dionysus." Available online: https://dc.uwm.edu/cgi/viewcontent.cgi?article=1000&context=rsso.

Kuhn, Christopher (1995), "Hemingway and Nietzsche: The Context of Ideas," in Manfred Putz, ed., *Nietzsche in American Literature and Thought*, New York: Camden House, pp. 233–8.

Marx, Karl (1852), *The Eighteenth Brumaire of Louis Bonaparte*, Marxist Internet Archive Library. Available online: https://www.marxists.org/archive/marx/works/1852/18th-brumaire/ch01.htm.

Morwood, J. H. W. (1981), "The Pattern of the Euripides Electra," *The American Journal of Philology*, Vol. 102, No. 4, pp. 362–70, *JSTOR*. Available online: www.jstor.org/stable/294324.

Nietzsche, Friedrich (1886), *The Birth of Tragedy*, trans. W. A. Haussmann, ed. Oscar Levy, [EBook # 51356] Project Gutenberg. Available online: https://www.gutenberg.org/files/51356/51356-h/51356-h.htm.

Pippin, Anne Newton (1960), "Euripides' 'Helen': A Comedy of Ideas," *Classical Philology*, Vol. 55, No. 3, pp. 151–63. Available online: www.jstor.org/stable/266350.

Putnam, Thomas (2006), "Hemingway on War and Its Aftermath," *Prologue Magazine*, Spring, Vol. 38, No. 1. Available online: https://www.archives.gov/publications/prologue/2006/spring/hemingway.html.

Raeburn, John (1998), "Hemingway on Stage: *The Fifth Column*, Politics and Biography," *The Hemingway Review*, Vol. 18, No. 1, pp. 5–16.

Reynolds, Michael S. (1981), *Hemingway's Reading: 1910–1940*, Princeton: Princeton University Press.
Thumiger, Chiara (2013), "Mad *Erôs* and Eroticized Madness in Tragedy," in Chiara Thumiger Sanders et al., eds., *Erôs in Ancient Greece*, Oxford and New York: Oxford University Press.
Vaill, Amanda (2014), *Hotel Florida: Truth, Love, and Death in the Spanish Civil War*, New York: Farrar, Straus and Giroux.
Valis, Noel (2008), "Hemingway's the Fifth Column, Fifth Columnism, and the Spanish Civil War," *The Hemingway Review*, Vol. 28, No. 1, Fall, pp. 19–32.
Willoughby, Harold R. (1929), *Pagan Regeneration*. Available online: http://www.sacred-texts.com/cla/pr/pr06.htm. Last accessed July 11, 2020.
Windham, Arielle (n.d.), "Significance of Names in The Old Man and the Sea." Available online: https://study.com/academy/lesson/significance-of-names-in-the-old-man-and-the-sea.html. Last accessed July 11, 2020.

6

The Early African American Theatre of Joshua McCarter Simpson during the Civil War

Lauri Scheyer

Joshua McCarter Simpson (c. 1820–1876) was an ardent African American antislavery activist, Underground Railroad conductor, civic leader, church elder, businessperson, and herbal doctor, as well as gifted writer and rhetorician.[1] He published two books in the throes of the American Civil War and during Reconstruction in the aftermath of the bloody conflagration that nearly tore America in two. Believed to be the first volumes solely devoted to the theme of abolition by an author of any race, both were labelled an "original composition" by the author whose name was affixed.[2] His writings were well-known and widely circulated during his lifetime—including by famed figures such as Harriet Tubman—though undeservedly overlooked today. Many of Simpson's writings were clearly intended as scripts for performance. He provides an early originating point for African American theatre as a vehicle for political protest and racial pride to serve the community, a theme that later became prominent in the New Negro plays of the Harlem Renaissance (1920s–1930s), the performative militancy of the Black Arts Movement (1960s–1970s), and the flowering of post-1980s live art and performance poetry in rap, hip-hop, and slam culture.

As noted by Bernard L. Peterson, Jr., "a good number" of the short-lived African American theatrical companies of the nineteenth century "belonged to the minstrel tradition that had been originated by white troupes to ridicule stereotypical images of poor, uneducated Southern blacks" (Peterson 1997: loc. 28).[3] In contrast, Simpson's goal was to eradicate cross-racial mockery of black culture through his bold writings designed to instigate social action in the years leading up to the Civil War. Instead of self-parody, Simpson aimed to counter the impulse of burlesque to "change the flow of those sweet melodies (so often disgraced by Comic Negro Songs, and sung by our own people,) into a more appropriate and useful channel" (Simpson 1854: v). The phrase "our own people" indicates inclusion of an African American audience, along with his aspiration that "this little work (the *first* of the kind in the United States,) may find a resting place and a hearty welcome in every State, community and family in the Union, and as far as a friend to the slave may be found" (Simpson 1854: vi). Simpson's hope might be viewed as braggadocio unless we scrutinize it carefully in context. In an era when it was still illegal to teach enslaved African Americans to read and write, when they were called chattel, ranked with work-animals, and bought and sold as possessions, Simpson addressed his brothers and sisters as literate and sentient human beings.

A unified America—racially or governmentally—was not universally supported in the nineteenth century, and Simpson was proposing his dream of a post-slavery America before the Civil War. He spoke to the whole American public in stating his political posture, using his own name, and claiming authority and responsibility for his words. He also invited others to use his words as moral instruments for public performance to engender change and solidarity by subtitling them "composed exclusively for the Under Ground Rail Road." This ethos of art as social agency is a forerunner of the proud and self-actualizing African American theatre of the twentieth and twenty-first centuries. Simpson's writing contains parodies of nationalistic and often racist American songs, verse miniplays with stage directions, and exhortatory lyrics for group performance anticipating the later theatrical productions of figures such as Langston Hughes, Ed Bullins, LeRoi Jones/Amiri Baraka, August Wilson, and Lynn Nottage.

His magnum opus, *The Emancipation Car, being an Original Composition of Anti-Slavery Ballads, Composed Exclusively for the Under Ground Rail Road* (1854), contains embedded scripts complete with character descriptions, settings, dialogue, stage directions, and authorial instructions. These verse plays blend the call-and-response structure of the orally performed African American spirituals with conventional, but ironically inverted, representations of classical Greek theatre, such as choruses to represent the voices of an oppressed and marginalized polis. His achievements are remarkable in their modernity and political brashness in using scripts and song lyrics as revolutionary palimpsests to perform blackness by overwriting popular, and frequently racist, white narratives, characterizations, and tropes.

The book opens with a Note to the Public in a supplication that frames the author as a prophetic intercessor emulating Moses: "Lord what can be done for my people" (Simpson [1854] 1874: III). The answer comes in the introductory preface as Simpson recognizes the "horrid pictures of the condition of my people, and something seemed to say, 'Write and sing about it—you can sing what would be death to speak'" (Simpson [1854] 1874: IV). The necessity for anonymous and clandestine performance of political insurgency echoes the operations of the spirituals, the foundational materials of African American culture which were delivered orally as communal performances of words, song, dance, and instrumentation. The performed verses of the spirituals were originally created by enslaved African Americans, most likely in the seventeenth century, and then used in the nineteenth century by conductors of the Underground Railroad who used secret tactics to help the enslaved people escape to freedom. As in the spirituals, Simpson realized he could share powerful messages through song to convey revolutionary ideas that might be dangerous in print. For their own protection, he encouraged Underground Railroad conductors and passengers to liberate his words from the page and perform them orally for strength and sense of purpose. He used live art to sustain community for the social and political benefit of what he protectively called "my people."

Simpson referred to many of his literary creations as "airs," a polysemous term whose meanings are elemental, literary, musical, temporal, spatial, and metaphorical, evoking the breath and an attitude. The airs that Simpson chose to counter-write were popular and immediately recognizable to audiences. The strength of his "ballads" lay in eradicating and overpowering songs of racist nationalism and answering the message by drowning it out. He used the medium of white culture just as white culture used African American labor, including his own, having spent much of his youth in indentured thrall. Being born and remaining legally free all his life, his animating and ventriloquizing of enslaved speakers was an act of informed imaginative conscience. Simpson chose political, moral, and historical themes to generate imagined empathetic scenarios in his vignette-like plays. *The Emancipation Car* is a hybrid work that contains elements of poetry, fiction, oratory, essays, autobiography, and political history with the interpellation of the theatrical and performative as dominant stylistic features.

Simpson wanted to provide a voice for the voiceless while still claiming authorship by calling his airs "original compositions." This was an era when it could be perilous for African Americans to put their names on their writing, when countless literary works appeared as "Anon.," under pseudonyms, or credited to white editors or transcribers. This circumstance is reflected in Simpson's piece "Dedicated to ____, An Aged Pioneer Who Now Resides Near Chatham, C.W.," where the blank protects the name and identity of the character whose life experiences are told in this work (Simpson [1854] 1874: 15). It is structured as a call-and-response, with a leader or speaker (the voice and perspective of the "aged pioneer") alternating with a refrain by a chorus. Simpson utilizes a hybrid form reflecting the history and needs of African American literature by combining cultural and political statements with communitarian ideals, signifying on mainstream culture, and utilizing words, movement, performance, group participation, and music to do so. As Vicki L. Eaklor emphasizes, although Simpson's writing contains ideas that were already circulating among abolitionists, he was in a unique position as a free black man to represent the emotions and attitudes of the enslaved. Eaklor hypothesizes his role as an Underground Railroad conductor was the source of these stories as he represented both individual and communal experiences in his characters. As a result, his writing provides special insight into how communication functioned in the clandestine operations of the Underground Railroad. That Simpson claims authorship by asserting that his works are "original" does not negate his desire for them to be used widely by others. They are inherently theatrical in calling for spectatorship and live participation in political, social, and religious arenas.

"The Final Adieu," set to the "air" of "I'm Bound to Run All Night" ("Camptown Races"), is an example of Simpson's theatrical devices. This call-and-response structure is performed by a leader and two speakers. The leader is an enslaved person on the verge of escaping to Canada. The scene opens with the call: "Come all my brethren now draw near– / Good-bye, Good-bye" where the empty signifier of "doo-dah" in the original song is replaced with the amplitude of meaning in "Good-bye." The response is allocated to First Voice and Second Voice whose interspersed dialogue unfolds the plot told as a distributed narrative: the leader plans to run all night and sleep all day until attaining freedom, and the First and Second Voice characters apparently will accompany the leader since they share in telling the same story. This performance evokes the group operations of the Underground Railroad as a dialogue among characters sharing the same dramatic and conceptual space as they act to take defiant control of their lives. This format is noteworthy for early African American theatre with an intriguing twist near the end. A fourth character is introduced parenthetically: "(A voice is heard in a low but distinct tone from the kitchen cellar, uttered by an old house servant.)" (Simpson [1854] 1874: 50). Reinforcing the intermedia relationships among text, song, score, script, and performance, the servant's speech—in quotation marks—opens by reciting the lyrics to the spiritual "Swing Low, Sweet Chariot," a song not from popular white culture but a plantation artifact, which would be more targeted toward an African American audience than the popular songs he overwrote:

"If you get there before I do,"
    Good-bye, Good-bye.
"Look out for me I'm coming too,"
    I'll soon be on my way.

In the last two stanzas, the house servant's words appear in quotation marks with the other three characters' speeches indented. The extraordinary introduction of a fourth character in a different space breaks the fourth wall and reflects the theatrical originality of this piece. All four characters sing the last two stanzas as a chorus which ends "I'm bound for Canada." The inventiveness and sophistication of "The Final Adieu" is a harbinger of modern literary and theatrical practices. Simpson experiments with form in a way that demands to be lifted from the page and performed as communal theatre.[4]

Simpson wrote theatrical scripts intended for public performance in order to counter the prevailing racism in a divided America where slavery remained legal. His creativity as a playwright is underscored by the fact that he was not presenting firsthand autobiographical experiences but narratives that were relayed to him or imagined. For example, "The Slaveholder's Rest" is a call-and-response theatrical vignette featuring a solo actor, Servant, and a chorus of Brethren. It opens with instructions for staging and characterizations: "A Song, illustrative of the true feelings of the slave, when a tyrant Master dies, sung by the body-servant and his field brethren, in a retired negro quarter" (Simpson [1854] 1874: 57). The script alternates between Servant and Brethren and ends in a crescendo where the body-servant and his field brethren "All join together." In terms of literary genre, this work cannot be interpreted as a static text or pure poetry but as a script intended for performance by multiple actors. A common theme of Simpson is unity, shown in a grand finale where all characters perform together. With every script set to a musical "air," these pieces are miniature operas combining song, settings, characters, plots, and moral messages of uplift.

In another gesture prescient of techniques yet to come in the following century, "The Colonization Society" can be viewed as an early form of tribunal theatre in using contemporaneous documents that were updated in each edition as Simpson's magnum opus evolved. Another novel script of pure imagination is "Queen Victoria Conversing with her Slave Children," a call-and-response between Queen Victoria as the leader and Slaves as the responding chorus. This verse play's plot consists of the Queen's inducements to the Slaves to flee to Canada where she stands "With open arms and stretched out hands" (Simpson [1854] 1874: 60). The Slaves explain the dangers of an attempted escape to "Mother Victoria," as the Queen contrasts the British government of "John Bull," supported by "The Lord," with "tyrant Columbia's land" ruled by American racism.

A minidrama to the tune of "The Infant's Dream" involves two characters, Child and Father. In this dramatic dialogue, the Father explains to the Child that his wife and the child's mother has been "sold"—the quotation marks are in the original—and they will never see her again. Another duet—by two groups of characters—is a fully developed script performed to the tune of "Ho! Boys, Carry me Back." It opens by introducing the emblematic fictionalized characters of Farmers and Mechanics. According to Simpson, it is "A song, illustrative of those persons who, as many say, cannot take care of themselves. But after a few years' trial in a land of equal rights, we find them, in many instances, at home, enjoying the benefits of industry, with a new song in their mouths" (Simpson [1854] 1874: 97). This script, as so many in *The Emancipation Car*, extols the Romantic and utopian combination of faith in God, industry, and equal rights for a renewed and healthy American society. The Farmers and Mechanics alternately argue that they each are the most satisfied, valuable, prosperous, and self-sufficient in their chosen labors. The banter and rivalry end in a harmonious group chorus:

We all have plenty to do,
And plenty of money in hand;
We are happy and free,
As the bird and the bee,
We're brethren all joined in a band. (Simpson [1854] 1874: 100)

The final line of this piece sung by Farmers and Mechanics together—representing the equal standing of modern industry and agrarian traditions—is "And Providence surely will smile" (Simpson [1854] 1874: 100). This post-slavery vision of the future is a fulfilment of the divine order.

"Fourth of July in Alabama" is similarly a performance by a fictional archetypal character. Performed to the tune of "America," it serves as a bitter counter-song to the hypocritical hymn which falsely extols America's devotion to upholding freedom for all. It opens with this epigraph: "The following piece is the meditation and feelings of the poor Slave, as he toils and sweats over the hoe and cotton hook, while his master, neighbors, and neighbors' children are commemorating that day, which brought life to the whites and death to the poor African" (Simpson [1854] 1874: 40). Simpson significantly refers to this work as "a piece" while the subtitle of the book is "ballads." These terms evoking music reveal his sense of the medium in which he was working. Simpson repurposed the performative, communal, and oral traditions of African American cultural products like spirituals to signify on the current moment in American history. He formalized the theatrical elements of his hybrid form by adding characters, plots, dialogues, settings, lyrics, and stage directions to create a form that was avant-garde for the antebellum period.

This chapter has aimed to demonstrate the theatrical intention of Simpson's brilliant and *sui generis* book to convey and preserve the national tone for African

Americans and "friends to the slave" in the nineteenth century. Written before the Civil War, *The Emancipation Car* contains vivid intimations—in the form of dreams, dramatizations, and predictions—of the bloodshed and violence ahead. There is ample evidence that Simpson's "airs" were publicly performed, especially in the antebellum period and war years, as encouragement to keep hopes alive for the anti-slavery cause. These performances were designed to express protest, fellowship, and optimism for the forging of a better and more just nation. In the twenty-first century, with increased public outcry for the rights of African Americans, it would be inspirational to stage them as an act of reclamation, retrieval, and respect for the history and power of African American theatre. By "singing what would be death to speak" in live performances for the benefit of the community, Simpson's *oeuvre* demonstrates the instrumental and longstanding role of theatre in forging an anti-racist vision of American national identity.

Notes

1. Because resources on Simpson are limited, Works Cited shares key critical materials on Simpson to aid further research. Though the resources are few, their quality is exemplary. Eaklor provides outstanding historical and political background, including excellent discussion of literal and metaphorical railroad imagery, and well-detailed biblio-biographical information on Simpson's life and writings. Marble's wonderful podcast offers a sensitive and expert musical analysis of Simpson's dialogues with contemporaneous songs. Mabry elaborates in excellent detail on the variety of literary and conceptual methods used by Simpson to counter and transform popular songs of the era. Sandler aptly places Simpson in the Romantic tradition while explaining the impact of race and nationalism on the autonomy of the lyric subject. Karlsberg's commentary on Simpson eloquently stresses his contemporary value and the references provide very helpful further resources. Sherman must also be mentioned for her brilliantly researched and insistent attention to nineteenth-century Black poets, including Simpson. See *Invisible Poets: Afro-Americans of the Nineteenth Century* (Sherman 1974) and *African American Poetry of the Nineteenth Century: An Anthology* (Sherman 1992).

2. The first volume, titled *Original Anti-Slavery Songs*, was attributed to "Joshua M'C Simpson, A Colored Man" (1852). The expanded volume, titled *The Emancipation Car: Being an Original Composition of Anti-Slavery Ballads Composed Exclusively for the Under Ground Rail Road* (1874) contains much of the material of the first volume and a substantial quantity of new poetry, prose, and hybrid forms. Authorship is attributed to J. Mc. C. Simpson. It's important to note important details in both titles: the first volume (only) identifies the author's race. The second volume acknowledges the Under Ground Railroad and political agenda of the contents. Both volumes boldly stress the word "original" and the author's name, emphasizing individuality and ownership, in an era when literacy and authorial claims were dangerous and equivocal for African Americans. While Simpson intended these works for public use and agency, he wished his claim of original creativity to be credited and preserved.

3   *The Routledge Companion to African American Theatre and Performance* (Perkins et al. 2019) offers an outstanding overview of the history, key issues, and current state of African American theatre that extends far beyond the capacity of this brief chapter, and provides excellent further context.
4   In *Slave Songs and the Birth of African American Poetry* (Ramey 2008), I discuss the perturbation caused by the spirituals because they were emotive, performative, musical, and communal. They were roundly criticized for their "primitivism" and lack of "propriety" as sacred music by critics such as George Pullen Jackson, Newman I. White, and John F. Watson. A major theme of *A History of African American Poetry* is that this genre is inherently theatrical—deriving from African survivals and the spirituals as the original African American cultural products—as live performances which combine interactivity, orality, physicality, music, words, and dance. Analysis of Simpson's writing appears on pages 76–7 and 89–90.

Works Cited

Eaklor, Vicki L. (1989), "Introduction to Joshua Simpson's *Original Anti-Slavery Songs*," *The Journal of Black Sacred Music*, Vol. 3, No. 1, pp. 14–21. Available online: https://doi.org/10.1215/10439455-3.1.14. Last accessed August 27, 2020.

Karlsberg, Jesse P. (2020), "To the White People of America (1854)," *Southern Spaces*, June 30. Available online: https://southernspaces.org/2020/white-people-america-1854/. Last accessed August 27, 2020.

Mabry, Tyler Grant (2011), "Seizing the Laurels: Nineteenth-Century African American Poetic Performance," Ph.D. Dissertation, The University of Texas at Austin, December.

Marble, Matt (2020), Secret Sound 16, "The Emancipation Car (Joshua McCarter Simpson)." Available online: https://mattmarble.net/blogs/secret-sound-a606f93d-a87d-4175-9c68-ff824542d887/posts/secret-sound-16-the-emancipation-car-joshua-mccarter-simpson-4286711f-1d2a-41a5-acd2-f09340f70d9e. Last accessed August 27, 2020.

Peterson, Bernard L., Jr. (1997), *The African American Theatre Directory, 1816–1960: A Comprehensive Guide to Early Black Theatre Organizations, Companies, Theatres, and Performing Groups*, Westport, CT: Greenwood Press. Kindle edition.

Perkins, Kathy A., Sandra L. Richards, Renée Alexander Craft, and Thomas F. DeFrantz (2019), *The Routledge Companion to African American Theatre and Performance*, London and New York: Routledge.

Ramey, Lauri (2019), *A History of African American Poetry*, Cambridge, UK: Cambridge University Press.

Ramey, Lauri (2008), *Slave Songs and the Birth of African American Poetry*, New York: Palgrave Macmillan.

Sandler, Matt (2020), *The Black Romantic Revolution: Abolitionist Poets at the End of Slavery*, London: Verso.

Sherman, Joan R. (1974), *Invisible Poets: Afro-Americans of the Nineteenth Century*, Urbana, IL: University of Illinois Press.

Sherman, Joan R. (1992), *African American Poetry of the Nineteenth Century: An Anthology*, Urbana, IL: University of Illinois Press.

Simpson, J. Mc. C. ([1854] 1874), *The Emancipation Car, Being an Original Composition of Anti-Slavery Ballads, Composed Exclusively for the Under Ground Rail Road*, Zanesville, OH: Sullivan & Brown; Miami: Mnemosyne Publishing Co. Reprint, 1969.

Simpson, Joshua M'C, A Colored Man (1852), *Original Anti-Slavery Songs*, Zanesville, OH: Printed for the author.
Simpson, Joshua McCarter (J. M'C. S.) (1848), "Strike, but Hear Me!," Letter to the Editor (Rev. M.R. Hull), *The Clarion of Freedom*, New Concord, OH, July 28. Available online: http://henryburke1010.tripod.com/id78.html. Last accessed August 26, 2020.
Simpson, J. McC., M.D. (n.d.), Identifier: A0286-00572, 7 Sheet Music Broadsides, Missouri Historical Society, Civil War Collection, Box 11, Sc-Te. Available online: http://collections.mohistory.org/resource/221476. Last accessed August 26, 2020.

7

Performing Trauma: Narratives of Rupture in Caryl Churchill's *Seven Jewish Children*

Mamata Sengupta

If words could effectively summarize the trauma of the Jewish existence, then one would resort to using terms like alienation, non-belonging, and deterritorialization. There can be little doubt regarding the severity, extent, and persistence of the crisis that the Jews were exposed to right from their distant origin in the Middle East. The seemingly eternal displacement, the never-arrived Promised Land, and the devastating wars have scarred their individual experiences and collective consciousness to such an extent that even today any representative Jewish reaction to life and the world exhibits profound traumatic imprints of fear and insecurity. The British playwright Caryl Churchill deals with this terrible identity crisis of the Jews in her 2009 play *Seven Jewish Children*. I shall re-read the play as a specimen of trauma documentation wherein a group of trauma victims ponder the necessity, propriety, and justification of constructing an official history of their community which can both inform the young generation about their heritage of loss and warn them of the many pitfalls lying ahead in time. I shall also discuss how narrating the story of the "ostracized" Jews provides Churchill with an opportunity to highlight the problems and the prospects of history-making—how power structures in society define, produce, and strategize knowledge through often arbitrary selection and organization of historical truths so as to serve the purposes or fulfill the aspirations of the dominant social group.

The word "trauma" can be defined as the real or perceived experience of some debilitating physical/psychological injury. Traumatic exposures at once disturb the victims' physical equilibrium by inflicting injuries and also disrupt their sense of selfhood through an acute awareness of purposelessness, non-belonging, and irreparable damage. Doris Brothers defines "trauma" as "a complex phenomenon involving both a shattering experience and efforts at restoration" (Brothers 2008: 48–9). According to Brothers, the "traumatized person" exists as "an exile, someone who is forced to live in a world that is no longer recognizable" (Brothers 2008: 46). In fact, trauma manifests itself more through its effects on the victims than through what it was caused by. As Richard B. Ulman and Brothers put it, "The full unconscious meaning of trauma is not completely captured by the shattering of self. Part of the meaning for the subject lies in the unsuccessful (faulty) attempt to restore the self as a center of organizing activity" (Ulman and Brothers 1988: 7). This fact or fear of failure to "restore the self" to its lost "centrality" is what generates in trauma victims an anxiety disorder, best known as Post-Traumatic Stress Disorder, which overpowers them with a profound doubt regarding their ability to survive the insurmountable odds of the world.

This loss of self-confidence generates a distrust of the world which both caused the trauma and anchored the self. As Kirby Farrell avers, "In trauma, terror overwhelms not just the self, but the ground of the self, which is to say our trust in the world" (Farrell 1998: xii). This rupture of trust makes the traumatic memory largely non-declarative whereby the conscious subject is temporarily spared from the terror of discussing the event. According to B.A. van der Kolk, this is a state of "speechless terror" in which the victim, in spite of remembering the incident, "lacks words to describe what has happened" (Kolk 1996: 203). This inability of the victims to express their sense of disruption in a coherent narrative, coupled with their need to express it, tortures them so greatly that it often leads to the blurring of the distinctions between the conscious and the subconscious memories. This blurring signals the breakdown of the victims' self-identity whereby repressed traumatic memories start infiltrating the realms of their consciousness and the victims compulsively revisit their experience of the trauma. This cycle further alienates the trauma victims from their world.

Written in response to the 2008-9 Gaza crisis, *Seven Jewish Children* was first performed at the Royal Court Theatre in London on February 6, 2009. It is a conversation play recording the voices of some anonymous guardians of Jewish children who attempt to retell their history to their wards. What problematizes this telling is the guardians' awareness that informing the children about Jewish history runs the risk of exposing them to the same trauma which scarred their own memory. The gender of the children here further complicates the issue. The fact that these "children" are all girls (as evinced by the guardians' use of the feminine pronoun) makes them vulnerable to the dual trauma of racial (as Jewish children) and racio-gendered (as Jewish *female* children) marginalization. Moreover, as Stef Craps claims, it is women's time-honored role as the preserver and transmitter of "traditions" and "cultural heritage" that causes the guardians to take "greater care" while telling things to them (Craps 2014: 189).

The guardians of Churchill's play agree to select and organize their history before it is passed onto the children. However, the more they engage in this process of history-making, the more fissures that develop in their narrative. As David Lane asserts, these guardians "are simultaneously heroes and villains. Their pride is at stake but they are aware of their own fallibility and therefore show a confused humility, rather than Machiavellian cunning" (Lane 2010: 51). This confusion becomes evident when the guardians start reconstructing their history beginning from the Holocaust and the immigration to Palestine through the creation of Israel, the expulsion of Palestinian Arabs, the 1948 Arab-Israeli War, the dispute over water, and the South Lebanon Conflict to the First and the Second Intifada, the building of the West Bank Barrier, the Palestinian suicide attacks, Hamas rocket attacks, and the Operation Cast Lead of 2008-9.

According to Michael Billington, *Seven Jewish Children* is a "heartfelt lamentation" (Billington 2009: n.p.). The play opens with a harrowing picture of the Nazi regime wherein the guardians are seen discussing the need to inform their children about the current danger. In a series of nineteen imperatives, the guardians build up the image of a community in crisis: "Tell her it's a game / Tell her it's serious" (Churchill 2009b: 1). According to Lane, "Charting the rise of a nation from the persecuted to the aggressor, the dialogue is comprised as a list of statements rife with internal conflict over honesty and versus the need to protect" (Lane 2010: 50). The guardians' plan to inform the children of the present situation in the guise of a game-strategy highlights their desperate attempt to palliate the harshness of the reality. This attempt, however, is thwarted by their need to warn the children about the seriousness of the "game." Similarly, the caution not to "frighten" the children gets nullified by the reality of silencing their happy songs (Churchill 2009b: 1).

The second segment of the play narrates a post–Second World War scenario wherein the guardians are seen to reconstruct the history of the Holocaust: "Tell her it was before she was born and she's not in danger" (Churchill 2009b: 2). The decision of the guardians to keep the children informed only about the abilities and achievements of their grandmothers and uncles but not about their deaths serves two purposes. It spares the children of the horror of the Holocaust and helps the guardians forget their traumatic past. However, the repeated emphasis on the "past"-ness of the crimes against the Jews, despite the culture of enforced silence, points up the possibility of a future recurrence.

The third and the fourth segments of the play concern the Jewish immigration to Palestine (1940s) followed by the creation of Israel as the Promised Land after the May 14, 1948 Declaration of David Ben-Gurion, "Tell her it's sunny there / Tell her we're going home" (Churchill 2009b: 2–3). The guardians' emphasis on the "sunny" aspect of the new land reflects their expectations during the creation of Israel. However, establishing their hold on Israel was no easy task. Just a day after Israel was born, it was attacked by the combined military forces of Egypt, Syria, Trans-Jordan, and Iraq, and within days the besiegers were joined by other Arab countries including Yemen, Morocco, Saudi Arabia, and Sudan. What the guardians, therefore, try to hide from the children is a twofold realization: the persistence of their fear of displacement and a newly developed frustration at the failure of the "Promised Land" to match their expectations.

The fifth segment of *Seven Jewish Children* alludes to Israel's victory in the 1948 Arab-Israeli War during which Jordan and East Jerusalem (renamed as the West Bank) were annexed to Israel while Egypt captured the Gaza Strip and a temporary border called the "Green Line" was drawn (Churchill 2009b: 4). In this section, the enemy whom the "we" of the play, that is, the Israelis, turn "back" from their land refers to the millions of Palestinians who were expelled from the "new land" (the captured territories) by the Israeli forces.

The sixth segment of the play highlights the 1960s dispute over water between Israel and the occupied Palestine: "Tell her it's our water, we have the right" (Churchill 2009b: 5). The section refers to a time when water was being rationed to the Palestinians, and they had no rights to drill wells and/or repair the already existing ones. The situation worsened with Israel's 1964 National Water Carrier project against which the Arabs launched their Headwater Diversion Plan to divert two of Jordan's water sources to the Yarmouk River. This provoked Israel to launch serial attacks on the Arab States which started the 1967 Six-Day War. This was followed by the devastating Operation Litani (1978) and the Lebanon War (1982) that established Israel as the new perpetrator of violence in the Middle East (Dunstan 2009). This is precisely the guilt that haunts the guardians throughout Churchill's play and accounts for their need to suppress certain portions of their history from the children.

The history that the guardians ultimately pass on to the children serves three different purposes. First, it establishes the right of the Jews on Israel. Second, it asserts their ability and right to protect their families. And third, it justifies all the Jewish atrocities against the enemies: "Tell her we're entitled" (Churchill 2009b: 5–6). However, the guardians' sense of guilt resurfaces again with the reference to the word "peace" in "Tell her we want peace," and they are immediately compelled to shift their attention to discussing happier prospects like going "swimming" (6).

Seven Jewish Children has been criticized for its putative "anti-Semitism." The BBC declined to air this play for "impartiality reasons" (Dowell 2009: n.p.). Critic Howard Jacobson condemned Churchill's "wantonly inflammatory" take on a serious issue (Jacobson 2009: n.p.). These accusations were primarily directed against the final section of the play where a series of thirty-five directives highlights the cause of the guardians' guilt ("tell her to be proud of the army"; "Tell her they want their children killed to make people sorry for them"). Churchill reacts to such accusations in her letter to the American playwright-director Ari Roth where she states, "the play faces charges that it shows 'a terrible historical irony, that Jews once under siege are now laying siege.' I'm not sure why that is a charge. It seems a fact" (Churchill 2009a: n.p.). Evidently, Churchill is responding to the Gaza Crisis, but her concerns as an artist extend far beyond the Palestinians or the Israelis to include the entirety of humanity. Like Arthur Rimbaud's "poet" who stands "responsible for humanity, even for the animals" (Rimbaud in Ellmann and Feidleson 1965: 204), Churchill here sees Gaza as a metaphor for the entire world where, as Craps has put it, power struggle reigns supreme and any particular group's "monopoly on victimhood" is supremely impossible (Craps 2014: 186). Churchill admits to this stance: "I am not going to pretend that I am not critical of Israel, or that the play was not written out of anger about Gaza. But it was also written out of a more complicated anguish about the whole history, which I know is shared by many Jewish people outside Israel as well as many Israelis" (Churchill 2009a: n.p.). The transformation of the Jews from victims to victimizers after the creation of Israel underlines the corrupting nature of power. As Churchill herself puts it, *Seven Jewish Children* is about "people who are aggressive because they (do) not surprisingly feel defensive" (Churchill 2009a: n.p.). The play works through shifting the audience's attention from one Jewish trauma narrative to another, and at the same time, suggesting the possibility of many other similar undocumented narratives through its reference to the guardians' apparent lack of interest in the sufferings of the Palestinians.

The final section of *Seven Jewish Children* highlights the condition of modern Israel from the Hamas attacks to the December 27, 2008 bombing of Gaza. It traces how Israel has become a virtual panopticon for its own children who are allowed to watch "cartoons" but not "the news" of the "rocket attacks" or "killings" (Churchill 2009b: 6). This injunction is more political than parental; for, it is prompted by the guardians' need to hide the Israeli atrocities on the Palestinians from the children. The next dictate that the children should not know about their cousins' refusal to join "the army" serves two purposes—a) it guards the children against an example of political disobedience (a citizen refusing to perform the national duty), and b) it allows the guardians to forget their own failure to control a socially "unwanted" behavior (6). Hence, recounting Israel's victory over the Hamas militants becomes the guardians' only tool to boost their self-confidence and sense of security.

As the guardians grow increasingly uncomfortable with Israel's new political stance, their commands become more self-contradictory. The play ends with a series of confused prohibitions regarding what should or should not be told to the children as explanations for the brutalities done by the Israelis to their opponents: "Tell her I don't care if the world hates us, tell her we're better haters" (Churchill 2009b 6). The guardians' repeated stress on distrusting the television news is not due to their fear of rumors but because the news might inform the children about the Israeli actions on the Palestinians—that the Gaza attack also killed innocent "babies" and the Palestinians did not "want their children killed" to draw political sympathy. Similarly, their desperate attempts to justify Israel's political stance, in statements such as the Israelis have "got nothing to be ashamed of," underline the guardians' own sense of guilt. The final lines of the play uttered by the guardians reiterate their long-felt need to safeguard the children from all traumatic exposures: "Tell her we love her. Don't frighten her."

Seven Jewish Children hints at trauma on three major levels—a) mythical (the Exodus), b) historical (the Jewish experience from 1880 to the Second World War), and c) personal (the Jewish experience from 1960s to 2008-9). To add to this, there is also a traumatic restraint on what and what not to share with the children. In fact, it is the guardians' awareness of their community's role in inflicting violence on the Palestinians which worries them regarding the mode and extent of narrating their history to the children. While an edited version of their history featuring the Jews as mere victims seems to resolve these issues, the guardians are insecure about the effect of this "telling" on the children. Since children are completely dependent on their guardians for their survival, any violent incident threatening their guardians' safety exposes the children to a similar kind of threat. Interfamilial sharing of personal stories often takes the form of what Efraim Sicher calls "working through trauma" whereby traumatic memories travel from one person/generation to another (Sicher 1998: 13). Marianne Hirsch names this transferred traumatic memory "postmemory" and explains it as an emotional experience that the "generation after" (the children, in this case) inherits from "the personal, collective, and cultural trauma of those who came before" (the guardians) (Hirsch 2008). The "generation after," comments Hirsch, who inherits this "postmemory," primarily "by means of the stories, images, and behaviors among which they grew up," compulsively carries it forward to the next generation, exposing them to a similar sense of insecurity and loss (Hirsch 2008).

It is this burden of "postmemory" that transforms the second and third generation trauma survivors into what Dina Wardi calls "Memorial Candles" with no identity or life of their own, only carrying on an extinguished existence (Wardi 1992: 28). Churchill here displays her creative multivocalism by merging multiple disrupted narratives of the Jewish trauma victims with often overlapping "silence-acts." If the speech of the guardians vocalizes the historical realities which formed and framed the present Israeli existence, then their studied "silence" about the Palestinian children constructs what Warren Motte calls a "negative narrative" that highlights issues that are unrecorded in history (Motte 2013: 56). The guardians' unwillingness to talk about the condition of the Palestinians' children and their frantic attempts to justify the Israeli military acts highlight their complicit and corrupt nature. Their silence in the play becomes Churchill's tool to register her protest against the Israeli violence: "Israel has done lots of terrible things in the past but what happened in Gaza seems particularly extreme" (Churchill 2009a: n.p.).

It is this capacity of Churchill, the playwright, to speak for different characters at the same time, what we call her "creative multivocalism," which distinguishes *Seven Jewish Children* as a study in trauma expression. Instead of taking sides with one at the cost of the other, Churchill attempts to see the play as what Eleanor Catton calls "purified version[s] of real life, an extraction, an essence of human behaviour that is stranger and more tragic and more perfect than everything that is ordinary about me and you" (Catton 2010: 127). *Seven Jewish Children* is extremely political in nature, as it strongly condemns the 2008–9 Gaza attacks. But this condemnation is neither political nor racial but humanitarian. Churchill herself clarifies that the play wants to "share" the "hope of peace and reconciliation through talking about these things, and through being able to disagree with each other with understanding" (Churchill 2009a: n.p.); for it is only through "disagreement with understanding" that we can hope to identify better alternatives for ourselves, and it is only through such alternatives that we can hope to survive in "peace" and progress.

Works Cited

Billington, Michael (2009), "Seven Jewish Children," *The Guardian*, February 11. Available online: https://www.theguardian.com/stage/2009/feb/11/seven-jewish-children. Last accessed September 6, 2019.

Brothers, Doris (2008), *Towards a Psychology of Uncertainty: Trauma-Centered Psychoanalysis*, New York and London: The Analytic Press.

Catton, Eleanor (2010), *The Rehearsal*, London: Granta.

Churchill, Caryl (2009a), Letter to Ari Roth, Theatre J Blog, March 24. Available online: https://theatrejblogs.wordpress.com/2009/03/24/caryl-churchill-speaks-part1/?blogsub =confirming#blogsubscription-3. Last accessed February 24, 2020.

Churchill, Caryl (2009b), *Seven Jewish Children—A Play for Gaza*, London: Nick Hern Books.

Craps, Stef (2014), "Holocaust Memory and the Critique of Violence in Caryl Churchill's *Seven Jewish Children: A Play for Gaza*," in Jane Kilby and Antony Rowland, eds., *The Future of Testimony: Interdisciplinary Perspectives on Witnessing*, Abingdon, UK: Routledge, pp. 179–92.

Dowell, Ben (2009), "BBC Rejects Play on Israel's History for Impartiality Reasons," *The Guardian*, March 16. Available online: https://www.theguardian.com/media/2009/ mar/16/bbc-rejects-caryl-churchill-israel. Last accessed August 9, 2016.

Dunstan, Simon (2009), *The Six-Day War 1967: Sinai,* London: Bloomsbury.
Farrell, Kirby (1998), *Post-Traumatic Culture: Injury and Interpretation in the Nineties*, Baltimore and London: The Johns Hopkins University Press.
Hirsch, Marianne (2008), "Columbia University Press Interview with Marianne Hirsch." Available online: https://cup.columbia.edu/author-interviews/hirsch-generation-postmemory. Last accessed June 28, 2020.
Jacobson, Howard (2009), "Let's See the 'Criticism' of Israel for What It Really Is," *The Independent*, February 18. Available online: http://www.independent.co.uk/voices/commentators/howard-jacobson/howardjacobson-letrsquos-see-the-criticism-of-israel-for-what-it-really-is-1624827. Last accessed March 22, 2013.
Kolk, B. A. van der (1996), "The Complexity of Adaptation to Trauma: Self-Regulation, Stimulus Discrimination, and Characterological Development," in B. A. van Der Kolk, A. C. McFarlane, and L. Weisaeth, eds., *Traumatic Stress: The Effects of Overwhelming Experience on Mind, Body, and Society*, London and New York: Guilford, pp. 182–213.
Lane, David (2010), *Contemporary British Theatre*, Edinburgh: Edinburgh University Press.
Motte, Warren (2013), "Negative Narrative," *L'Esprit Créateur*, Vol. 53, No. 2, pp. 56–66.
Rimbaud, Arthur (1965), "Letter to Georges Izambard and Paul Demeny [1871]," in Richard Ellmann and Charles Feidelson, Jr., eds., *The Modern Tradition: Backgrounds of Modern Literature*, New York: Oxford University Press, pp. 202–5.
Sicher, Efraim (1998), "Introduction," in Efraim Sicher, ed., *Breaking Crystal: Writing and Memory after Auschwitz*, Champaign: University of Illinois Press, pp. 1–16.
Ulman, Richard B. and Doris Brothers (1988), *The Shattered Self: A Psychoanalytic Study of Trauma*, London and New York: Routledge.
Wardi, Dina (1992), *Memorial Candles: Children of the Holocaust*, trans. Naomi Goldblum, London and New York: Routledge.

8

Two Truths and a Lie: Theatrical Form, Plays about Terrorism, and the Search for Understanding

Lindsey Mantoan

Since 9/11, there has been a surge in verbatim theatre pieces investigating international violence and terrorism. In the UK, especially, at least a dozen documentary plays examine the 2003 invasion of Iraq, the war in Afghanistan, the trauma experienced by veterans, and radicalism. The rise of verbatim theatre has in turn led to an abundance of scholarship about the documentary form and its effects, including *Get Real: Documentary Theatre Past and Present* (edited by Alison Forsyth and Chris Megson, 2009), *Dramaturgy of the Real on the World Stage* (edited by Carol Martin, 2010), and *Political and Protest Theatre After 9/11* (edited by Jenny Spencer, 2012).

This chapter looks closely at three plays investigating why people become terrorists: Gillian Slovo's *Another World: Losing Our Children to the Islamic State*, Robin Soans's *Talking to Terrorists,* and Omar El-Khairy and Nadia Latif's *Homegrown*. Formally, *Another World* and *Talking to Terrorists* are verbatim plays—the actors strive for realistic representations of existing people; they speak verbatim words; and the multimedia elements of the performance investigate the ways journalism and social media influence, and are influenced by, terrorism. *Homegrown*, however, is an immersive, site-specific experience in a high school. I argue that realistic verbatim theatre is broadly perceived as the safest methodology for investigating the mind of a terrorist, and I evaluate its usefulness against another theatrical mode that might be riskier, but holds the potential to teach audiences about terrorism in different and important ways. The dramaturgy of verbatim plays relies on the conflict inherent in terrorism and radicalism, and hearing actual words spoken by terrorists and their families can be profoundly instructive. And yet, the devised nature of *Homegrown*, its staging of Islamophobia, its exploration of youth culture, and its focus on audience interaction are more artistically interesting and potentially politically useful.

This chapter doesn't dismiss the value of verbatim theatre—on the contrary, it delves into the most profound moments of these two verbatim plays—but it does ask what focusing on this one theatrical form might miss. I ultimately posit that theatre artists seeking to engage in activism or reconciliation should consider other forms besides verbatim theatre.

Gillian Slovo's *Another World: Losing Our Children to Islamic State*

The UK's National Theatre produced Gillian Slovo's *Another World: Losing Our Children to Islamic State* in 2016, two years after Abu Bakr al-Baghdadi announced a caliphate stretching from Aleppo in Syria to Diyala in Iraq. As verbatim theatre drawn from interviews, the play features stories from three Belgian women whose children joined Daesh.[1] The play also includes testimony from counterterrorist activists and scholars, a US general in charge of combatting Daesh, British Prime Minister David Cameron, and four anonymous university students in the UK who speak about the recruiting tactics they've witnessed.

The play puts forward a range of suggestions about why and how young people can be so easily radicalized, most of them focused on the brutality of the Assad regime in Syria and the appeal of any organization resisting Assad, the geopolitical hegemony of the United States, and the discrimination that Muslims in Europe and the United States face. In the play, young Muslims living in Europe discuss feeling alienated from their communities, being treated with fear while on public transportation, and experiencing surveillance by teachers who are required by law to report any student who might be remotely suspicious. Following lines from David Cameron, then-Prime Minister of Britain, about British values and respect for democracy, these students say, "[Those values] are shared all around the world. Why do we have to put a label on it that this is British," and "it's making us feel more segregated" (Slovo 2016: 44). Juxtaposing speeches from public figures with responses by Muslims in Europe, the play suggests that a decades-long war with Islam by the West played a large role in creating the conditions in which young men and women joined Daesh.

As the problem is more generally with theatrical responses to twenty-first-century military conflicts, there was little formal or aesthetic innovation in *Another World*. As a piece of staged journalism, the play offers new insights into the historical conditions that gave rise to Daesh, from the Sykes-Picot agreement to the Cold War. Much of Nicolas Kent's staging at the National Theatre involves actors seated in rolling office chairs positioned in front of a series of screens onto which archival videos are projected. In her review of the National Theatre production, Aleks Sierz at *The Arts Desk* finds the production inert: "No one interrogates anyone, and no one asks why some Islamists become violent killers. There's a real failure of the liberal imagination in this play" (Sierz 2016). Thus, the audience might be watching a trial or taking in a series of compelling stories, but their spectatorial position remains passive.

In analyzing verbatim theatre, Carol Martin finds that "The result is a genre that can invite contemplation of the ways in which histories are told—a form of Brechtian distancing that asks spectators to simultaneously understand the theatrical, the real, and the simulated, each as its own form of truth" (Martin 2010: 22). Indeed, Slovo's approach to the play seems to be that of a scholar on a fact-finding mission to unearth the roots of radicalization. The stories represented in *Another World* educate audiences about what is arguably the most dangerous terrorist organization of the twenty-first century. And unlike Sierz's review, Sarah Hemming of the *Financial Times* called the National Theatre's production an "absorbing, painstakingly composed evening that offers some insights into one of the gravest challenges of our age" (Hemming 2016). Thus, it's possible the piece can be both inert and also offer vital insights.

The play's unique contribution to the conversation about Daesh comes from the perspective of the mothers who have lost their children to the caliphate. The guilt they feel about not recognizing the signs sooner, or not understanding what their children were missing that they filled with Daesh's philosophies, is haunting. When Samira (likely a name Slovo changed to protect anonymity) explains how it felt to learn her daughter Nora had gone to Syria, she says, "It took me 18 years to bring her up. And in a few months, they completely changed her. Completely" (Slovo 2016: 20). The play encourages audiences to identify with parents whose misunderstood children seek out new communities for connections—a mundane phenomenon that suddenly has violent consequences when the community is a terrorist organization. In this way, the play avoids allowing audiences to simply dismiss the radicalized children as "bad eggs." The play concludes with Geraldine, the mother of Anis, explaining that her son had gone to Syria to help people, and eventually when Daesh asked him to participate in violence and he refused, they shot him. In this way, the play ends not on a hopeful note but with the implication that terrorism might be impossible to escape.

The central question *Another World* considers, why would anyone join a terrorist organization, has no easy answer and requires self-reflection and a nuanced understanding of global politics. *Another World* foregrounds instruction over a more expressive, affective theatrical experience. Global emotional fatigue, the result of two decades facing international terrorism after 9/11, has left many artists and audiences with little capacity to grapple with its roots. Given the global breadth of Daesh's terrorist attacks, perhaps positioning audiences to *feel* about the organization instead of *think* about it would be too much for a piece of theatre to ask. But I wonder whether incorporating emotions into the historiographical project behind plays like *Another World* might hold more political potential.

Talking to Terrorists by Robin Soans

Robin Soans spent a year researching his play *Talking to Terrorists*, which premiered at the Royal Court in 2005. Given the challenges of attempting to interview active terrorists, the play focuses on ex-members of various terrorist groups, including Uganda's National Resistance Army (NRA), the Kurdish Workers Party (PKK), the Irish Republican Army (IRA), the Ulster Volunteer Force (UVF), and the Al Aqa Martyrs Brigade (AAB), and these characters are signified in the script by the initials of the organization of which they were members. With such a diversity of geographical, religious, and political contexts of these groups, the play puts forward multiple origin stories for radicalization. IRA's grandparents were both in the organization, so joining felt natural for him. Some of the former terrorists suffered bullying, unjust imprisonment, or domestic abuse, and these experiences left them both jaded and vulnerable to influence. Drugs played a role in ensuring loyalty to terrorist organizations and enduring violent tendencies. The ex-terrorists, the Ambassador character, and the

Colonel character share stories about children abducted, forced to kill their parents, and subsumed into the life of a child soldier.

Similar to *Another World*'s argument that radicalization cannot simply be attributed to some kind of innate evil, this play demonstrates the ways in which circumstances drive terrorism. The Colonel describes an epiphany he experienced at age twenty-eight: "I realized that if I had been [somewhere else], I would have been a terrorist. And that's an understanding every soldier should have. None of this is personal" (Soans 2005: 35). These former terrorists lacked control over their lives, whether because of governmental upheaval, poverty, or racial/sectarian violence. Most of the stories represented in the play involve a loss of bodily autonomy, either through abduction, imprisonment, or torture. Characters describe getting captured by law enforcement or a terrorist organization, beaten and raped, drugged, and ultimately indoctrinated into an ideology that inspired feelings of superiority and personal invincibility.

Unlike Slovo's *Another World*, this play delves into the emotions a terrorist feels during an act of violence—and is generally a more emotional play. Edward, listed in the play simply as "a psychologist," testifies that "Terrorists certainly aren't thinking about the day after tomorrow. They're enjoying the moment. Even if it's ghastly, it's invigorating. It's what's called a 'peak experience'" (Soans 2005: 19). Perhaps unsurprisingly, he asserts, "the key to the ideology of violence is to see your enemy as sub-human" (Soans 2005: 35). While *Another World* suggests that emotional connection drives Muslims to Daesh, *Talking to Terrorists* argues that dehumanization lies at the root of radicalization. On the surface, these arguments might seem at odds; taken together, a clear "us versus them" ordering of the world roots terrorism as an ideology in the minds of young people.

As with most verbatim theatre, the theatricality of *Talking to Terrorists* rests primarily in the editing, ordering, and juxtaposing of interview text. The main focus of Act 2 is the 1984 Brighton hotel bombing, told through the perspective of IRA, Ex-Secretary of State 2 (S.S.2), and His Wife, wheel-chair bound after the blast. The layering of this testimony and the way this event unfolds denies the audience an easy conclusion about the players involved. Having heard in Act 1 about IRA's torture at the hands of three military policemen who nearly shattered his spine, the audience has already gone through the exercise of sympathizing with him. Learning in Act 2 about his role as the "Brighton Bomber" (the character clearly represents Patrick Magee), and hearing from two of his victims, unsettles presumptions about the man who, in another play, might facilely occupy the position of villain. Instead, IRA describes sitting down and talking with Jo Berry, the daughter of one of his victims. Questions of forgiveness and reconciliation haunt the ending, which includes a meeting between IRA and UVF, former members of two organizations whose primary objective was to obliterate the other. The play title's emphasis on "talking" drives its conclusion, which posits discourse as vital to counterterrorism.

Reviews of the Royal Court's production of *Talking to Terrorists* were mixed, with Michael Billington calling it in *The Guardian* "the most important new play we have seen this year" (Billington 2005) and Matt Wolf of *Variety* dubbing it "necessary and important. And, rather more surprisingly, fairly dull" (Wolf 2005). Given its lack of surreal visuals, expressionist soundscape, or other compelling aesthetic strategies, the most fascinating claim verbatim theatre—whether *Talking to Terrorists* or *Another World*—makes involves the relation between objective truth and personal experience. The postmodern assertion that the truth is unstable, subject to manipulation, and always unknowable, opens a lacuna in what audiences can ever truly know. Verbatim theatre, Carol Martin believes, represents not only a desire for something stable to hold onto, but also the very real ways in which people organize world views around "the assertion that there is something to be known in addition to the dizzying kaleidoscopic array of competing truths" (Martin 2010: 4). Essentially, *Another World* and *Talking to Terrorists* put forward subjective experiences as a pathway toward meaning, as unstable and contradictory as those experiences might be. These plays rehearse the kinds of conversations that hold more potential than military violence to uproot the conditions that give rise to terrorism.

Homegrown

Originally commissioned by the National Youth Theatre of London in 2015, the immersive and site-specific play *Homegrown* is the product of Omar El-Khairy and Nadia Latif's research and writing, along with devised work done in rehearsals with over one hundred students between the ages of fourteen and eighteen. Set in a high school, *Homegrown* attempts to excavate the racial, class, and gender dynamics that might lead a young person to join Daesh, with scenes of shocking Islamophobia juxtaposed with exchanges between multiple Muslim characters who complicate the representation of their faith and identity. The piece shares formal similarities with Maria Irene Fornes's play *Fefu and Her Friends*, with the audience divided up into groups and ushered by "tour guides" to witness simultaneous performances. Unlike *Fefu*, the performances only happen once and audience members in different groups see different content, "So you'd have to have conversations at the end," says Latif. "There was no way to say everything we wanted to say in an hour and a half so the audience had to converse for us" (qtd in Jupp 2017). The highly theatrical nature of *Homegrown* differs significantly from the verbatim pieces I've analyzed above; there, audiences were framed as jury, here they are framed as active participants in a culture that misunderstands, demeans, objectifies, and oppresses Muslims. *Homegrown* then transforms this complicity into the catalyst for young people embracing extremism.

The original production of *Homegrown* was shut down two weeks before its scheduled opening, with the National Youth Theatre citing "a lack of quality and the need to protect the young people involved in the project" (Gardner 2017). An email from Mark Roseby, the artistic director of the National Youth Theatre, obtained through the Freedom of Information Act, indicates that Roseby wrote to the Arts Council of England saying the creators of *Homegrown* "failed to meet repeated requests for a complete chronological script to justify their extremist agenda" (qtd in Gardner 2017). Roseby's censorship of the performance also seems linked to police involvement, especially given that police officers attended rehearsals and there was a suggestion that they might attend performances in plain clothes.

El-Khairy and Latif's commitment to the project, matched by the cast members, inspired the group to finish rehearsing the show in secret, but attempts to locate other producers were fruitless. The publisher originally slated to print the play withdrew, citing fears of becoming "another Charlie Hebdo" (El-Khairy and Latif 2017: 14). In 2017, El-Khairy and Latif published the play themselves, and in March 2017, forty-four members of the original cast performed an extract of the play at an Index on Censorship event in London; the event also celebrated the script's publication. To date, the play has never seen a full production.

Unlike verbatim theatre, which regularly touts its own realness in the script, *Homegrown* begins with deception: while the audience is gathered in the lobby waiting for the performance to begin, three actors storm through the space and out the front door, ranting things such as "this is bullshit," "I'm done, man," "fuck this show," and "technical difficulty, yeah?" After their exit, the audience remains in the lobby for an uncomfortable amount of time until a voice on a loudspeaker announces that the show has been delayed and inviting people to take a tour of the school while they wait. Tour guides pair with groups designated by colored wristbands (people arriving together are typically separated), and they lead their groups in varying directions into classrooms and other spaces, where audiences experience ten scenes before the voice on the loudspeaker instructs them to come to the theatre for "the show," five final scenes the audience experiences as a single community.

The censorship of *Homegrown* has been well-documented, and Roaa Ali's 2018 article in *The Journal of Applied Theatre and Performance* details not only the police visits to *Homegrown* rehearsals and the conflicting messaging from the National Youth Theatre and the Arts Council, but also the history of censorship in the UK. What I'm primarily interested in here is the play's form and the difference between theatrical excavations of terrorism through verbatim drama and devised immersive performance. Through framing the bulk of the show as a diversion filling time while a technical difficulty is resolved, the creators suggest that audiences are watching every-day life; given the obviousness of this fiction, audiences must then suspend disbelief in a way that verbatim theatre avoids asking of them. Their physical proximity to the actors, and the lack of lighting separating a clearly delineated performance space from a safely protected audience space, generates an intimacy that is both uncomfortable and a new ingredient for engaging with extremism absent from verbatim theatre. Having large portions of the piece devised by the students performing them generates an authenticity that, surprisingly perhaps, cannot be found in verbatim theatre where professional actors play real people.

Homegrown stands as one of the few plays to engage with terrorism through a form other than verbatim. Possibly its censorship has deterred other artists from replicating similar theatre. And arguably, performance as a broad field engages with Muslim representation, radicalization, scapegoating, and Western imperialism more than theatre does. An article in iNEWS chronicles the censorship of *Homegrown* and describes subsequent creative works with similar themes, including Comedian Shazia Mirza's stand-up show *The Kardashians Made Me Do It* about three UK girls who joined ISIS in 2015, Negin Farsad's film *The Muslims Are Coming!*, and Chimene Suleyman's poetry collection *Outside Looking On*. It's worth noting that only one of the pieces the article mentions, Annemiek Van Elst's *Becoming Mohammed*, is a play, and it focuses on family drama rather than radicalization. Artists are hesitant to use theatre as a methodology for studying extremism, and when they do, they rely on the words of experts, victims, or perpetrators. Indeed, the recent *Faceless*, Selina Fillinger's 2019 play based on the real-life trial of a white US woman engaged in an online romance with an ISIS fighter who joins the organization herself, is one of the few original plays to delve into the roots of terrorism.

Questions of authenticity haunt any discussion of terrorism, in part because terrorist acts such as car bombs, IEDs, and suicide bombers, undermine trust in the reality of everyday situations. In the search for a stable truth about terrorism, playwrights and audiences typically turn to verbatim theatre in the hopes that real words by real people might hold a deeper truth than those crafted by artists. This view fails to account for the possibility of unreliable narrators in verbatim pieces, and, as Amanda Stuart Fisher reminds us, "the testimony of traumatized subjects, which verbatim theatre exploits, places great pressure on such literalist construals of truth and authenticity. The 'truth' of the traumatic event is arguably not transparent, knowable or even communicable" (Fisher 2011: 112). If violent incursions into the everyday unsettle expectations of safety—and even truth—retreating to safe theatre that asserts certain truth-claims might not exclusively hold the answers that a community is looking for. Perhaps dangerous theatre—site-specific, durational, improvisational, or otherwise non-traditional—holds important answers as well.

Note

1   Nomenclature for this organization can be hard to pin down. As I wrote in my book *War as Performance*, "Europeans favored the name ISIL, or the Islamic State in Iraq and the Levant; the US news media favored ISIS, or the Islamic State in Iraq and Syria. Some, including me, prefer 'Daesh,' a label with pejorative undertones that irritates the group's leaders" (Mantoan 2018: 13).

Works Cited

Ali, Roaa (2018), "*Homegrown* Censored Voices and the Discursive British Muslim Representation," *Research in Drama Education: The Journal of Applied Theatre and Performance*, Vol. 23, No. 3, pp. 373–88.
Billington, Michael (2005), "Talking to Terrorists," *The Guardian*, July 6. Available online: https://www.theguardian.com/stage/2005/jul/06/theatre. Last accessed January 8, 2020.
El-Khairy, Omar and Nadia Latif (2017), *Homegrown*, London: fly Пrates.
Fisher, Amanda Stuart (2011), "Trauma, Authenticity, and the Limits of Verbatim," *Performance Research*, Vol. 16, No. 1, pp. 112–22.
Gardner, Lyn (2017), "Shut Down But Not Silenced: Isis Play Homegrown Demands to be Staged," *The Guardian*, March 8. Available online: https://www.theguardian.com/stage/theatreblog/2017/mar/08/isis-play-homegrown-national-youth-theatre. Last accessed January 9, 2020.

Hemming, Sarah (2016), "Another World: Losing Our Children to Islamic State, National Theatre (Temporary), London—'Thoughtful, Absorbing'," *Financial Times*, April 18. Available online: https://www.ft.com/content/7fdf2d94-055b-11e6-a70d-4e39ac32c284. Last accessed November 20, 2017.

Jupp, Emily (2017), "Homegrown: The Isis Drama That Was Too Hot to Handle," April 25. Available online: https://inews.co.uk/culture/arts/homegrown-the-isis-drama-that-was-too-hot-to-handle-635422. Last accessed January 9, 2020.

Mantoan, Lindsey (2018), *War as Performance: Conflicts in Iraq and Political Theatricality*, Basingstoke and New York: Palgrave Macmillan.

Martin, Carol, ed. (2010), *Dramaturgy of the Real on the World Stage*, Basingstoke and New York: Palgrave Macmillan.

Sierz, Alekx (2016), "Another World: Losing Our Children to the Islamic State," *The Arts Desk*, April 16. Available online: http://www.theartsdesk.com/theatre/another-world-losing-our-children-islamic-state-national-theatre. Last accessed November 20, 2017.

Slovo, G. (2016), *Another World: Losing Our Children to Islamic State*, London: Oberon Books.

Soans, Robin (2005), *Talking to Terrorists*, London: Oberon Books.

Wolf, Matt (2005), "Talking to Terrorists," *Variety*, July 13. Available online: https://variety.com/2005/legit/reviews/talking-to-terrorists-1200524514/. Last accessed January 8, 2020.

Section Two

Global Perspectives on Theatres of War

1

Unremaking the War: Theatrical Historiography in Alfian Sa'at's *Tiger of Malaya*

Kevin Riordan

The 1943 Japanese propaganda film *The Tiger of Malaya* (*Marai no Tora*) mythologizes the historical figure of Tani Yutaka. The Fukuoka-born Tani moved to British Malaya as a child and became an outlaw-agitator against British rule and eventually an agent for the Japanese Empire. The film narrates his rise to notoriety and concludes with Tani's supposed martyrdom in 1942. But this death is rendered differently in two versions of the film. In the first, ostensibly for Japanese audiences, the final moments focus on Tani's isolated and noble death. Alternatively, in the Southeast Asian version the same death is intercut with the faces of the Malay characters whose lives he affected, played by Japanese actors in brown face. These two endings capture two of the main goals of Japan's "film war," that is, to bolster home-front morale and to frame Japanese aggression in Asia as a liberation from European imperialism. With the second ending director Koga Masato conveys that Tani sacrificed himself for this just Pan-Asian cause; the Japanese were not aggressors but liberators.

Alfian Sa'at's play *Tiger of Malaya* dramatizes five performers' efforts to reconstruct and respond to this film on stage. It was first performed in 2018 by Teater Ekamatra in The Drama Centre Black Box in Singapore's National Library Building. This site lends a useful way of understanding the play's relationship to history and the archive, as Corrie Tan stresses in her review essay: "It's a play within a film within a play, it's a piece of film criticism, it's a research paper on history and representation strutting about in clever theatrical disguise" (Tan 2018). *Tiger of Malaya* is all of these things, though it begins with a simple and familiar premise, of actors gathering to put on a play; dramaturgically, this group is not unlike Shakespeare's Rude Mechanicals or Pirandello's author-searching characters. According to the first-scene exposition, the Asian Film Archive (also housed in the building) has recently restored Koga's 1943 film. As an acknowledgment of the film's historical importance and its troubling legacy, these actors have been commissioned to respond to it in the present.

Following this conceit, the three Singaporean and two Japanese actors discuss and reenact the film's representations. In the early scenes of the play, they talk through the practical challenges of a common language, of casting the parts, and of recreating the film's locations in a modest black box. Before long they stumble on the source material's more complex provocations, asking one another about facts and context and airing personal discomforts in how this Japanese film portrays the invasion and occupation of Malaya. They improvise voices and try out provisional postures, variably assuming the roles of war criminals, victims, and bystanders. At times, they turn their backs to watch the film footage unfold with the audience; more often the 1943 images are screened across their performing bodies. As Tan suggests, the performers' bodies become sites of projection, agents of transmission, and even their own alternative archives—in *Tiger of Malaya*'s strongest moments, the audience's bodies too feel pulled into the piece's present historical reckoning.

In *Performing Remains: Art and War in Times of Theatrical Reenactment*, Rebecca Schneider studies American Civil War reenactors to understand a similar process, what it means to encounter and transmit a history of war through the body. She shows how these nineteenth-century battles are revisited, embodied, and revised in the present using familiar forms of theatrical repetition. Schneider's reenactors recreate the battles in intricate detail, while the performers in *Tiger of Malaya* work at a greater distance: they work in a theatre space, not on the battlefield; they do not stage war itself but its contemporary representations, the early and influential record. While war reenactors value getting closer and closer to the event itself, to almost feel and touch it, Alfian's dramaturgy accentuates the distance and difference of the past that the film invokes. In this play he shows how national histories and traumas are primarily understood through and accessible as already-mediated representations. For better and worse then, they are the more pliable for ongoing evaluation, confrontation, and transformation.

As the characters work through the source film chronologically, *Tiger of Malaya* seems to conclude with the death of Tani Yutaka, but the actor comes back to life—only to die a second time (for the film's other ending). This coup de théâtre provides a clever ending and a parable for the work of theatrical re-enactment. It literally scripts how the historical record can be repeated differently and shows how the present is charged as the pivotal site for revisiting, reinterpreting, and even remaking the record. In Alfian's *Tiger of Malaya*, however, there is still another ending, and with it another death. For the final scene, the stage is cleared and the actor-characters hold a makeshift tribunal. Beyond the film's logic they speak more candidly. They confront one another's complicity in having played these parts.

Stepping into this final scene the character playing Tani Yutaka explicitly comments on the ongoing work: "WHAT YOU CANNOT UNMAKE YOU MUST REMAKE" (the line is displayed in all caps on the surtitle screens) (Alfian 2018: 70). Another character adds, and the screen revises the syntax: "WHAT YOU CANNOT REMAKE YOU MUST UNMAKE" (Alfian 2018: 71). To speak is to rewrite the record. These two provocative statements seem to complement and contradict one another. Yet, in this final scene, more important than their sequence or relative veracity is these statements' co-existence, their compossibility, in and as theatrical performance. These embedded statements on method capture Alfian's commitment to the messy and always-unfinished work of a theatrical historiography, one that blends making, remaking, and unmaking, one that ultimately exposes history as heterogeneous, reiterative, and participatory. In this final scene, with the characters confronting their own actions, the question of history—which had seemed to reside with the 1943 material—is shifted to the tenuous performed present. In this reckoning, this unremaking, there is a shared sense of responsibility, a shared affirmation that the past is not something to represent and remember (or to remember and represent) but something to respond to.

History in the Screening Room

The fiftieth anniversary of the Battle of Singapore in 1992 marked a turning point in how Singapore remembers the Second World War. Singapore's political history was turbulent across the mid-twentieth century and its experience with combat comparatively brief—the subsequent, brutal Japanese occupation is remembered as the primary trauma of the war. A strategic port in British Malaya, Singapore first saw fighting when the Japanese bombed the island on December 8, 1941. The British anticipated the island's subsequent invasion, but were nonetheless caught off-guard when the Japanese came by land rather than sea. They arrived over the Malayan peninsula with many of their troops on bicycles. The bicycle infantry became iconic for this theatre of war, and it is featured in the closing images of *The Tiger of Malaya*. The archival footage of troops heading south to Singapore is spliced with images of the film's characters smiling and waving Japanese flags. This same footage is projected at the play's close, as the two Japanese performers make a final cross and the Singaporean actors smile and wave Singapore flags.

Japanese forces crossed the Straits of Johor on February 8, 1942, and the British surrendered a week later at the Ford Factory near Bukit Timah. Winston Churchill described the battle as the "worst disaster and largest capitulation in British history" (Churchill 1948: 41). The Japanese controlled Singapore (renamed Syonan-to) until 1945, and as they continued to fight on other fronts, their occupation was extractive and characterized by food shortages and cruelty. The military police targeted ethnically Chinese men in particular, the group most likely to threaten their rule. As the characters in *Tiger of Malaya* themselves discuss in the trial scene, 50,000 civilians were massacred in the first weeks of this occupation. The longstanding Singapore Prime Minister Lee Kuan Yew believed 70,000 were killed; the Japanese acknowledge a number closer to 5,000. On stage, as in history, the numbers are named but never quite reconciled.

In *Tiger of Malaya*'s opening scenes, the characters collectively determine the parameters for bringing this film's story into the embodied present. As the film's opening credits are projected, Yudai addresses the audience in Japanese: "In the spirit of sincerity we have come to your country to learn from the past. To trace where the present might split into two different pasts. Or to follow where a single shared past then splits into two different presents" (Alfian 2018: 11). The first sentence offers customary politeness, before the second and third start to grapple with the complexity of the task at hand. In naming the performers' motives, Yudai is uncertain whether it is the past or the present that is shared or split; his lines drift into the inevitable temporal flux of reenactment. When Rebecca Schneider describes similar ideas in her book, the reader can patiently and recursively reckon with their contours and consequences: "Touching time against itself, by bringing time *again and again* out of joint into theatrical, even anamorphic, relief presents the real, the actual, the raw and the true as, precisely, the zigzagging, diagonal, and crookedly imprecise returns of time" (Schneider 2011: 16). With Yudai's quickly spoken lines, the other characters and the audience are not entirely sure if something was lost in translation or whether he himself knows what he means. As with much of the non-English dialogue, the lines are projected on surtitle screens, at which the characters—to comic effect—join the audience in peeking, in order to understand one another.

In the early scenes, the characters' first divergences from the film concern different versions of the truth but not yet on the level of history; their concerns are about their own acting, about character and psychology. In playing a Japanese mother who sees her daughter die, for example, Faridah insists on redoing the scene in Malay, "Crisis. Pain. Stress. That's why I need to use my Mother Tongue. I tangkap the feeling first" (Alfian 2018: 32). Having agreed to this significant revision, the other characters begin to advocate for their own adjustments. Teck objects to murdering the daughter with such little motivation. While the others will not allow his mooted back story, they do agree to shift the staging, to reframe the gunshot death as accidental; doing so seems more psychologically plausible. The actors start to lean into making adjustments to the film, realizing that as the process becomes messier it also becomes more their own.

There are inevitably tensions in this remaking. For one, to comment on or correct a scene is to draw attention to it and therefore to reproduce the ostensibly objectionable representation; to unmake is to remake, and versions of the past proliferate in the play. As they meddle with details like a murderer's motives, Yudai wonders, "if [the killer] becomes less of a villain, does it mean Yutaka also becomes less of a hero?" (Alfian 2018: 36). As they repeat scenes, they "touch time against itself," bringing these events into what Schneider calls anamorphic, theatrical relief. Yudai is the first to realize that their revisions to the past will transform (or will have already transformed) their present in unanticipated ways; he is like a time traveler first sensing the butterfly effect. But the question he asks is left hanging: Saiko already has begun narrating the next film sequence, "We find ourselves now at the Kota Bharu police station" (Alfian 2018: 36). As if subjected to the projector's mechanical motion, the actors must keep up with their source material.

In presenting the footage, the staging style comes to resemble early-twentieth-century film narration. In Japan and Korea in particular, performers called *benshi* and *pyonsa* narrated, translated, and commented on silent films. They often were the cinema's real stars, regardless of the incidental, often imported films playing behind them. In *Tiger of Malaya*, the characters play a similar role, providing necessary information while also becoming more compelling than the film itself with their irreverent commentary and exaggerated impersonations. The characters rarely sync up with their images and instead play against the record. They are less interested in getting it right than in seeing what is produced by getting it wrong. The result is a dense staged montage, in which sounds and images produce something beyond their individual significations. By exposing the very incongruities between the film and the performance, this conceit clears space for the play's stronger statements about historiography, about the performers' unremaking.

After Tani Yutaka leaps out of the Kota Bharu police station window—having realized British complicity in the escape of his sister's killer—Faridah carries the audience across an abrupt transition: "We cut to a scene of Malays dancing around a campfire in the forest. There are musicians playing the violin, the gendang and the gong. What is this scene doing in the film?" (Alfian 2018: 39). This narratively extraneous scene becomes the next source of contention. Yudai and Saiko point out that since the plot revolves around Japanese, Chinese, and British characters, this interlude is a welcome glimpse of Malay characters and culture. Adnan, a Malay Singaporean, bristles at the tokenism, "Why can't they show Malay people as farmers, or boat builders, or teachers? The movie is supposed to be anti-British but it does the same thing the British do. All we tropical natives do is sing and dance" (Alfian 2018: 40).

Despite Adnan's misgivings, Faridah proceeds to sing the film's song, in which she later is joined by Saiko in Japanese. This song, "Terang Bulan," has its own zigzagging history, and further disrupts the company's grasp on what they are transmitting or critiquing. The song's melody is derived from a nineteenth-century French song; it would later resurface in the state anthem of Perak and, in 1957, in Malaysia's national anthem. But in the early 1940s, "no one working on the film would know this. That scene is haunted by the future" (Alfian 2018: 42). Here the characters score the unpredictable cross-currents that their 2018 reenactment of a 1943 film illuminates and disturbs. With the memory of war the present is clearly haunted by the past, but as theatre theory has long insisted, hauntology works in unexpected ways. In this play, the chronological echoes, glitches, and hiccups unmoor the characters' sense of working through the contested past from the relatively stable ground of the present; they begin to recognize the present itself as a haunted history or an imagined future. Yudai's initial cryptic statement about split-presents and shared-pasts retrospectively attains dramatic shape.

In response to this future-haunting melody, Yudai breaks the language convention and speaks in English, "I have a question" (Alfian 2018: 42). He asks the Singaporean characters what has lurked underneath this well-meaning collaboration, "Do you think the Japanese helped Asia to become free?" (Alfian 2018: 42). Their responses differ: "They did plant the idea that Asians could beat the West;" but someone else adds, "They defeated the British but they didn't do it for us … They came to Southeast Asia to steal our natural resources" (Alfian 2018: 42). Yudai asks if this is what is in the history books in Singapore; Teck isn't sure. For the moment print records and conflict are deferred, but they will resurface in the final scene. For now, Adnan helps Yudai into Malay dress for the scene to follow. He is on his way to die, though for neither the first nor last time.

Scenes of Surrender; or, History's Table Read

After Tani Yutaka's second death the stage is mostly cleared, aside from two tables. The Singaporean performers sit at one, the Japanese performers at the other. They have removed their film costumes leaving only the theatre baseline of all black; they could be out of character or in rehearsal or stage hands. Yet even this stripped-down stage picture triggers other associations. In her essay, Corrie Tan notices her own associations, her own projections, taking shape—this is how "our lithe, slippery histories have solidified into static objects" (Tan 2018). These tables on a National Library stage, she explains, carry her elsewhere, to the "scene from the British surrender to the Japanese—a scene hammered into my mind ... by social studies school trips to the ghostly waxworks in the Surrender Chambers at Fort Siloso" (Tan 2018). This scene, this memory, and these tables are all surrogates of others, enmeshed in what Schneider calls theatre and history's "temporal tangle" (Schneider 2011: 10).

The Surrender Chambers at Fort Siloso were constructed in the 1970s. As Paul Rae has written, these wax scenes are also theatrical copies, built from incomplete photographic records. Representing the early 1940s, these 1970s displays introduce another time signature and another contested juncture for Japanese influence in Singapore; after paying a "blood debt," in the 1970s Japan became Singapore's largest foreign investor and trade partner (Rae forthcoming). This haunting wax exhibit represents the Second World War in Malaya as the interval between two scenes of surrender, the British to the Japanese, and the Japanese to the British; as Rae notes, Singaporeans are absent from, as well as anachronistic to, these pivotal scenes. More recently, the National Heritage Board has supplemented these Surrender Chambers with a Surrender Room in a newer museum at the Former Ford Factory. The Former Ford Factory's siting makes up in spatial authenticity what it lacks in wax; *this* room was the actual site of the British surrender. Yet the table in the Surrender Room is an understudy: the actual table is in the Australian War Museum in Canberra (although it has recently been on loan to the National Museum of Singapore). Post-imperial war stories get tangled up with national ones; even the physical markers seem to move.

In *Tiger of Malaya*'s final scene the performers find themselves outside of the film, seated at these tables. They now look at one another and more patiently consider their roles in the unremaking. They have been collaborators—the script plays on the artistic and wartime senses of that word—but they now find themselves apart, spatially opposed. After the dynamic multimedia performance, this final scene is considerably more staid but also more charged; less theatrical in its artifice, it is more dramatic in its acted intensity. The Singaporean characters pursue a formal line of questioning about what they all have just made. Yudai responds to an initial question thoughtfully and Teck curtly counters: "Just answer with a yes or no" (Alfian 2018: 72). The earlier congenial tone falls away. The two Japanese characters, and particularly Yudai (who played Tani), are accused of misrepresenting the war to insidious ends. This courtroom dialogue seeks to fix the facts. Its staging implies that it too will be a scene of surrender.

Challenging the film's representations, and consequently the play's, the prosecution makes the case for still another version of the Tani Yutaka history. They cite accounts that he had converted to Islam, becoming Muhammad Bin Abdullah. When he was twenty he failed a test for Japanese conscription because he could not recognize the Emperor as divine. So they question Yudai as to whether Tani would have joined the Japanese during the war. They defer to other records that suggest that Tani did not bomb a bridge protected by the British (the climactic act of heroism depicted in the film). They name still another account to suggest that he did not die fighting the British at all, but "caught malaria and died in a hospital in Singapore" (Alfian 2018: 72); there is a plaque corroborating this fate in the Japanese Cemetery in Singapore. Accounts and records are spoken of but never summoned. Still, their repeated invocation, coupled with this mise-en-scène, lends this last version of Tani Yutaka a storytelling gravitas that Yudai and Saiko cannot counter, especially with only yes-or-no answers to leading questions. While stripped of the reenactment's theatrical trappings, this scene still follows a familiar script, a set of political theatre conventions understood by the participants and the audience alike. The final scene of *Tiger of Malaya* invokes the uneasy juncture between the sincere and the artificial, the historical and the fictional, at once deploying and critiquing the power of formalized public proceedings. As theatre theorist Herbert Blau puts it, "There is still (as old actors used to tell me) nothing more dramatic than a trial" (Blau 1982: 25).

If the present had seemed the neutral and unmarked time from which to address the 1943 film, this trial casts the present's own historicity in theatrical relief. When Yudai is accused of misrepresenting the past, the specific language of accusation is "fake news" (Alfian 2018: 72). In performance in 2018, the phrase received a laugh and a cringe of recognition, as it dragged the play into the present. While "fake news" gained worldwide traction in 2016 after the American election, it remains a flashpoint in Singapore; according to critics, the spectre of fake news has prompted the government to tighten control on free speech. A couple of months before *Tiger of Malaya*, the historian Thum Ping Tjin was called before Parliament to speak about "Deliberate Online Falsehoods," but was questioned instead for six hours regarding an academic article he wrote on Operation Cold Store (a covert 1963 operation in which 113 people suspected of communism were arrested without trial). In its first performances, *Tiger of Malaya*'s references to "fake news" and the insistence on "yes or no" answers pointed to that recent scene in which academic history was put on trial.

If the waxworks depicting 1945, viewed in 2018, are marked by the interpolated concerns of the 1970s, then "fake news" and what Tan calls the play's "social justice jargon" (Tan 2018) become *Tiger of Malaya*'s own carbon datings for future retrospect. While the contemporaneity of this final scene risks dating the play with its more presentist concerns, Yudai's dissenting speech reexpands the time frame and the historical scope of the trial. In *Tiger of Malaya* he is eventually given the chance to speak. Referring to the Tokyo Trials, he does not dispute the guilt of war criminals but questions the narrative certitudes of a victor's justice. He makes a distinction regarding the function of these trials, between establishing guilt and establishing truth: "I am trying to mount a defence of history itself," because "It is my understanding that history dies in the courtroom" (Alfian 2018: 78). In a theatrical court like this one, history might die—but it can die more than once, and differently, like Yudai's own character. He ends his speech insisting that the historical record receives the same treatment, that it must be unremade. Like theatre, it "must be open to an endless process of revision" (Alfian 2018: 78). With the bicycle infantry and flag-waving footage still to come, this history play does not quite end with this testimony. It remains subject to other crossings and other projections, to its own irreverent unremakings. This performed moment of reckoning must be left ajar, to new hauntings from both the future and the past.

Works Cited

Alfian, Sa'at (2018), *Tiger of Malaya*, unpublished play script.
Blau, Herbert (1982), *Take Up the Bodies: Theater at the Vanishing Point*, Urbana: University of Illinois Press.
Churchill, Winston (1948), *The Hinge of Fate*, Boston: Houghton Mifflin Harcourt.
Rae, Paul (forthcoming), "Work Over Time: The Waxing of Surrender in Singapore," unpublished chapter.
Schneider, Rebecca (2011), *Performing Remains: Art and War in Times of Theatrical Reenactment*, New York: Routledge.
Tan, Corrie (2018), "'Tiger of Malaya:' The Body Remembers What the Archive Cannot," *Arts Equator*, September 27. Available online: https://artsequator.com/review-tiger-of-malaya-teater-ekamatra/. Last accessed January 27, 2020.

2

Ferenc Molnár's *The White Cloud* and the First World War

Márta Pellérdi

Is there such a thing as a true war story? What is the truth about war that is so impossible to tell? Tim O'Brien's short story about the Vietnam war "How to Tell a True War Story" (O'Brien 2009: 64–81) tackles the impossibility of telling a true war story except through fiction. But can a play performed on stage tell a true war story? It may be even more difficult than in prose. The Hungarian playwright Ferenc Molnár, however, attempted to do so more than 100 years ago with a play about dead Hussars meeting their children in the heavenly white clouds. His attempt was part success and part failure. Back in 1916, during the premiere of Molnár's *The White Cloud* at the National Theatre of Budapest on February 25, more than one reviewer noted the misty eyes and frequent use of handkerchiefs (Kosztolányi 1916: 12; Porzsolt 1916: 9). More than eighteen months into the First World War, all layers of Hungarian society found themselves directly or indirectly affected by the continuous news of losses suffered by the Austro-Hungarian troops on the Galician frontlines. Regarded as a powerful and moving play at the time by those who praised it, and as one of Molnár's less successful plays by those who were more critical of its tear-jerking scenes, *The White Cloud* explored the tension between the legendary glory of war and its stark reality, and turned out to be unlike any of the highly popular comedies and dramas that Molnár wrote before. A playwright of international reputation by 1916, Molnár had behind him an impressive career and could boast of a long run of hit plays on the stages of New York, Budapest, and Vienna. *The Devil*, for instance, was played simultaneously by four theatres in New York in 1908. *The Guardsman* (1910) and *The Wolf* (1912) also proved to be international successes. *Liliom* (1909), although initially a failure in Budapest, soon became Molnár's most famous play abroad upon which Rodgers and Hammerstein's future musical *Carousel* (1945) would later be based. The First World War, however, curbed Molnár's dramatic talents; he returned to journalism, the activity which launched his whole writing career.

In a sketchy résumé of his life, Molnár marked 1914, when the First World War broke out, as the year when he "became a war correspondent" (qtd in Behrman 1965: 194). From November 1914 until the end of the following year, Molnár worked behind the Galician frontlines for the Hungarian newspaper *Az Est* (*The Evening*). The war reports were finally compiled into a book and were published in 1916 under the title *Egy haditudósító emlékei* (*Memoirs of a War Correspondent*) when the end of the war was still nowhere in sight. *The White Cloud* was written in the beginning of 1916 at army headquarters (at an undisclosed location) before returning to his former life in Budapest and "bec[oming] a playwright once more" (qtd in Behrman 1965: 194). By tackling the uncommon theme of war on stage and focusing on Hungarian Hussars of peasant background and also their families at home in the village, Molnár was condensing his own impressions into a short one-act play and raising questions of political importance. Furthermore, he was paying tribute to the self-sacrificing Hungarian cavalry, the Nádasdy Hussars, for example, who played a major role in winning the important Limanowa battle in December of 1914, albeit at the cost of great losses.[1] Although *The White Cloud* was successfully performed throughout 1916— Molnár was even awarded the prestigious Vojnits Prize from the Hungarian Academy of Sciences and the Franz Joseph Order the following year—it was quickly forgotten amidst the violent turmoil of the war and the eventual disintegration of the Austro-Hungarian Monarchy. But back in 1916, Molnár's short play was effective in revealing a truth about the war which dispelled all the illusions that might still have remained and succeeded in commemorating the soldiers who were fighting the bloody battles. Although the contemporary success of the play can be attributed to the emotional response of the audience, who were very much in need of Molnár's palliative miracle at the time, *The White Cloud* also points out that the days of the famous Magyar Hussar are over, and with it the old safe world of the Belle Époque, as Molnár and his contemporaries knew it, was disappearing forever.

The White Cloud is a miracle play. Consisting of five scenes, they reveal the striking conflict between the romantic swashbuckling image of the Hussars and bloodstained reality. As the introduction to the play by translator Louis Rittenberg points out, it is "devoted to a simple analysis of how legends are born and destroyed" (1929: xix). By raising questions about the causes behind the war, and focusing on the victims—the soldiers, the women, and the children at home—Molnár subtly criticizes war propaganda and manages to point to the truth about Hungary's tragic role within the play. The form of the miracle play, however, also opens up religious dimensions. By making use of a spectacular stage set to present an otherworldly atmosphere, introducing the character of the angel, and employing children and music for reaching the highest emotional (and sentimental) effect, Molnár cleverly plays upon the heartstrings of the audience. Rather than presenting the martyrdom of a saint, as would be the case in a traditional medieval miracle play, the focus in *The White Cloud* is on the martyrdom of the Hungarian (Magyar) Hussar. The heroic reputation of the Hussars has to be preserved even after their death for the sake of those at home, especially their children. It is, however, only with divine intervention that their romantic image can be upheld.

In the opening scene exhausted Hussars are sleeping in the trenches of the Galician front the night before the battle. There is a brief dialogue between the Lieutenant Colonel and the sentinel. Although the scene is short, there is tension between the peace of the camp fireside and the knowledge that the next day may be their last. As the final scene at dawn returns to the sentinel who guards the sleeping men in the trenches, it becomes clear that the in-between scenes can be interpreted as the dream of one, or all, of the men. Molnár had already experimented with dream techniques in the action of *The Wolf* (1912), reaching a "dramatic effectiveness [which] is heightened by the same sort of celestial scenery as is called for in 'Liliom'" (1909) (Rittenberg 1929: xix). The dream and the otherworldly atmosphere are combined in the intermediate scenes to express the political and social problems inherent in a war that was forced upon Hungary through the political copartner Austria. The hussar and his family are victims of higher and irresponsible political powers.

The second and third scenes serve the function of acquainting the audience with the poor but respectable peasant families of the Hussars. In the first of the dream sequences, one of the wives back home in the village has received a letter from a commanding officer informing her about the death of her husband. She has to surrender her painful emotions to propriety, which demands that she should write a reply. Still unconsoled and weeping, the illiterate young widow dictates her true feelings in simple language to another war widow who knows how to write. The latter, however, is only willing to put down the meaningless clichés formality dictates. The special Hungarian idiom used by the women, who are at cross purposes, creates a semi-comic situation, which earned the praise of the judges of the Vojnits Prize ("A Vojnits Díjat" 1917). The children lying in bed overhear the two women talking about the story of the dead Hussars in the white cloud (a white lie invented by adults to console the children), and decide to visit their fathers. They are joined by other orphans. The audience can see a miracle happening, which even the widows in the village cannot believe: children are climbing up the mountain to the white cloud to meet their fathers, who, they expect, will be riding on beautiful horses in decorated uniforms and brandishing glittering sabers.

In the fourth scene—still part of the dream—it becomes clear that reality proves to be different from stories and legends. The once valiant and proud Hussars who have just died in battle can be seen in the clouds, bareheaded, on foot, halfway between earth and heaven. They look more relaxed and calm but hearing the news about their children coming to visit them worries rather than pleases them. Revealing the truth to their children about the war and the conditions under which they have lost their lives places them into a conflicting and embarrassing situation. The Hussars, who have a long and proud military history behind them, have to appear before their children not as idealized heroes on horseback, but as they died: as the unfortunate victims of a massacre, dying in ditches or on the muddy battlefield. The mountainous terrain and trench warfare of Galicia have made horses useless:

CORPORAL.   How can I tell them that I fell on foot, and in the mud?
FIRST HUSSAR.   Or that we lived in a ditch? And that we had spades in our
    hands … (Molnár 1929: 253)

For hundreds of years, the proud hussar, mounted on a charger, wore a flamboyant colorful uniform and had a sabre for a weapon, but in the Great War the uniforms became dull-colored, and horses and sabers became superfluous. Molnár emphasizes the changes in modern warfare in this scene and the tragic fact that the Austro-Hungarian Army had a shortage of modern weapons. The idealized, fairy-tale-like stories Hussars used to tell their children and the romanticized letters they wrote home about their life on the front helped preserve the false heroic image. A strong sense of pride and honor are at the root of a hussar's motivation:

SERGEANT.   Back home … the village … thinks … that … [He is stuck.]
CADET.   Thinks what?
SERGEANT. [quietly, fairly abashed]   It's all bugles and flowers … shiny swords … colored shawls … flags … and gold trappings …
CADET.   That's too bad … The hussar's real worth is right in his heart, not in his outfit. (Molnár 1929: 253)

The Hussars talk to an inquisitive angel (played by Gizi Bajor in 1916, a prominent actress at the time) who appears and warns them that their children are coming. She embarrasses them with her uncomfortable questions. The questions are also intended to make the audience ponder over the cause the war was fought for and to emphasize that neither the hussar nor the country have anything to gain from it. In other words, the play raises sensitive political questions not only about war in general, but about the highly disproportionate land ownership structure of Hungarian society and the multi-ethnic structure of the dual Austro-Hungarian Monarchy. The angel wishes to know why the men had to die; she repeats the answers she receives for emphatic effect and interprets them (for the audience):

CORPORAL.   For the land.
ANGEL.   For the land?
CORPORAL.   That's right.
ANGEL.   You mean you … had to defend the land?
CORPORAL.   That's what we did.
ANGEL.   Which land?
CORPORAL.   That there down below. You can still see it over the rim. It's the land … on this side of the mountain.
ANGEL.   Who lives there?
CORPORAL.   Hungarians. [Pause.] That's the land we defended. (Molnár 1929: 249)

The Angel assumes that if the Hussars were willing to die for the land, then it must have belonged to them. She finds out that they "hadn't any land at all" (Molnár 1929: 249); and even the farmland they used to plow at home was never in their possession but belonged to their landlords. Still, the patriotic Hungarian Hussars of mostly peasant background are willing to sacrifice their lives and thrust back the offensive Russian troops in Galicia (where there are no Hungarians) in order to defend the Hungarian historical borders. It is a paradoxical situation, however, that even though Galicia constitutes a part of the Austro-Hungarian Monarchy, it does not lie on the territory of historical Hungary. It is a foreign land for the Hussars who have died there. Why, then, die in a foreign land for a cause which can never fully be theirs? The unexpected answer is "honor," as the men emphasize, "It's honor that counts" (Molnár 1929: 250).

ANGEL. Well … but is there such a thing … honor … everywhere?
SERGEANT. Yes, lovely little white angel, there was every place we went.
ANGEL. And … did you always know where you were going? … When you started out … did you know where you were bound? …
SERGEANT. Nobody told us. Not even the officers knew where the train was taking us. (Molnár 1929: 250)

Thus the popular and idealized image of the Hungarian Hussar is reinforced, according to which he is bound by "aristocratic" honor (despite his low social background) when obeying commanding officers and fighting not only for his own country but for the entire Austro-Hungarian Empire in the war. One of the Hussars tells the Angel that he used to be a shepherd and watched over "two thousand lambkins" (Molnár 1929: 249). In the same manner as the hussar who shows "overflowing affection" for his sheep, Molnár cannot help but display his admiration for the heroism of the Hussars (Molnár 1929: 249). But he makes it clear that their sheeplike innocence and ignorance also led to their destruction (Györgyey 1980: 100). It is finally, through divine intervention, that the Hussars can appear in their formal and glorious attire before their children, as in the tales. The scenes in which the twenty-seven children appear and the sentimental encounter that takes place between the Hussars and their offspring have been harshly criticized by the Molnár scholar Clara Györgyey: "[t]he encounter in heaven conveyed nothing more than sentimentality, a tearjerking gimmick that reduced the action to sugarcoated, heartrending melodrama … appeal[ing] only to a naïve, undemanding audience 'overdoped' by bombastic propaganda" (Györgyey 1980: 100).

But writing a drama which reveals the truth about the war, and seeing it performed on stage while the war is still raging, produces a different effect from reading it, or seeing it performed in time of peace. In other words, it is a "Zeitstück," most effective on stage only at the time when it was written (Csáki 2014). Also, as O'Brien's narrator points out, "A true war story is never moral" (O'Brien 2009: 65). In Molnár's play there is certainly a degree of criticism but there is no moral in tow. Molnár's purpose in the middle of the First World War in 1916 was not to be profoundly politic; he did not intend to satirize, or be woundingly ironical, but to illustrate the huge difference between romantic legends and cruel reality and to show his respect for the self-sacrifice of the Hussars on the Galician front. It is only in retrospect that the irony in the First Hussar's words on the future partition of Hungary in 1920 can be detected: "They wanted to slice up our beautiful Hungary … but didn't succeed" (Molnár 1929: 247). The intention to write the truth about Hungarian Hussars in the First World War transpires through the supernatural and the sentimental. Although Molnár was only a war correspondent witnessing the events and not taking part physically in the battles, he nevertheless makes it clear that the romance of war is nonexistent in reality or in dreams, as the idealized village and cloud scenes demonstrate. Miracles are necessary even in the otherworld.

With the war over and the catastrophic defeat and dissolution of the Austro-Hungarian Monarchy, public attention was intent on facing the menacing future rather than looking back. This explains why the play was not performed between the two

World Wars. Nor was it reproduced during the Second World War, by which time the proud Hungarian cavalry proved to be completely obsolete and Molnár was living in New York City. The play was revived only in 2014 by the National Theatre in Budapest when the centenary commemorations of the outbreak of the First World War made it once more of topical and historical interest, if not a popular success. Despite the stage director Attila Vidnyánszky's attempt to recreate the atmosphere of the times, it failed to capture the imagination of the twenty-first-century audience.[2]

"[A] true war story," as O'Brien points out, "is never about war ... It's about the special way that dawn spreads out on a river when you know you must cross the river and march into the mountains and do things you are afraid to do. It's about love and memory. It's about sorrow" (O'Brien 2009: 81). In the final scene, dawn is breaking, the sentinel pokes at the fire and the cannonballs are thundering from afar and soldiers somewhere in the distance are singing. This day for the Hussars is going to be about death and doing what they are "afraid to do" (O'Brien 2009: 81). Despite the banal elements (children and music), Molnár's *The White Cloud* is of historical interest today, as the prominent Hungarian poet and writer Dezső Kosztolányi at the time prophesied it would be (1916: 12), successfully demonstrating that the days of the Hungarian Hussar were over, and it was "love and memory" and "sorrow" that remained (O'Brien 2009: 81). These feelings also resonated in the hearts of the contemporary audience in February 1916—the year when Hungarian optimistic public opinion concerning the outcome of the war was replaced by doubt, grief, and fear. And the Great War was only the overture to the future horrors of twentieth-century Hungarian history, ominously foreshadowing that even worse was yet to come.

Notes

1   Molnár wrote about the shock he experienced after visiting the battlefield of Limanowa in 1914 in his memoir about the war (Molnár 1916: 69–82). The action of the play, however, takes place one year later.
2   *The White Cloud* was never produced in England or the US, only in Hungary. Hungarian critics have also tended to neglect this play. The most recent articles on *The White Cloud*, written by István Kornya, were published in the promotional magazine of the National Theatre in Budapest, describing the production directed by Attila Vidnyánszky in the Fall of 2014 (Kornya 2014: 13–15). Vidnyánszky's production received few, mostly negative, reviews. See Tarján (2014) and Csáki (2014).

Works Cited

"A Vojnits—jutalmat Molnár Ferencnek ítélték" (1917), *Budapesti Hírlap*, January 30. Available online: https://adtplus.arcanum.hu/hu/view/BudapestiHirlap_1917_01/?query=feh%C3%A9r%20felh%C5%91%20moln%C3%A1r%20ferenc%20tudom%C3%A1nyos%20akad%C3%A9mia&pg=489&layout=s. Last accessed April 20, 2020.

Behrman, S. N. (1965), *The Suspended Drawing Room*, New York: Stein and Day Publishers.
Csáki, Judit (2014), "Esőre áll," *Revizor: A kritikai portál*, October 3. Available online: https://revizoronline.com/hu/cikk/5232/fekete-eg-a-feher-felho-nemzeti-szinhaz/. Last accessed April 20, 2020.
Györgyey, Clara (1980), *Ferenc Molnár*, Twayne's World Author Series, Boston: Twayne Publishers.
Kornya, István (2014), "Mirákulum a frontról," *Nemzeti Magazin*, September–October, pp. 13–15. Available online: https://adtplus.arcanum.hu/hu/view/Szinhaz1968_2014/?query=kornya%20istv%C3%A1n%20mir%C3%A1kulum&pg=548&layout=s. Last accessed April 20, 2020.
Kosztolányi, Dezső (1916), "A fehér felhő: bemutató a Nemzeti Színházban," *Világ*, February 26. Available online: https://adtplus.arcanum.hu/hu/view/Vilag_1916_02/?pg=423&layout=s&query=kosztol%C3%A1nyi. Last accessed April 20, 2020.
Molnár, Ferenc (1916), *Egy haditudósító emlékei*, Budapest: Franklin Társulat.
Molnár, Ferenc (1929), *The Plays of Ferenc Molnár*, ed. and tr. Louis Rittenberg, New York: The Vanguard Press (Macy-Masius).
O'Brien, Tim (2009), "How to Tell a True War Story," in *The Things They Carried*, Boston: Mariner Books/Houghton Mifflin Harcourt, pp. 64–81.
Porzsolt, K. (1916), "A fehér felhő," *Pesti Hírlap*, February 26. Available online: https://adtplus.arcanum.hu/hu/view/PestiHirlap_1916_02/?query=SZO%3D_Cs%C3%A1ky%20J%C3%B3zsef_&pg=604&layout=s. Last accessed April 20, 2020.
Rittenberg, Louis (1929), "Introduction," in *The Plays of Ferenc Molnár*, ed. Louis Rittenberg, New York: The Vanguard Press (Macy-Masius), pp. xi–xxii.
Tarján, Tamás (2014), "Itt is fáj, ott is fáj: Fekete ég/Molnár Ferenc: A fehér felhő—kritika," *Színház.net*, September 30. Available online:http://szinhaz.net/2014/09/30/tarjan-tamas-itt-is-faj-ott-is-faj/. Last accessed April 20, 2020.

3

Presenting *Picasso Presents*: Exploring the Process of Crafting and Staging Historical Docudrama

Annika C. Speer and Begoña Echeverria

On April 26, 1937, Hitler's Condor Legion bombed Gernika (the Basque spelling), the sacred city of the Basques—the first civilian target in history decimated by aerial bombing (Clark 1979: 70). Terrified, parents sent their children away to allies of the fledgling democratically elected government of Spain, such as France, Mexico, Russia, and England. The United States refused to take the child refugees, in part because their families' left-leaning politics fed into the anti-Communist fears of the time (Legarreta 1984: 182–3).

Although this evacuation of Basque children preceded the *kindertransport* of Jewish children from Nazism, a library database search of "kindertransport" yielded upwards of 300 sources compared to only about twenty for "evacuation of Basque children." Echeverria knew little about it, even as the daughter of Basque immigrants named after Our Lady Begoña of Bilbao, the port city from which the refugee children departed.

An off-hand remark made by the daughter of another Basque immigrant brought this event to the fore. In the 1990s, Echeverria lived in Donostia (San Sebastian) in Gipuzkoa, the province adjacent to Bizkaia of which Bilbao is the capital. Her British neighbor Manuela[1] had moved to Donostia after marrying Paco, a Basque native, whom she'd met while he studied in the UK. Manuela mentioned to Echeverria that, as children, her father Alejandro and his brother had been evacuated to England during the Spanish Civil War (1936-9). Eventually, the boys' mother requested that Alejandro's brother be returned to her in Spain; but she did not ask for Alejandro. "My father never forgave his mother for that," Manuela explained. He lived the rest of his life in England, never learning why his mother had not also called him home.

Echeverria knows nothing more of this story. Manuela and she never discussed this painful familial event again. Unfortunately, it presaged refugee crises that continue to this day. From this seed, her docudrama play *Picasso Presents Gernika* surfaced over twenty years later. After crafting the script, Echeverria partnered with theatre scholar Speer to stage a reading of the play in May 2019. The staged reading integrated audience engagement with the historiography of the event and its current relevance, while also allowing the actors to breathe life into the fictional narrative. Working with a team of student designers, Speer and Echeverria negotiated the dramaturgical process of incorporating salient historical documentation in the form of theatrical audio visuals.

This chapter discusses the process of crafting and staging a new docudrama script and balancing pedagogy with artistry while engaging with issues of temporality and gender.

Docudrama blends primary source materials (media footage, newspaper quotations, trial transcripts) with fiction. *Picasso Presents Gernika* weaves primary source material stemming from myriad sources (e.g., newspapers, radio programs, letters, photographs, paintings) with a fictionalized reimagining of the experience of one family. Drawing from Manuela's anecdote about Alejandro and his brother, the play follows brother and sister pair, Aitor ("testimony" in Basque) and Andrea (meaning "woman"), whose parents sent them away for safety. The mother calls only for Aitor to return home after the war and Andrea, who becomes a psychiatrist specializing in child refugees, spends a lifetime navigating her own trauma, isolation, and devastation from feeling abandoned. The familial scenes intertwine with scenes from Picasso, who acts as the narrator, and uses historical material to provide clarity and context through direct address to the audience.

While much of the script's pathos stems from the fictionalized story of the family, the title, *Picasso Presents Gernika*, plays linguistically with the multiple meanings of "present." Picasso's world-famous painting *Guernica* illustrates the atrocities of war, and anyone familiar with this painting has immediate connotations for the concepts explored within the play. And yet, the events that inspired *Guernica* are less familiar to most people than the painting itself. To "present" means to introduce information, to bring forth, to submit. Picasso not only presents his portrait through exhibition, he also introduces the audience to little-known material from this historical event. Picasso acts as audience raconteur and teacher, a fitting role, given the documentary theatre's pedagogical function. Documentary scholar Gary Fisher Dawson points out that *docui* is the Latin root "to teach" (Dawson 1999: 19). But what are the lessons? Why engage with them now? And how can they be staged theatrically?

A homonym with a plurality of meaning, "present" connotes gift or offering, but also "this moment," the here and now. Speer and Echeverria began the process of moving the script from page to stage, continuously faced with the ways in which this story about a mother who "chose" (among limited choices) to send her children away during heightened political crisis parallels or intersects with the 2019 political moment. The staged reading of the play at Chino Community Theatre on May 19, 2019, fell between Mother's Day and the eighty-second anniversary of the Basque children's arrival to Southampton on May 23, on which date news broke that a sixth migrant child had died while in US custody (Goodkind 2019).

Indeed, the unfortunate resonance of the Gernika evacuation with current events impacted considerations of the multimedia display that accompanies the docudrama. In the final scene of the play, Andrea (now in her eighties) meets her brother's grandson (also named Aitor) at a reunion in England for child evacuees who remained there. Grandnephew Aitor brings newspaper clippings, photographs, and other ephemera that Andrea's mother had saved for her. While the characters Andrea and Aitor are fictional, the documentation that Andrea examines (projected for the audience) is real. The documents showcase the difficult conditions in which women and girls lived under the Franco regime: the Second Republic that preceded the Spanish Civil War had granted suffrage to women as well as men in 1931, as well as free secular education. But the Franco regime's (1939–75) "True Catholic Motherhood" ideology erased those gains.

The headlines Andrea reads include the General Director of Education's proclamation (1942) that "We must keep women away from the university. The place of a woman is at home" (Morcillo 2000: 44); the Decree of March 31, 1944, stating: "Married women need their husbands' permission to practice any 'trade or industry'" (Morcillo 2000: 36); the Decree of July 29, 1948, stating "No woman of any age may be employed at night" (Morcillo 2000: 36); and the 1955 high school manual for girls, *Amor*: "Prepare yourself to assist men ... Be housewives, not learned women" (Morcillo 2000: 96). These documents demonstrate that Andrea's mother believed life would be more difficult for a girl under a dictatorship than for a boy, hence why she "left" Andrea behind. As Andrea examines the documents, a song plays that Echeverria wrote (in Basque) titled "My Children," expressing the mother's anguished hope that she made the right choice. Andrea weeps at this realization of the sacrifice her mother made.

In discussing the ending, Speer suggested to Echeverria that this "lesson" of the play might have more pedagogical punch if it were brought up to date more explicitly, that is, made "more present." For example, in addition to the archival materials Echeverria had gathered about how the Gernika bombing, evacuation, and civil war had affected the Basque population, Speer proposed images be included to show the particular violence women writ large suffer as a result of war, displacement, and political instability. Contemporary events provided ample relevant material. Director of the Traprock Center for Peace and Justice, H. Patricia Hynes (2004: 431), has noted the "unique harm[s] of war for women [in] military brothels, rape camps ... sex trafficking ... [and] increased domestic violence, all of which is fueled by the culture of war, male aggression, and the social and economic ruin left in the wake of war" (Hynes 2004: 431). According to Professor of International Law and Human Rights Chaloka Beyani, political instability even within countries continues to disproportionately harm women. In addition to being at greater risk for rape and sexual violence, internally displaced women face greater obstacles than men when it comes to securing assistance, housing, healthcare, training, education, livelihoods, and access to decision-making resources (Beyani 2014: 1). While time constraints prevented the inclusion of images illustrating such gendered harm during the play's premiere, such images can be integrated to reflect the circumstances and contexts wherever the docudrama is produced.

These choices about what and how to make more present the seemingly distant events of 1937 illustrate Dawson's argument that interpreting and staging a documentary play requires responding to a past event in a way that makes "the full consequence of [that] event ... known" (Dawson 1999: 168) or "more present" to contemporary audiences.[2] But consequences of such atrocities are incalculable. The cost of war exceeds any body count, and the trauma caused to separated families and children is similarly boundless. This holds true both in 2019–20 for families being separated on the US border and for the transgenerational trauma of people affected by the long-since-concluded event of the bombing in Gernika (in 1937). While the play text grounds its narrative in a definitive time and historical event, the act of staging the script is less anchored in its specificity. Creating a production from the text requires collaborative devising; the staging explores the then in the now, the both/and.

The fluidity of temporality resonated with Speer and Echeverria as they staged the play. Echeverria's training in sociolinguistics, which notes the socially constructed and contested nature of identity and language, intersected with Speer's training in theatre and gender studies. Identities are not fixed, and neither is a theatrical production which inevitably engages with the ephemerality of staging, and the plurality of productions/performances. Speer and Echeverria anchored their discussions about staging to the docudrama structure of the script, which includes abundant primary source materials. Such structure lent itself to a desire to move between the embodied narratives of the siblings on stage and the multimedia potential of incorporating historical images and materials from the period and event.

Much like the construction of a docudrama script in which an author engages in editing, arrangement, and selectivity while weaving the material with original fiction, the slideshow as mediatized performance runs in tandem with the live bodies on the stage. Projected onto the back wall of the stage, the slideshow works with Picasso's narration to contextualize historical detail as well as to invoke pathos with its imagery. Unlike the fixed play text, the slideshow can shift dependent upon time, location, or directorial decisions. The crafting of the slideshow involves combing through myriad historical documents with attention to how the visual material will best serve the individual scenes, the title slides, and the production in its entirety. The process is both archival in its mining of the past and discursive in Speer and Echeverria's collaborative effort to shape a production that will resonate with contemporary audiences.

The slideshow needed to balance the mediatized material with the live bodies of the actors on stage. In an age of infoglut and media consumption, Speer and Echeverria understood that any media projected onto the back wall of the stage would pull audience attention from the live human presence of the actors. Arguing in opposition to ontology, performance studies scholar Philip Auslander states: "Whereas mediatized performance derives its authority from its reference to the live or the real, the live now derives its authority from its reference to the mediatized, which derives its authority from its reference to the live, etc." (Auslander 2008: 43).

In creating the slideshow, Speer and Echeverria faced this exact predicament. The slideshow pulls from the primary source material; thus, the slideshow taps into the reference to the live or real events. The slideshow highlighted the "doc" in docudrama and its references to this lived material deliver some of the play text's powerful pathos as well as components of its historicity. And yet, the live bodies onstage, the actors performing the fictional account, are the reason this script exists as a theatrical production and not a PowerPoint, academic article, or alternate form of pedagogical documentation. The live actors are not less *real* than the mediatized account of the events, and it undermines their performances and the broader goals of the play to upstage them with media footage. A challenge of the slideshow was balancing the *doc* with the scripted *drama*.

Additionally, through conversations and engagement with the materials, Speer and Echeverria discovered the central role gender played in the staged reading. Although Picasso narrates the story inspired by Alejandro's experience with his brother, Echeverria deliberately made the siblings a brother and sister pair with Andrea as the sibling left behind so the script could explore the gendered effects of war. While historical accounts celebrate the men who declare, fight, and die in wars, they rarely discuss the sacrifices made by and suffering of women (and children). What would it take for a mother to send her children off to a foreign country in the (perhaps vain) hope that they would have a better life? And then make the agonizing decision to only ask for one child back, never to see her daughter again?

In exploring gender-based suffering, Echeverria also wanted to highlight the physical toll war and political violence can have on women in particular. *Guernica* features primarily women figures (one, weeping for her dead baby): could this be one of Picasso's points in making the mural? By going back and forth between the story of the children and the journey of the painting, Echeverria hoped to show that the meaning of the painting is multivocal. She began by allowing herself her own interpretations of the *Guernica* mural, dispensing with the voluminous scholarship on the painting, its maker, and its context, and instead giving herself creative permission for the fictional story to emerge.

Echeverria attempts to center the voices of women storytellers in Basque culture whose contributions have frequently been relegated to supporting rather than leading roles. Although Alejandro had the lived experience, his daughter Manuela disseminated the initial kernel to Echeverria. Echeverria's research on Basque oral literature demonstrated that while women often related folktales and songs to male compilers, citations often only acknowledge the latter (Echeverria 2021). Hence the decision to employ Picasso as the narrator, whose presence operates simultaneously as a memorialization and a critique of androcentrism in Basque culture. Picasso's painting foregrounds women's suffering, and yet, women's experiences and narratives also receive less attention than Picasso and other male artists and culture makers of this period. This aligns with the androcentric patterns that Echeverria's (2003) research has uncovered; portrayals of Basque culture and identity privilege male speakers of the language who participate in traditional domains that are male dominated (Echeverria 2003).

Indeed, Echeverria has personally experienced such androcentrism even in the diaspora and worked against this bias explicitly in her script. Every Basque festival held throughout California opens with the singing of the "Gernikako Arbola" (The Tree of Gernika), led by a bugle corps called the Klika, whose membership is predominantly male. Such performances reinforce public displays of Basque identity, as well as patriotism, as a male domain. Yet Echeverria's research showed that girls also sang and danced at the fundraisers for their upkeep as evacuees to England. Indeed, souvenir stamps to raise funds featured a little girl, the youngest evacuee of all. The Tree of Gernika graced the cover of one such event, which was deemed "a most successful way to raise money" (Legarreta 1984: 126). The script reflects these facts in several ways. First, in the scene set in the refugee camp in England, Andrea rather than her brother Aitor leads the children in the singing of "Gernikako Arbola." Second, Andrea's British foster mother opens Act 2 by playing "Gernikako Arbola" on the piano in an attempt to reconnect a rebellious teenaged Andrea with her Basque roots. Third, like the transmission of the initial story told from Manuela to Echeverria, the process of staging the script was also multigenerational and gendered. The production team that Echeverria and Speer supervised to create the multimedia display during the first staged reading was composed of undergraduate students, all of them women.

In this sense, the off-hand remark made by Manuela to Echeverria resembles the kind of informal storytelling between women that has been key to transmitting cultural information that would otherwise be lost. This moment of understanding between two neighbors resonated with Echeverria and ultimately became the inspiration for her docudrama script. In her article, "The Feminist Potential of Docudrama," Speer argues that an underappreciated merit of docudrama lies in the imaginative and pedagogical potential of the material for which no public record exists (Speer 2013: 3–4). Numerous documentary scholars and practitioners, individuals who already acknowledge the complexity and shortcomings of privileging primary source material, have nonetheless argued against docudrama precisely for how it weaves preexisting material with fiction (Speer 2013: 2–3).[3] According to this view, fiction alongside "fact(s)" deliberately misleads spectators. Yet, no one simple set of facts reigns, nor does docudrama intend to adhere rigidly to data from the original event. Whose version would we even tell? How much public information is there for the women and children who survived? The moment between Echeverria and her neighbor resonates, not only because of the empathy both women felt for Alejandro's circumstances but also because such a moment, raw in its humanity, happens privately between two people in an unrecorded or informal setting. Such discourse can be a particularly rich space for sharing between women, who have often been excluded from public fora for creative or cultural expression (Smith 1975; de Beauvoir [1952] 1989). An intimate conversation between women clearly differs from the discursive circumstances of a trial transcript, mediatized event, or other form of public record. The conversation stayed with Echeverria for over two decades, opening numerous questions and ultimately leaving them unanswered. Less interested in the logistics of the bombing of Gernika, Echeverria focused on the human experience.

So, what lessons does *Picasso Presents Gernika* present? To weave the roots of the Latin *docui* into the current parlance about "teachable" moments, Speer and Echeverria found the process of collaboratively staging this script presented opportunities to engage with historical narratives about gender and cross-generational trauma in ways that would not necessarily have been available in other pedagogical forms. The scholarship on *Guernica* is substantial and the mural is among the most famous works of art ever created. Most viewers of *Guernica* might come to understand its connection to the bombing of Gernika. But few likely make the connection between *Guernica* and the 20,000 children evaluated as a consequence of the bombing (Legarreta 1984: ix). Fewer still would consider the suffering it engendered for the children and their loved ones; while the fate of The Gernika Generation does not loom large in the public imagination, the facts are well-documented for those who seek them out,[4] and embodied performance can be an edifying medium for promoting further engagement.

The *drama* of *docudrama* provides audience members with special emotional affordances that allow such connections to be made and the "lessons" about the gendered effects of war to be more legible. Autobiographies or individual narratives are powerful; stories such as *The Diary of Anne Frank* use the lens of an individual to illuminate the human cost of war. It is more memorable to engage with the in-depth narrative of one human experience than to read a textbook about the event itself. *The Diary of Anne Frank* is salient for many reasons, not least of which is its uniqueness as a surviving record of a young woman's experiences, thoughts, and trauma in her own voice.

Docudrama taps into this pathos-based pedagogical potential, with an understanding that there is frequently a lack of public record or data for the voices of women and other marginalized subjects. By presenting *Picasso Presents* theatrically, Speer and Echeverria hope to bear testimony to the intergenerational sacrifices made and violence endured by women and girls in times of war and political instability whether behind the scenes, on the home front, in the heat of battle, or crossing a border. Docudrama offers a means for engaging with and recognizing the lasting impacts and continuing relevance of such violence and survival. The docudrama creates a space for alternatively and imaginatively documenting or remembering the past, considering how it shapes the present, as well as creating community through artistic practice and building hope and resilience for the future.

Notes

1 Names are pseudonyms.
2 Speer (2013) has also addressed such issues of documentation for ongoing events as they pertain to docudrama scripts that deal with the continuing debates around reproductive rights.
3 Further information on documentary theatre and docudrama can be found in Will Hammond and Dan Steward (2008: 152); Eric Bentley (1985: 51–2); Alison Forsyth and Chris Megson (2009: 1–6).
4 An excellent resource from which much of the documentary evidence for the script draws is basquechildren.org.

Works Cited

Auslander, Philip (2008), *Liveness: Performance in a Mediatized Culture*, London: Routledge.
Bentley, Eric (1985), "Writing for a Political Theatre," *Performing Arts Journal*, Vol. 9, No. 2–3, pp. 51–2.
Beyani, Chaloka (2014), "Improving the Protection of Internally Displaced Women: Assessment of Progress and Challenges," Washington, D.C.: The Brookings Institute.
Clark, Robert P. (1979), *The Basques: The Franco Years and Beyond*, Reno: University of Nevada Press.
Dawson, Gary Fisher (1999), *Documentary Theatre in the United States: An Historical Survey and Analysis of Its Content, Form, and Stagecraft*, Westport: Greenwood Publishing Group.
de Beauvoir, Simone ([1952] 1989), *The Second Sex*, New York: Vintage Books.
Echeverria, Begoña (2021), *"Witches" and Wily Women: Saving "Noka" Through Basque Folklore and Song*, Reno: The University of Nevada Reno's Center for Basque Studies.

Echeverria, Begoña (2003), "Language Ideologies and Practices in (En)gendering the Basque Nation," *Language in Society*, Vol. 32, No. 3, pp. 383–414.
Forsyth, Alison and Chris Megson, eds. (2009), *Get Real: Documentary Theatre Past and Present*, New York: Palgrave Macmillan.
Goodkind, Nicole (2019), "Trump Officials Acknowledge Sixth Migrant Child Death in US Custody in 6 Months after None in Previous Decades," *Newsweek*, May 23. Available online: http://www.newsweek.com/border-family-separation-child-death-democrats-investigate-1434591. Last accessed July 17, 2020.
Hammond, Will and Dan Steward (2008), *Verbatim Verbatim: Contemporary Documentary Theatre*, London: Oberon Books.
Hynes, H. Patricia (2004), "On the Battlefield of Women's Bodies: An Overview of the Harm of War to Women," *Women's Studies International Forum*, Vol. 27, No. 5–6, pp. 431–45.
Legarreta, Dorothy (1984), *The Guernica Generation: Basque Refugee Children of the Spanish Civil War*, Reno: University of Nevada Press.
Morcillo, Aurora G. (2000), *True Catholic Womanhood: Gender Ideology in Franco's Spain*, DeKalb: Northern Illinois University Press.
Smith, Dorothy E. (1975), "An Analysis of Ideological Structures and How Women Are Excluded: Considerations for Academic Women," *Canadian Review of Sociology* Vol. 12, No. 4, pp. 353–69.
Speer, Annika C. (2013), "The Feminist Potential of Docudrama: Destabilizing the Primacy of Primary Sources through Paula Kamen's *Jane*," *Frontiers: A Journal of Women Studies*, Vol. 34, No. 3, pp. 1–26.

4

War, Tyranny, and Political Sacrifice in Luis Vélez de Guevara's *Más pesar el rey que la sangre y blasón de los Guzmanes*

Alani Hicks-Bartlett

A preoccupation with proper governance and the qualities and actions that make an "effective" leader is significant to discussions of political vigor and national integrity in early modern Spanish literature. Considerations of power utilized positively often take priority, yet analyses of tyranny and failure are equally helpful to understanding theorizations of political strength. Thus, tyrannical kings and their alignment with political theories regarding weak leadership, violence, and chaos become prime illustrations of the miscarriages of power and poor governance that propel conflict.

Taking the descriptions of bellicosity that open Luis Vélez de Guevara's *Más pesa el rey que la sangre y blasón de los Guzmanes* (*The King weighs more than blood, and the blazon of the Guzmáns*, 1621)[1] as the point of departure, this chapter examines how tyranny and the testing of political devotion raise wider questions about power during periods of war. For the Andalusian playwright (1570–1644), the rigid way in which rulers assert control initially seems to provide the foundation for national fortitude and political strength. Indeed, the rulers represented in *Más pesa el rey que la sangre* explicitly articulate their objectives of increasing their power while expanding the borders of their respective domains.

However, Vélez de Guevara offers an acerbic commentary on political authority by demonstrating how the same rigidity that initially appears to reinforce national identity also serves as a tool to control and manipulate subjects, and ends up encouraging tyrannical postures that ultimately undermine national strength. Although his critique has vast implications for the idea of national fortitude prevalent when he was writing, particularly as reflected in the proliferation of political manuals and *specula principum* published during the medieval and early modern periods, and for the thorny historical intrigue his play teases out, it also offers a more pointed argument. That is, Vélez de Guevara stresses the risks of tyrannical behavior in his representation of kings and leaders who are so irascible they are unable to properly identify their political and ideological allies. Arguing for prudence, reliability, and loyalty, he critiques the political rashness and volatility that prevents rulers from appropriately assessing the allegiances that would actually strengthen their rule, serve as their most helpful assets in war, and help extend their power. Instead, these problematic rulers malign those who would have been most loyal to them. In so doing, they neglect opportunities to strengthen their bond with the very characters who could have better served the nation and its rulers had their skills and unflagging loyalty been utilized more appropriately.

A fictionalized account of historical events, *Más pesa el rey que la sangre* offers an interpretation of a series of Reconquista episodes that took place during the reign of Sancho IV el Bravo, King of Castile (1258–1295). Due to internecine family politics and deep ideological clashes, Sancho, the second son of Alfonso X of Castile (1221–1284), opposes his nephew (the son of his late brother Ferdinand de la Cerda) in order to forcibly accede to the throne and replace his father.[2] Nicknamed "The Wise" for his intellectual resolve and encouragement of court culture, for his advancement of Castilian maritime influence and the Castilian language, along with other forms of cosmopolitan advancement, Alfonso X was often viewed in contradistinction to Sancho, particularly given the "precipitous campaign" his son launched to "build his own rebellious faction" and dispossess his father of ruling power (Kinkade 2020: 241–4). Opposed to his father's elitist bent, Sancho had majoritarian support, which increased during the final years of his father's reign (Pepin 2013: 813–16).

One of Sancho's fiercest detractors, however, was his younger brother Juan of Castile (1262–1319), a "turbulent and unprincipled warrior" who contrived against him (Spofford 1906: 149), until Sancho imprisoned Juan and executed many of his supporters. After Juan's release, another contention between the brothers transpired when Sancho annexed Tarifa (Agrait 2015: 144; Giménez 1930: 20), and Juan aligned himself with Islamic troops and began to plot against Sancho. Although he had earlier fought for Alonso X and opposed Sancho, the nobleman Alonso Pérez de Guzmán (known as Guzmán el Bueno, 1256–1309) installed himself in Tarifa to support Sancho. In his attempt to besiege the city, Juan tried to force Guzmán to surrender by taking his son captive and threatening to kill him unless Guzmán relinquished power. As the chronicles recount, not only did Guzmán accept that his son would be killed, he threw his dagger to his son's assailants to facilitate their bloody task (Spofford 1906: 149). Guzmán viewed this action as one that exemplified honor and loyalty.[3] He was thereby able to show his fidelity to Sancho while upholding his own reputation and name; he was able to hold Tarifa against assault; and Juan's plan for takeover failed.

Más pesa el rey que la sangre loosely follows these events,[4] though its plot focuses primarily on virtuous and tyrannical models of conduct during bellicose confrontations, while revealing how heroism, despite frequently being attached to one's name, is more aligned with the individual than with rank. To this end, Vélez de Guevara juxtaposes the tyrannical comportment of Sancho IV and that of the play's other despotic rulers—Sancho's rebellious brother Enrique, and Sancho's adversary, the monarch Abén Jacob—with the exemplary behavior of a vilified character of lower rank. How these tyrannical rulers struggle with properly adjudicating and weighing the worth of others is equipoised by their dramatic clashes with the upstanding and entirely faithful Don Alonso Pérez de Guzmán, and Guzmán's concluding Abrahamic sacrifice of his son. Given that the political errors Sancho commits in his tyrannical dealings with Guzmán are the first to occur in the play and motor of the dénouement, they are the focus of the present discussion.

The play's opening scenes present a vision of Sancho's court as one that is unstable, with Sancho being portrayed as a volatile and arbitrary ruler. Though Sancho's troops have gained control of Seville and festivities are underway, Sancho is brooding and hostile. He participates in the celebration and "se deja lisonjear" (I.57, "he allows himself to be praised"),[5] but his attentions turn darkly to Guzmán el Bueno. Possible reasons for the King's antipathy are suggested in the monologue of the clown Castanilla, which opens the play and immediately offers portraits of the worth and heroism of both Sancho and Guzmán. Castanilla begins with Sancho's merits, which he treats briefly in comparison to his lengthier praise of Guzmán. Thanks to God's grace and his own skills, Sancho is:

A quien por ser valeroso
el Bravo en Castilla llaman
siendo mayores los hechos
aunque es tan grande la fama
(I.17–20, "who, for being brave, is called 'the Brave' in Castile, given that his feats are even greater than his great fame").

Castanilla then goes on to describe Sancho's legacy, exalting the magnificence of his father, Alfonso X, and the marvels of Seville, before turning to Alonso Pérez de Guzmán. Described as having "heroica sangre guzmana" (I.82, "heroic Guzman blood") Guzmán's worth and heroism are amplified by the presence of a lion, who fights ferociously alongside him in battle, but otherwise humbly follows his every step, "doméstica y mansa," and "amigo y camarada" (v.102, "tame and docile," and "both a friend and a brother in arms") (Manson and Peele 2011: 22; Vega 1997: 355). In addition to this wondrous accompaniment attributed to "celestial influencia / virtud o secreta causa" (I.99–100, "celestial influence, virtue, or [a] secret reason") that associates Guzmán with the biblical Daniel who emerges unscathed from the lion's den, it is Guzmán's excellence in war—daring and courageous like that of his lion—that further highlights his singularity, granting him a superiority that Sancho resents:

[….] es león
de los caballeros hasta
tener de los disfavores
del Rey […]
(I. 105–8, "he is so much the lion of the knights that he earns the antipathy of the King").

Indeed, despite how consistently and diligently Guzmán has served both Sancho and his father, he has never received the recognition and praise that he deserves—though they have been generously, and unfairly, extended to those who have done far less than he to further the King's political strength.

As the celebration wanes, those who are gathered partake in a vassalage ceremony. While Sancho kindly receives those who have fought for him, he is tyrannical in his dealings with Guzmán and Guzmán's son Pedro, both of whom have accomplished many prodigious feats in his name. Offering an early example of his inconstant behavior, Sancho greets father and son tersely, and with "extraño despego," "desvarío," and "gran desdén" (I.330-2, "strange detachment," "absurdity," and "great disdain"), despite heaping praise on lesser vassals. Although Guzmán initially attributes Sancho's pithiness to the loftier mind of kings that occasionally renders royal judgments impenetrable, Sancho's cruel behavior is clear to others, especially since Guzmán is identified as the strongest and most valiant of Sancho's men.

An early climactic moment dramatizing Sancho's mistreatment of Guzmán and irascibility arrives when the King wants to know which of his men were most impressive in a tournament. The answer, of course, is Guzmán, which further incites the King's ire. Sancho initially makes a poor attempt at dissimulation, pretending not to understand "a quién se debe ese aplauso" (I.378-9, "to whom this applause is owed"), and to which "Don Alonso Pérez" the tournament's judge might be referring. Yet when Guzmán attempts to explain how ardently he has battled for Sancho, the King has no desire to listen—"De vuestra soberbia / [...] estoy cansado / muchos días ha" (I.392-4, "I've been fed up with your arrogance for many days")—and he openly announces that he is purposefully being spiteful: "este lance he deseado / porque delante de todos / os quise hacer este agravio" (I.397-9, "I wanted to have this quarrel, so that I could do you this wrong in front of everyone"). Although Guzmán has professed his loyalty to Sancho numerous times, both formally and informally, Sancho continues to mistreat him.

Sancho finally admits that a political slight underlies his rage: Guzmán previously had favored Sancho's nephew for king until Sancho took it upon himself to usurp the normal line of succession to gain control and install himself in Seville.[6] With this confession, Guzmán finally becomes enraged himself for he has been unfailingly loyal once Sancho became king. Citing Sancho's ingratitude and immature behavior ("en vez de hacerme mercedes, / me hacéis públicos agravios" [I.435-58, "instead of granting me favors, you publicly humiliate me"]), he denaturalizes himself. Instead of granting him the standard thirty-day allowance for preparing his departure, Sancho orders Guzmán from the region that very night, threatening him with decapitation if he resists.

Along with the stark contrast between the king's irascibility and Guzmán's faithfulness and honor, Sancho's "classically" tyrannical behavior—his lack of morals, and his abusive, fickle nature—is overtly critiqued in the text (Giménez 1930: 376; Sánchez-Blanco 1988: 401). For example, when Guzmán prepares to leave Sancho's court, according to the "custom" of Castile and Leon, all of his men refuse to let him go alone. Although Guzmán insists that he is prepared to depart with only his son and his faithful lion, "everyone" follows him, which Sancho takes as another great affront: "Todos tras él han salido. / ¡Notable resolución! / [...] No es justa la ley / y todos me han indignados" (I.490-1, 496-7, "Everyone has gone after him. Noteworthy resolve! [...] The law is unfair, and everyone has outraged me"). That Sancho's attention quickly leaves Guzmán and falls instead on a "law" and "custom" that is frequently practiced, and which he deems "unfair" since it is not in his favor, again emphasizes the petulance that characterizes his tyranny.

Furthermore, when Sancho's brother Enrique attempts to placate the King, he cites the prevalence of the "custom" and Guzmán's men's understandable respect for the "vasallo más fiel" (I.504, "the most faithful vassal") as reason for their departure. In doing so, Enrique uses the verb "templar"—"si yo […] / no llego a templaros ¿quién / lo ha de intentar?" (I.520–1, "if I am unable to calm you down, who would dare try?"])—thereby introducing Hippocratic and Galenic models of humoral theory that were in vigor during the medieval and early modern periods. Rather than using "tempered" as an action conditioning a direct object like "behavior" or "mood," Vélez de Guevara describes Sancho as actively needing to be "tempered," thus proposing even a physiological hypothesis for the tyrannical fits that dramatize his unsuitability as King. Given that Enrique's attempts to "temper" his brother fail, since Sancho's anger toward Enrique escalates to the point that he threatens him with a dagger, Sancho's poor humoral complexion and the suggestion of dyscrasia show how poorly suited he is for fair arbitration, and how his tyranny only serves to introduce chaos in his court.

Finally, Sancho's tyrannical conduct becomes critiqued even more harshly via intertextual dialogue with the *Siete partidas*, the encyclopedic treatise of Alfonso X, Sancho IV's father representing humanist values and offering "a panoramic view of thirteenth-century Castilian society" (O'Callaghan 2019: 244).[7] In "Que quiere dezir Rey, e por que es assi llamado" (2.1.6, "What the Word King Means, and Why He is So Called"), kings are defined as not only having the ability to lead, but to arbitrate and adjudicate: "el rey non tan solamente era guiador e cabdiello de las huestes" he was also "juez sobre todos los del reyno" ("the king was not only the leader and commander of armies" [he was also], "the judge over all those in the kingdom [272]").[8] More than failing to serve as an appropriate king by definition, Sancho shows profound lapses in judgment in his treatment of his best man, especially given how he overrides the judgment of others who accurately appraise Guzmán's strengths, loyalty, and virtue.

Sancho's faults grow more apparent when his methods of obtaining power are read against those delineated in the *Siete partidas* for true and noble kings: "Verdaderamente es llamado Rey aquel que con derecho gana el señorio del Reyno" (2.1.9, "He is legitimately called King, who justly obtains the sovereignty of a kingdom" [274]). Being benevolent and kind towards his subjects is another characteristic that kings "should" have, yet Sancho's derisory treatment of the noble Guzmán and the lengths he goes to publicly shame him fall quite far from the imperative for kings to "amar […] a cada vno segund su estado" (2.1.9, "to love everyone according to their station" [274]). Since numerous characters confirm Guzmán's epic attributes; since Guzmán's loyalty never wavers, even when he temporarily exiles himself; since he serves as a model of knightly and religious exemplarity; and, since the lion that guards him links his heroism to the marvelous, Sancho's denigration of Guzmán and threat to murder him fall squarely within what constitutes tyrannical behavior.

The description of tyrants that Alonso X offers in "Que quiere dezir tirano, e como vsa su poderio en el Rey no despues que es apoderado del" (2.1.10, "What the Word Tyrant Means and how the Tyrant Makes Use of His Power in a Kingdom, After he has Obtained Possession of It") provides a strong intertextual condemnation of Sancho's behavior:

Tirano, tanto quiere dezir, como Señor, que es apoderado, o por traycion. E estos a tales, son de tal natura, que despues, que son bien apoderados en la tierra, aman mas de fazer su pro, maguer sea daño de la tierra que la pro comunal, de todos, porque siempre biuen a mala sospecha, de la perder.

("A tyrant means a lord who has obtained possession of some kingdom, or country, by force, fraud, or treason. Persons of this kind are of such a character, that after they have obtained thorough control of a country, they prefer to act for their own advantage, although it may result in injury to the country, rather than for the common benefit of all, because they always live in the expectation of losing it." [274–5])

Just as tyrants act tyrannically, stolen power begets rash extremes to preserve it. The *Siete partidas*' emphasis on power taken improperly—that is, "by force, fraud, or treason," which was precisely what came to pass in the historical Sancho IV's overthrowal of his father and nephew—creates an intertextual denunciation of the unkinglike behavior of Vélez de Guevara's Sancho.

Ultimately, if the king "usasse mal de su poderío," that is, if he were to make "a bad use of his power," then people are completely correct to consider him a tyrant: "en esta ley que pueden dezir las gentes tirano: e tomarle el señorio que era derecho, en torticero" ("people can denounce him as a tyrant, and his government which was lawful, will become wrongful" [275]). Sancho's volatility, his jealousy-based judgments, his disregard for the opinion of those who counsel him, along with his denigration of a high-ranking official, and obsession with power accentuate the many ways in which he abuses the *raison d'état*, while those around him—like Guzmán and Guzmán's family—hold it in the highest regard. Indeed, Sancho's villainy develops in stark contrast to the political heroism and exemplary status upheld by Guzmán, who, in the play's final scenes, sacrifices his son to preserve Sancho's power and political control despite suffering harsh mistreatment and despite being torn between the "weight" of his love for his son and the "weight" of his devotion to Sancho. As such, Sancho's inconsistency and the irrational judgments that lead him to vilify his greatest military asset, reinforces how political solvency in *Más pesa el rey que la sangre* is consistently undermined by volatile behavior, by the failure to effectively reason and follow appropriate courses of action, and by the inability to control tyrannical, destructive desires.

Notes

1. While 1621 is the date upon which most scholars of Luis Vélez de Guevara agree (Manson and Peale 2011: 17; Peale 2003: 81), convincing arguments have been made that situate the play anywhere between 1621 and 1635 (Kennedy 1964: 101), or less commonly, after 1635 (Ziomek 1979: 238).
2. As Ferdinand de la Cerda was first in line for the throne, upon his death, ruling power would normally pass down to his eldest son. Sancho opposed this, and had the support of many nobles; however, dispossessing his nephew and replacing his

3   As the "Crónica de la provincia de León" explains: "Ni las ofertas, ni las amenazas más crueles del infante D. Juan, pudieron quebrantar su fidelidad; llevada á tal punto su virtud que desde el muro vio el sacrificio bárbaro y cruento de su propio hijo." ("Neither the Prince Don Juan's bargaining, nor the cruelest threats could break his [Guzmán's] loyalty. His virtue was tested to such an extent that from the castle walls he saw the barbarous and cruel sacrifice of his own son.") (García de la Foz 1867: 70, translation mine).

father was an infringement of the rules regarding the order of succession established by Alfonso X himself in the encyclopedic statuary code, the *Siete partidas* (The Seven Divisions of Law or Seven-Part Code).

4   A modification the play makes that bears mentioning is its recasting of Sancho's brother Juan (in name only), as "Don Enrique." Many have hypothesized about this change, particularly given that Sancho and Don Juan's troubled relationship was well known. Both Kennedy (1964: 102) and Bianco (1979: 17, 29) read the intrigue surrounding the character Enrique as a thin veil for Vélez de Guevara's exploration of contemporary history and defense of the third Duke of Osuna, Pedro Téllez-Girón (1574–1624). During the early years of Philip IV's reign (1621–1640), Téllez-Girón had gained the disfavor of the government, was treated poorly, and imprisoned until his death, which Manson and Peele, citing Bianco, put in alignment with Enrique and Pedro's mistreatment by the fictionalized and historical (Sancho 2011: 25).

5   All citations of Vélez de Guevara are taken from Díez Mediavilla's 2002 edition, based on the editions of Antonio Sanz (1745) and Joseph Thomas de Orga (1774); all translations are mine.

6   Following the problem undergirding the historical example of Alfonso X and his sons and nephew, the normal line of succession would go from: King removed from the throne, to eldest son, to eldest child of the eldest son.

7   The *Siete partidas*, full of "reflective historico-moral disquisitions" was likely written at the behest of Castilian jurists with the aim of promoting a national identity and unifying the kingdom of Castile. See Burns (1990: 7); Craddock (1990: 182–97); García-Gallo (1976, 1984); MacDonald (2014: 181).

8   All citations of the *Siete partidas* are taken from Fradejas Ruedas's (2017) digital critical edition of the original and Scott's (2001) translation, edited by Burns, with page numbers from Scott provided.

Works Cited

Agrait, N. (2015), "Por la guarda de la mar: Castile and the Struggle for the Sea in the Thirteenth and Fourteenth Centuries," *Journal of Medieval Military History*, Vol. 13, pp. 139–66.

Bianco, F., ed. (1979), *Más pesa el rey que la sangre*, Barcelona: Puvill.

Burns, R. (1990), "Stupor Mundi: Alfonso X of Castile, the Learned," in R. Burns, ed., *Emperor of Culture: Alfonso X the Learned of Castile and His Thirteenth Century Renaissance*, Philadelphia: University of Pennsylvania Press.

Craddock, J. (1990), "The Legislative Works of Alfonso el Sabio," in R. Burns, ed., *Emperor of Culture: Alfonso X the Learned of Castile and His Thirteenth-Century Renaissance*, Philadelphia: University of Pennsylvania Press, pp. 182–97.

Díez Mediavilla, A., ed. (2002), *Más pesa el rey que la sangre* y *Reinar después de morir*, Madrid: Ediciones Akal.
Fradejas Rueda, J. M., ed. (2017), *7 Partidas Digital. Edición crítica digital de las Siete Partidas*, Valladolid: Universidad de Valladolid. Available online: http://7partidas.hypotheses.org/. Last accessed March 10, 2020.
García de la Foz, J. (1867), "Crónica de la provincia de León," in Rubio, Grilo y Vitturi, eds., *Crónica general de España: Historia descriptiva de sus provincias, poblaciónes más importantes y posesiones de ultramar*, Madrid: Rubio y compañia.
García-Gallo, A. (1976), "Nuevas observaciones sobre la obra legislativa de Alfonso X," *Anuario de Historia del Derecho español*, Vol. 46, pp. 509–70.
García-Gallo, A. (1984), "La obra legislativa de Alfonso X. Hechos e hipótesis," *Anuario de Historia del Derecho español*, Vol. 54, pp. 97–162.
Giménez, I. M. (1930), "Guzmán el Bueno en la historia y en la literature," *Revue Hispanique*, Vol. 78, pp. 311–488.
Kennedy, R. (1964), "Literary and Political Satire in Tirso's *La fingida Arcadia*," *Smith College Studies in History*, Vol. 44, pp. 91–110.
Kinkade, R. (2020), *Dawn of a Dynasty: The Life and Times of Infante Manuel of Castile*, Toronto: University of Toronto Press.
MacDonald, R. (2014), "Law and Politics: Alfonso's Program of Political Reform," in R. Burns, ed., *The Worlds of Alfonso the Learned and James the Conqueror*, Princeton: Princeton University Press, pp. 150–202.
Manson, W. and C.G. Peale, eds. (2011), *Más pesa el rey que la sangre y blasón de los Guzmanes*, Newark: Juan de la Cuesta.
O'Callaghan, J. (2019), *Alfonso X, the Justinian of His Age*, Ithaca: Cornell University Press.
Peale, C. G. (2003), "Estudio introductorio," in W. Manson and C.G. Peale, eds., *El águila del agua* de Luis Vélez de Guevara, Newark: Juan de la Cuesta.
Pepin, P. (2013), "A Case Study: Contract and Its Consequences for the Kingdom of Castile-León," *The Historian*, Vol. 75, No. 4, pp. 806–19.
Sánchez-Blanco, F. (1988), "Transformaciones y funciones de un mito nacional: Guzmán el Bueno," *Revista de Literatura*, Vol. 50, No. 100, pp. 387–422.
Scott, S., trans. and R. Burns, ed. (2001), *Las Siete partidas: Volume 2: Medieval Government, The World of Kings and Warriors*, Philadelphia: University of Pennsylvania Press.
Spofford, A., F. Weitenkampf, and J.P. Lamberten (1906), "Guzmán the Good," in *The Library of Historic Characters and Famous Events of All Nations and Ages*, Vol. 7, Boston: J.B.Millet, pp. 145–50.
Vega García-Luengos, G. (1997), "Luis Vélez de Guevara en la maraña de comedias escanderbescas," in A. R. Lauer and H. Sullivan, eds., *Hispanic Essays in Honor of Frank P. Casu*, New York: Peter Lang, pp. 343–71.
Ziomek, H. (1979), "An Historical Background and Interpretation of Luis Vélez de Guevara's *Más pesa el rey que la sangre, y blasón de los Guzmanes*," in S. Bowman and B. Damiani, eds., *Studies in Honor of Gerald E. Wade*, Madrid: Porrúa Turanzas, pp. 229–40.

5

Women and War: Seeing Trauma with Theatre

Oana Popescu-Sandu

We first meet Matei Vişniec's[1] characters from the play *The Body of a Woman as a Battlefield in the Bosnian War* (1996) in a sanatorium on the German-Austrian border where they struggle with suffering (Dorra) and witnessing (Kate) the sexual abuse trauma and the genocidal aftermath of ethnic warfare in the former Yugoslavia. Kate is an American psychologist who suffers from post-traumatic stress disorder (PTSD) after working with the personnel processing victims from common graves in Bosnia. Dorra has been savagely raped during the conflict and is now pregnant with a baby she at first loathes. The play is a series of monologues followed by conversations between the two women and it uses non-linear, non-chronological flashbacks traversing several geographical and ideological locations. The storyline goes back and forth from the present to the time of Dorra's trauma, and even further back to the story of Kate's grandfather who emigrated from Ireland to the United States, the fragmented form echoing the characters' traumatized psyche.

This chapter argues that theatre works to give embodied visibility and voice to victims of trauma. Visibility occurs because the stage and the dramatic form externalize the characters' inner conflicts and help the audience visualize and confront the traumatic past and present. The play achieves this by showing how discursive screens unravel because they replicate obsolete professional, social, national, and gender power/knowledge articulations (Foucault 1980: 51–2), and by dramatizing a critique of Western psychiatric approaches to Bosnian women's trauma. Moreover, the play shows how characters remake their identity by assessing their immediate and distant past as well as their participation in the dominant discourses of their cultures and their professions. I argue that it is only when the characters can move into the space of a different discourse that they are ready to literally move out of their confinement and out of static and restrictive identities.

The Role of Theatrical Embodiment

In this play, historical trauma is sublimated to the interaction of only two characters, while the dramatic form externalizes the characters' inner conflicts. The stage action and the stage directions help the audience and the reader visualize the simultaneous existence of the characters' past and present, and the interplay of voice and silence. At first, as Kate is reading entries from the journal which she wrote in different camps in Bosnia and Croatia, we do not know that she is also a patient in the clinic (we will find that out in Scene 26 out of 30). Next, she is having one-sided conversations with Dorra, who initially keeps silent and does not respond to questions, and we think Kate is treating Dorra. In private, Dorra speaks to herself and then to her baby, feeling hate and being conflicted about the fate of her pregnancy. Dorra's dialogue with her baby dramatizes the stages of her psychological evolution. She vacillates, thinks about abortion and suicide, and also considers adoption. She feels conflicted at the demands the fetus makes on her body, making its presence known. Her acceptance of the baby comes late in her pregnancy, in a way that almost feels accidental, but it is the end of a long process of negotiating her new understanding of herself and her position in the world.

Moreover, in the play we see how women's bodies are mistreated based on how culture and conflict are weaponized against women. The play educates audiences about the role of women's bodies in war through Kate's monologue in Scene 9: "The body of a woman who is his ethnic enemy becomes a battlefield in its own right, and he thrusts himself into it, regarding rape as a weapon of war. […] In today's ethnic conflicts, rape is a kind of *blietzkrieg*, and nothing can destabilize the enemy more than the rape of his women" (Vișniec 2015: 77). While Kate makes her theoretical observations, we see Dorra as a silent participant in the scene, indicated through the stage directions ("Throughout the following monologue, Dorra continues to look at herself in the mirror and to sing" [Vișniec 2015: 77]). The play does not allow the audience to treat Kate's observations as mere theory, and it highlights the presence of the body inflicted with pain.

Why are women chosen to dramatize historical trauma? Vișniec reveals from the title the political weight of his message that has to do with the way women's bodies are misused and abused in wars. In the introduction to the play he mentions that his work was directly inspired by Velibor Čolić's work "Chronique des Oubliés—Bosnie 1992–93."[2] Furthermore, Vișniec's work is motivated by both his journalistic and his writerly selves. In his *Chronicle of Stirring Ideas,* he describes the meeting point of these two professions:

> Taken separately, both [professions] are extraordinary. However, when performed together, they become contrasting, up to rushing violently against each other. Literature somehow succeeds in raising one towards eminence, towards the sublime nature of the human being. Journalism, on the contrary, especially when involving a daily basis, strikes one against the ground, against reality, against the present time. (Vișniec quoted in Prus 2013: 53)

Thus, this play seems to be at the intersection of informing and also influencing the reader, with the potential for literature to inspire people. Narrowing the narrative down to two characters is a way to sublimate the story, reduce the chaos, and make the events more intimate and thus more powerful.

Moreover, making two female characters the center of the play focuses the story and shows how literature can fill a representational void. In her analysis of the life of rape survivors, Nikolić-Ristanović remarks that "raped women have traditionally remained socially invisible—absent from the historical records that inscribe the victories, defeats, and heroic battles that primarily reflect men's experiences of war" (quoted in Snyder et al. 2006: 186).[3] Scholars also observe the "social rejection and marginalization [of women] enforced by family members and society" (Hashamova 2012: 234). Hashamova emphasizes that although many Western scholars have seen raped women as voiceless and helpless, several works of literature and films from the region (e.g., Slavenka Drakulić's *S. A Novel about the Balkans* [1999] and Jasmila Žbanić's film *Grbavica: Land of my Dreams* [2006]) engage in a discussion of agency in women carrying war rape pregnancies (Hashamova 2012: 236).

Similarly to Vişniec's play, Drakulić's narrative focuses on S., a pregnant raped Bosnian woman, who gives birth to her child. Hashamova interprets S.'s act through the lense of Julia Kristeva's notion of motherhood as an instinctual memory circumventing the Symbolic. For Kristeva, motherhood is a transgression of the boundary between the semiotic (preverbal creative) fullness and the symbolic. Mary Caputi explains Kristeva's view by saying that "This birth, this heretical gesture of disobeying the law, is therefore ethical given that it pushes culture to its limits, forcing it to resist the totalizing claims to truth which characterize the Symbolic" (Caputi 1993). Birth can enable the raped woman to change her relationship with the symbolic, that is the repressive conditions of the cultures that reject her and her unborn child. Therefore, the birth marks S's act as "an autonomous agent with power over her own life" (Hashamova 2012: 239). Dorra also decides to keep her baby and form an attachment to it, an act that expresses her own agency and decision, and which establishes a sense of attachment which she no longer has with her country as a space and culture.

Identity and Discourse

The play focuses on the discursive screens that characters use to attenuate their pain; these screens become useless because they replicate obsolete professional, social, national, and gender power/knowledge articulations (Foucault 1980: 51–2). When we first encounter Kate she is reading from her journal, using the professional language of the psychologist about the role and suffering of women in armed conflicts: "An attempt to apply psychoanalytical concepts to the autopsy of horror. This interethnic violence could perhaps be better understood by the use of Freudian terms" (Vişniec 2015: 69). The character uses lists to navigate the unknown; she relies on knowledge and discourses from her previous geographical and cultural spaces in order to prepare a response to the present. She overuses the psychologist's scientific discourse to cover up her trauma and this deepens her breakdown. Moreover, she reads old diary entries, but does not write new ones. She is stuck as she does not have a new language to process her psychological state. She was the one who was supposed to have the answers as a team psychologist, but she feels she has failed.

Kate identifies with her professional identity and, at first, she seems to approach Dorra as a professional. Dorra resists that until Kate is able to open up more and explain that she is Dorra's equal in a sense: they are both victims. Dorra does not want to feel like a patient interrogated by the Western psychologist and keeps her silence until Kate's motives become clearer. In her monologues, Kate goes to the source of her trauma while also educating the audience on the process of uncovering mass graves. Up to this moment, the language she uses in her monologues is professional, clinical, and distant. Kate is obsessed by a particular list that becomes like a litany:

> What do you do if you're in a forest near Srebrenica and you find the following objects in a clearing, scattered in the grass over an area of about 10 yards: 247 cartridges/a bicycle wheel/a teat from a baby's bottle/a beret with the letters U.N. barely decipherable [...] three packets of Drina cigarettes/ 11 empty cans of Croatian beer/a broken alarm clock/ [...] An Elvis T-shirt [...] there's a 50/50 chance that you're in the vicinity of a mass grave. (Vișniec 2015: 114–15)

When Kate stops ignoring her emotions, she starts to make progress but also to question her own allegiance to the process:

> there's now something else that's taken over my life: to excavate, excavate, excavate, to excavate mass graves in Bosnia in the name of the United States of America, in the name of the Allies, in the name of western civilization, in the name of the UN, in the name of justice, in the name of truth, in the name of the past and of the future. It's hard to carry such burden on your shoulders, Kate McNoil, but you'll never be able to regain your balance of mind unless you understand *why*. (Vișniec 2015: 106, italics in the original)

Yet the characters' previous experience, in the West or the East, proves inadequate to deal with the extremes of their new realities. The characters are caught between normative identities—the Western psychologist, the Balkan woman, the rape victim.

Dorra resists becoming a nameless victim. When Kate explains to her where they are, Dorra notices "the letters 'USA' stamped on everything" (Vișniec 2015: 91): "There's also an inventory number: 6632D. So, America has sent a chair for me, number 6632D?" (Vișniec 2015: 91). Vișniec dramatizes an element of critique against Western psychiatric approaches to Bosnian women's trauma. According to Azra Hromadžić, "[...] psychosocial and medical discourses do not take into consideration that individual victims suffer not only from rape-induced PTSD. Their experiences are shaped by a complex dynamic of 'cultural countering of memory and historiography'" (Hromadžić 2006: 176). The play aims to point to this intersection of physical trauma and the socio-historical dynamic.

While focusing on the ideological and cultural space in which the trauma is embedded, Hromadžić also disagrees with the use of the generalizing label of "powerless raped Bosnian women" as homogenizing, erasing the individual identities and experiences of women. Kate, unwittingly, is part of this process. Because, at first, she cannot yet speak about her own trauma in her own words, Kate employs the discourse that is most familiar to her, that of the Western educated psychologist. She translates Dorra's and her own trauma from lived experience into psychological jargon, from the first to the third person, therefore removing its authenticity and inserting distance between the victim and the story. In her beginning monologues we do not gain access to Kate's interiority, but she reads from her journal:

> See if the following concepts can better explain the sources of ethnic violence in Bosnia:
>
> Nationalistic libido
> Libidinous nationalism
> Infantile ethnic sadism
> The fantasy world of a national minority
> Nationalist neurosis. (Vișniec 2015: 69)

Only through her conversations with Dorra, after getting over her initial impulse to diagnose her, can Kate start to talk about her personal trauma and inability to continue her work in Bosnia or return to her work in the United States.

In their conversations, Dorra mimics and dramatizes a number of Eastern European ethnic stereotypes. However, it is not Dorra herself speaking: she is more like a mouthpiece for memory and history, and age-old cultural processes. In the stage directions, Vișniec writes: "In the following monologues, it isn't really Dorra who speaks, but her memories and her life experience. Each time, she really enters into the skin of the 'Balkan Man' who churns out, year in and year out, those same old clichés, those same over-used insults, and those spiteful comments directed at his 'Balkan brothers' of another nationality" (Vișniec 2015: 93). One after the other, the Gypsies, Albanians, Bulgarians, Turks, Jews, Serbians, Croatians, Greeks, Hungarians, Romanians, and Bosnian Muslims are "lovingly" portrayed. For example, when talking about the Gypsies, Dorra says:

> I do like gypsies; I've really got absolutely nothing against them. Come on gypsy, give me a song. No, don't get me wrong, gypsies are really great. They go back a long way; they have something about them that's deep and mysterious, but at the same time light-hearted and joyful. But, let's face it, they're all thieves [...]. (Vișniec 2015: 93)

In one short passage, the text praises and exoticizes a group of people using many of the available stereotypes revealing the racial prejudice that the voice is trying to hide by saying, "I like them, I have nothing against them." Here, Dorra shows how destructive national stereotypes can be used by nationalistic discourse, especially if it is weaponized in war. To show that this phenomenon is universal, Kate employs the same stereotypical discourse for "Blacks," "Indians" (Native Americans), "Mexicans," "Puerto Ricans," "Aztecs," and "Patagonians." Their map becomes more and more imaginary; it shows that the formula can be replicated infinitely and the representations it produces are fictional. At some point, both Dorra and Kate participate in the production of the stereotyping narrative, a narrative that has the ability to travel across borders and continents:

> DORRA. So, what about the Mexicans? I like the Mexicans …
> KATE. Yes, the Mexicans are nice …
> DORRA. They wear big hats …
> KATE. They're called sombreros …
> DORRA. And they have ponchos …
> KATE. And guitars …
> DORRA. But … […]
> KATE. But, they all want to come and live in *my* country, the goddamn fucking Mexicans, in *my* United States of America, those bastard Mexicans. Every day, every single day, thousands of them sneak across the border to come and work illegally in my country, taking jobs […] (italics in the original, Vişniec 2015: 103–4)

The discourse of "Balkanism" as a quality describing an essentially backward, underdeveloped, barbarous yet exotic behavior is applied here to the rest of the world, matching every single nationalistic discourse out there. With Kate and Dorra mimicking every national stereotype they can think of, and to such extent, the reader is faced with the absurdity of such stereotypical thinking.

Remaking Identity

The play dramatizes the breakdown of language as part of processing traumatic memory. Dorra's lack of language at the beginning of the play is indicative of trauma and the inability of language to express it.[4] What is required is learning a new language, a new discourse together with a new way of being in the world. The multiple geographies in the play, from Ireland to the United States, from Srebrenica and the United States to the German-Austrian border, imply multiple cultures and ways to perform identity. Multiple geographies provide multiple occasions to show that connections to one's past remain strong and are not dependent on a particular cultural space. However, a different geography, physical and cultural, is also seen as an opportunity for change and both characters take this opportunity. This is the reason Kate feels the need to go as far back as narrating her grandfather's immigration from Ireland to the United States in the process of remaking her identity. In the end, Kate returns to her family in the United States. Her home is still her home, unaffected by war, at least not this war. However, Dorra finds it impossible to return. She keeps her baby and attempts to find a new home through immigration, in Canada, Australia, South Africa, but not America. She provides an extensive list of reasons why she cannot return to Bosnia starting with: "I don't have a home anymore" (Vişniec 2015: 120). She ends with, "My country is a dog thrown alive into a well, in a burnt and abandoned village. Before giving up its ghost, the dog howls for three whole days" (Vișniec 2015: 122). Dorra makes it exceedingly clear that she does not want to return. War has destroyed her life, her identity, but also a whole community; however, through the power of changing narratives and discourses and the renewing power of the body, she can go on.

Notes

1. Matei Vișniec (born in 1956, Romania) was an active and recognized poet and playwright. In 1987, he asked for political asylum in France, where he continues a flourishing playwriting career. For an introduction to his work and aesthetic beliefs, see Josephina Komporaly's Introduction to the 2015 collection of Vișniec's plays *How to Explain the History of Communism to Mental Patients*. The play discussed here was written in late 1996, in French, with the title "La femme comme champ de battaille dans la guerre en Bosnie." In this chapter, I used the translation by Alison Sinclair from the above-mentioned collection.
2. Velibor Čolić (1964–) is a Bosnian-born author who emigrated to France in the 1990s.
3. Snyder et al. also review the extent to which rape was used as a weapon in the war in Bosnia: "Rape spread terror across the conquered territories; many eyewitness accounts attested to the brutality with which it was inflicted. It often involved gang rapes that were performed in public places as a spectacle that would terrorize the local population and induce them to flee the region. Rape victims tended to be of childbearing age, and some of them were young (Bernard 1994). Girls younger than age 15 who were consecutively and viciously raped frequently died or suffered permanent reproductive damage, resulting in infertility. Mothers were often raped in the presence of their husbands and children, and daughters were raped in the presence of their parents (Meznaric 1994). Women were also transported from rape camps to the front lines for the entertainment of soldiers. Women in the camps were raped frequently, with an alleged strategy by their captors to impregnate them in an effort to breed Serbian children" (Snyder et al. 2006: 190). For an account of women's lives as war refugees, see Nikolić-Ristanović 2003.
4. Nena Močnik analyzes silence as a symptom of trauma in female survivors of the Bosnian War. In a process that mirrors Kate's, she suffered from her own traumatic silence and sought to alleviate the silence and trauma by using methods borrowed from theatre: "The experience of working with applied drama is rather holistic: it is not simply 'individual and imaginary but also social and corporeal' (Nevitt 2013: 12). Narrating or framing the traumatic experience through the embodied action is not necessarily identified 'prima facie by their testimonial function' (Bennet 2005: 2), but has a potential to expand the understanding of the individual experiences through the broader context we live in" (Močnik 2018: 25).

Works Cited

Bennet, Jill (2005), *Empathic Vision. Affect, Trauma, and Contemporary Art*, Stanford: Stanford University Press.

Bernard, C. (1994), "Rape as Terror: The Case of Bosnia," *Terrorism and Political Violence*, Vol. 6, No. 1, pp. 29–43.

Caputi, Mary (1993), "The Abject Maternal: Kristeva's Theoretical Consistency," *Women and Language*, Vol. 16, No. 2, Fall, p. 32. Available online: https://login.lib-proxy.usi.edu/login?url=https://search-proquest-com.lib-proxy.usi.edu/docview/198811511?accountid=14752. Last accessed April 7, 2020.

Čolić, Velibor (1994), *Chronique des Oubliés—Bosnie 1992-93*, Quimperlé: Editions la Digitale.

Foucault, Michel (1980), *Power/Knowledge. Selected Interviews and Other Writings, 1972-1977*, New York: Pantheon Books.

Hashamova, Yana (2012), "War Rape: (Re)defining Motherhood, Fatherhood, and Nationhood," in Helena Goscilo and Yana Hashamova, eds., *Embracing Arms: Cultural Representation of Slavic and Balkan Women in War*, Budapest: Central European University Press, pp. 233–52.

Hromadžić, A. (2006), "Challenging the Discourse of Bosnian War Rapes," in Janet E. Johnson and Jean C. Robinson, eds., *Living Gender after Communism*, Bloomington: University of Indiana Press, pp. 169–84.

Meznaric, S. (1994), "Gender as an Ethno-marker: Rape, War and Identity Politics in the Former Yugoslavia," in V. Moghadam, ed., *Identity Politics and Women: Cultural Reassertions and Feminisms in International Perspective*, Boulder, CO: Westview, pp. 76–97.

Močnik, Nena (2018), "(Un)Canning the Victims: Embodied Research Practice and Ethnodrama in Response to War-Rape Legacy in Bosnia-Herzegovina," *Liminalities*, Vol. 14, No. 3, pp. 23–39.

Nevitt, Lucy (2013), *Theatre and Violence*, London: Palgrave Macmillan.

Nikolić-Ristanović, Vesna (2003), "Refugee Women in Serbia: Invisible Victims of War in the Former Yugoslavia," *Feminist Review*, No. 73, pp. 104–13. www.jstor.org/stable/1395995.

Prus, Elena (2013), "Matei Visniec and 'The Quicksands' of Journalism," *International Journal of Communication Research*, Vol. 3, No. 1, pp. 53–9.

Snyder, Cindy S., Wesley J. Gabbard, J. Dean May, and Nihada Zulcic (2006), "On the Battleground of Women's Bodies: Mass Rape in Bosnia-Herzegovina," *Affilia*, Vol. 21, No. 2, pp. 184–95.

Vișniec, Matei (2015), "The Body of a Woman as a Battlefield in the Bosnian War," trans. Alison Sinclair, in *How to Explain the History of Communism to Mental Patients*, New York: Seagull Books, pp. 60–123.

6

Wartime Gender Advocacy and Revival of Theatre in Afghanistan

Bahar Jalali

Introduction

Unlike other foreign invasions, the US-led military intervention in Afghanistan, following the horrific attacks in the United States on September 11, 2001, was welcomed by the Afghan people as a rescue mission (Barfield 2010: 276). The long-suffering Afghan population had witnessed decades of devastation, brutalization, and political, social, and economic degradation by power-hungry internal warring factions and regional actors. The exhausted and war-weary people of Afghanistan were eager to see the international community intervene militarily in what became known as the Global War on Terror. Afghanistan was catapulted to world prominence, and its most glaring and controversial issues became subject of worldwide debate. The Global War on Terror witnessed the revival of normal life in Afghanistan and the re-emergence of women in the public sphere. Like so many other aspects of society that were resurrected from ruin, the revival of theatre was part of broader efforts to revitalize the arts in Afghanistan after decades of repression. The development of theatre as a form of art in Afghanistan can be traced back to the court sponsorship of King Amanullah (1919–29). In his efforts to thoroughly modernize Afghanistan in the 1920s, Amanullah introduced the country to art from around the world. During his reign, staged performances of Western classics took place for the first time. His program of rapid modernization did not succeed but laid a durable foundation for reform and forward-thinking ideas. In the 1950s, the Turkish theatre practitioner Farouk Efendi traveled to Afghanistan and taught various theatrical techniques (Tordjman 2006: 12). A visiting American official in the 1950s on a trip to conduct a study of Afghan theatre remarked that all the Afghans he spoke to concluded that the practice of not including female actors on stage seriously impeded the development of theatre in Afghanistan. At that time, a step in this direction was already achieved in the formation of a producing group in the Women's Welfare Organization, which was subsidized by the government and apparently had the best moving picture theatre in Kabul. Male and female actors worked side by side. The female Director of the Women's Welfare Organization stated that the practice of using female actors on the public stage would be the finest step which could be taken toward the emancipation of women in Afghanistan (Quinby 1960: 200–4).

During the late 1950s two leading Afghan theatre practitioners, Dr. Farhan and Khaizadah, went to Germany and the United States, respectively, to study theatre. They returned to teach a generation of artists privately as there was no theatre school at that time. In the early 1960s, a state-of-the-art, German-designed National Theatre opened in Kabul, with a revolving stage, an orchestra pit, and seating for 700. In addition, provincial theatre companies were also set up in Mazar, Herat, Jalalabad, Kunduz, and Faryab to bring theatre to the provinces. During the 1970s these groups also began to include music and singing by men and women. At this time, the National Theatre Company of Afghanistan staged plays by Shakespeare, Brecht, and Chekhov. By all accounts, that was an exciting time for theatre in Afghanistan. The Afghan actress Torpekai Osna, from Kabul, acted in films and then transferred to the National Theatre Company. She learned her craft from her fellow actors, as there was no university course at that time. Theatre did not disappear as an art with the rise of the Communists in the late 1970s. During the Soviet-Afghan War (1979–89), Kabul's police and firemen even had their own theatre groups (Tordjman 2006: 19). But the Mujahidin (holy warriors) militias who drove out the Communists from power in Afghanistan in 1992 did away with theatre. Afghanistan was once progressive, but decades of war witnessed regression and curtailment of artistic activity, especially for women. The US-led military intervention in Afghanistan in 2001 brought theatre back to life and allowed women to take center stage.

This chapter will shed light on the subject of Afghan women's rights as portrayed by the revival of theatre in the Global War on Terror. It is argued that advocacy by the international community to promote women's rights in Afghanistan was a positive development in the war along with support for the revival of the arts. Support and sponsorship by foreign donors were critical for women's rights to become a serious factor in law and policy making. Despite critical scholarly and popular assessments of the Western savior complex approach vis-à-vis Afghan women (Kim 2003: 137–60), who are often portrayed as victims in need of rescue by outside forces, there is no doubt that international wartime advocacy for gender mainstreaming in Afghanistan had significant impact in re-integrating women in society. Undoubtedly, as the issue of Afghan women's rights became the focus of world attention, domestic and foreign exploitation did occur. Women's empowerment programs mainly benefitted elite Afghan women and those with access to opportunities, some of whom became overnight global celebrities. International forces invoked women's hardships under the Taliban as a politically and ideologically expedient justification for the US-led coalition to launch the war (Lindsey 2008: 140–9). Nevertheless, these shortcomings should not deflect from the constructive developments that took place in the area of women's affairs as a result of foreign intervention and ensuing domestic efforts.

The return of onstage performances to Afghanistan, many of which centered on the theme of raising awareness on gender issues and re-emergence of women in the public sphere, was inextricably linked to the world's fascination with the War on Terror being waged in the Central Asian country. One of the most visible signs of women's re-emergence in public space occurred through the revival of theatre in Afghanistan. Wartime gender advocacy by the international community not only aided in the resurrection of the arts, but educated audiences on women's issues through a medium that was accessible to a broad spectrum of society in a country with a high percentage of illiteracy. Theatrical performances by female Afghan actors were vivid examples of the new status of women in post-2001 Afghanistan. Efforts by Western theatre companies to collaborate with their Afghan counterparts and artists exemplified how the war on terror restored culture along with the resumption of women's participation in society. Collaborative artistic projects were also showcased for international audiences, and this raised the visibility of the situation in Afghanistan. Through an analysis of several plays that were staged in Afghanistan and abroad, it is argued that theatre served as a tangible symbol of wartime gender advocacy. Although the buzz of the last two decades has been quieted by the deterioration of security, waning international presence and support, and resurgence of the Taliban, it is hoped that the world continues to build on the progress in elevating the women of Afghanistan since 2001.

Afghan Women and the War on Terror

The peace deal between the US administration and the Taliban, which was signed in February 2020, aims to reduce violence and end the war in Afghanistan. However, there is natural anxiety about how gains made by women in the post-2001 era will be impacted. Nearly twenty years after the US-led military intervention, the subject of Afghan women's rights has faded from the international radar and has not been a factor in efforts to end the war. But sustaining the advances made in the first two decades of the twenty-first century remains a critical issue for women in Afghanistan. The plays that will be discussed in this chapter were staged in the early 2000s when the war in Afghanistan was also seen as a battle for the rights of women. Ever since the Trump administration began negotiating with the Taliban in 2019 to end America's engagement in Afghanistan, there has been a sense of urgency to sustain the hard-won rights that were gained as a result of the war and subsequent donor support for women's empowerment programs. The deal between the United States and Taliban could potentially pave the way for a lasting peace that Afghans desperately seek. However, there are major risks for women's rights in the process. Women have suffered deeply in Afghanistan over four decades of war, and they yearn desperately for peace and normality. At the same time, they fought fiercely for equality in the years since the fall of the Taliban government and have achieved notable gains. Afghanistan in the post-2001 era produced women ministers, governors, ambassadors, artists, judges, soldiers, and police (Barr 2020).

But Afghan women's rights activists have faced resistance from the Afghan government. President Ashraf Ghani's decision to appoint more women to high level positions is an attempt to present himself to the international community as a feminist leader. It does not reflect a serious commitment by the government regarding women's empowerment. These appointments at the elite level are divorced from a broader program of social change that could impact and bring change in the lives of the majority of women in Afghanistan. In 2015, this author established the first Gender Studies Program in Afghanistan in order to institutionalize the study of gender within an academic context (Friends of the American University of Afghanistan 2015). Male and female students enrolled in these courses and lively debates took place in classrooms on gender inequality in Afghanistan. For many students, it was the first time they had a platform to discuss such issues, which was so immediate in their lives. The establishment of the American University of Afghanistan, which is another significant development of the Global War on Terror, made it feasible for the first Gender Studies program in the country to be created. The university, which is mostly funded by the United States Agency for International Development (USAID), was founded in 2006 and is viewed by many as the only higher education institution in Afghanistan that offers a standard of learning that is on par with international models. Female education has been a central focus of the university. However, support from international donors in terms of advocacy and financial assistance for Afghan women's empowerment, which was so vocal in the early 2000s, has given way to prioritizing efforts to reach a deal with the Taliban and end the war, even perhaps at the expense of the gains made by women.

The Taliban were ousted from power in 2001. But they were not defeated and have re-emerged as a formidable political force. Although the arrival of foreign troops offered a new opening for Afghanistan and women, there is no military solution to ending the war. The reality is that a tangible peace cannot occur without a political settlement with the Taliban to refrain from violent attacks in an effort to end the war. Furthermore, the Taliban have been emboldened by the manner in which the Trump administration conducted peace talks. The United States entered into direct negotiations with the Taliban without the involvement of the Afghan government. This has undermined the authority of the national administration in Kabul and given undue leverage to the insurgent group. The US-Taliban deal is focused on foreign troop withdrawal and preventing Taliban support for international terrorism attacks. It also initiates "intra-Afghan" talks between the Taliban, the Afghan government, and other factions. But women's rights were not included in the deal. The reason for the omission is not clear and worrisome given that improving the lives of the women of Afghanistan served as a justification in the launch of the war in 2001. Zalmay Khalilzad, the lead US envoy to the talks, has recurrently stated that women's rights—and other issues relating to human rights, political structures, and power sharing—should be resolved through the subsequent intra-Afghan talks (Doucet 2020). This has been a source of frustration and consternation among Afghan women's rights activists. The exclusion of women's rights from the peace deal is viewed by many as an abandonment of support by the United States which had championed the cause of Afghan women's empowerment throughout much of the Global War on Terror (De Luce 2020).

Afghan women activists have repeatedly asserted that they will not return to the dark days of the Taliban era. One of the purported justifications for the US-led military intervention in Afghanistan following the horrific terrorist attacks on September 11, 2001, in the United States was to rescue Afghan women from the brutally misogynistic policies of the Taliban. Under the Taliban regime, women in Afghanistan were deprived of accessing education, employment, and seeking medical treatment from a male doctor. Other restrictions included mandatory wearing of the burqa, which is an all-enveloping garment, and prohibitions on freedom of movement. Violation of Taliban laws included public flogging and execution. In the wake of the 9/11 attacks on the American homeland, the Taliban's draconian measures against women emerged as a major ideological plank of the case for war. Then-First Lady Laura Bush made an extraordinary radio broadcast from her ranch in Crawford, Texas during which she stated that "the fight against terrorism is also a fight for the rights and dignity of women" (German 2008: 142–3). In the same vein, Cherie Blair, the wife of then-British Prime Minister Tony Blair, was depicted in a London newspaper as being on a campaign to liberate Afghan women (Ward 2001). These public appeals by the spouses of mega-powerful world leaders catapulted the plight of Afghan women onto the global stage and triggered a flurry of debate on the correct approach in responding to gender-based discrimination and violence in Afghanistan.

Wartime Gender Advocacy and Theatre

As the subject of women's rights in Afghanistan made international headlines during the Global War on Terror, one medium through which the stories of Afghan women's lives reached broader audiences was theatre. Bond Street Theatre, based in New York, began working in Afghanistan in 2003. Its goal has been to introduce theatre-based educational programs with special emphasis on targeting women and girls, who have few outlets for creative expression. Like so many other theatre groups that flocked to Afghanistan in the post-2001 era, it sought to revitalize the performing arts after a long period of cultural repression. One of Bond Street Theatre's major projects was a collaboration with Kabul's Exile Theatre, which became the first Afghan-American joint theater project after the launch of the War on Terror. The centerpiece of Bond Theatre's work in post-9/11 Afghanistan was the acclaimed production, *Beyond the Mirror*, depicting Afghan life in wartime as told through first-hand stories. Joanna Sherman, artistic director of the Bond Street Theatre and co-director of *Beyond the Mirror*, remarked that people's fascination with the war in Afghanistan served as a primary impetus for bringing stories of Afghan people to international audiences. The production starts with the invasion by the Soviet Union in 1979, continues through the reign of the Taliban regime, and ends with the post-2001 period.

The late Afghan actress, Anisa Wahab, from Kabul's Exile Theatre, is featured in *Beyond the Mirror*. Wahab was one of the few women in Afghan theatre with a long and successful career prior to Taliban rule. Wahab began performing as a child on Afghan television. She first gained prominence on Afghan TV in the 1960s, where she sometimes played the roles of boys. She performed on stage, television, and in films in Afghanistan until 1992 when she was forced into exile due to prolonged war in her homeland. When the Taliban ruled over Afghanistan and deprived women of the right to access education and employment, Wahab moved to Peshawar, Pakistan. During her years in exile, she performed in projects for the BBC and also became involved in programs supporting children's rights. She co-founded Theatre Exile in Pakistan, a theatre company created by exiled Afghan performers. Following the collapse of the Taliban regime in the autumn of 2001, Wahab returned to Afghanistan and resumed her acting career in a climate of renewed hope for the future. She pointed to the ability of Afghan artists, especially women, to once again work without any opposition. She attributed this development to better conditions for women in Afghanistan after the US-led military intervention toppled the Taliban and to support for gender equality by the international community. For example, Wahab's ability to appear on TV and on stage without incurring any problems for her family was cited as reflection of a relaxed environment for women. Moreover, Wahab noted that not only was there no pressure from the government on actors not to perform but there was even support for artistic activity (Krastev 2005). War is often seen as the antithesis of cultural revival and women's empowerment. But, in Afghanistan, progress and development not only worked in tandem with the waging of war but were made possible by it.

Beyond the Mirror emanates from the personal stories and first-hand accounts of ordinary Afghans striving to survive during decades of constant warfare. Each story depicts the outside structures that were imposed on the people of Afghanistan and their struggle to adapt, survive, and maintain their cultural identity. Woven through myths and memories, family histories and first-hand accounts, traditional dances and live music, storytelling and filmed montages, it vividly captures the essence of so much that was lost during decades of war. In one scene, Wahab is cradling a baby in her arms as she sings a lullaby, but shortly after, the baby falls from her embrace and has apparently lost its life. In another scene, a small child is placed in her lap to replace the one she lost. The play garnered first prize at the first Kabul International Theatre Festival in 2003. *Beyond the Mirror* toured the United States and Japan.

In 2004, a play written by sixteen-year-old female playwright/director Naseeba Ghulam Mohammad called *Toward Brightness* was featured in a national theatre festival in Kabul. The play, which was about the brutal suppression of women under the Taliban regime, featured female actors. The teenage artist confidently remarked that "to those people who want to keep us away from the stage, I say: You have no right to interfere" (Rahman 2004). Theatre became a transformative mechanism through which women were able to purge deep-seated tension.

In September 2005, the actress Corinne Jaber directed a production of Shakespeare's *Love's Labour's Lost* in Kabul as part of a summer-long festival: Kabul Theatre Summer and 2nd Afghan National Theatre Forum. The production ran five nights as part of efforts toward the revival of theatre in Afghanistan. Theatre groups from France, Germany, UK, United States, Estonia, and Tajikistan participated and financial sponsors included the British Council, Centre Culturel Française, Goethe-Institut, Kulturstiftung des Bundes, and US Embassy. In Summer 2006, Jaber returned for a revival in Kabul, and to tour the production in two other cities, Herat and Mazar-i Sharif. In 2005, the performances in Kabul were held in the sixteenth-century Babur Gardens, where Zahiruddin Muhammad Babur, founder of the Mughal Empire, lies buried. In Herat in 2006, the play was performed within the walls of the old citadel. The performance in Mazar-i Sharif in 2006 took place in a public square. The composition of the audiences varied substantially with each location. In Kabul (2005), the audience was extremely mixed. There were all the workmen from the Babur Gardens, who stayed beyond their work hours in order to see theatre for the first time. Members of the Afghan royal family were also in attendance in addition to VIPs including ambassadors and other dignitaries. Finally, there were attendees who had been invited. By contrast, in Mazar-i Sharif the audience consisted of only two women. The number of women in the audience for performances of *Love's Labour's Lost* in Herat was 30 percent, which was higher than in Kabul. For the 2006 Kabul performance, the audience was limited to invited guests (including six women) because of security concerns.

The performances of *Love's Labour's Lost* in Afghanistan, which were part of the much larger cultural project launched by the international consortium of agencies, marked a significant—and now, perhaps, short-lived—moment in the effort to return Afghanistan to some of its pre-1979 cultural status. For the Afghan audience, to see women on a stage simply with their faces visible signaled the re-emergence of women in the public sphere. The sight of female and male actors flirting and laughing on stage displayed a new openness. The 2005/6 production of *Love's Labour's Lost* was a key moment in the history of theatre in Afghanistan and in the long struggle for women's rights (Carroll 2010).

Conclusion

The war on terror in Afghanistan brought promise of a new chapter in the life of the country. The revival of theatre represented efforts to renew the arts by staging plays that sought to educate domestic and international audiences on social problems, political upheavals, economic hardships, and personal trauma of a long-suffering nation. For Afghan women, the war brought promise of reasserting their rights and regaining their dignity. The War on Terror became an outlet for free expression, challenging social stigmas, airing grievances, and cultural critique. In spite of critics who argue that the war in Afghanistan was a waste of blood and treasure, developments in the area of women's rights, albeit imperfect, can be counted as a positive achievement that would have been unfathomable had the United States and its allies not intervened militarily in Afghanistan.

A resurgent Taliban remain highly misogynistic and untrustworthy. Even after signing a deal with the Trump Administration in the presence of the Afghan government, the Taliban continue to carry out violent attacks (Faiez 2020). During the period of Taliban rule in the late 1990s, culture in Afghanistan was destroyed and women had no place in society. The significant investment by the international community in Afghan women's rights and rejuvenation of arts and culture should not be allowed to diminish for the sake of a flawed deal that may lead nowhere and risks reversing the achievements of two decades.

Works Cited

Barfield, Thomas (2010), *A Cultural and Political History of Afghanistan*, Princeton and Oxford: Princeton University Press.

Barr, Heather (2020), "A Crucial Moment for Women's Rights in Afghanistan," *Human Rights Watch*, March 5. Available online: https://www.hrw.org/news/2020/03/05/crucial-moment-womens-rights-afghanistan. Last accessed July 18, 2020.

Berry, Kim (2003), "The Symbolic Use of Afghan Women in the War on Terror," *Humboldt Journal of Social Relations*, Vol. 27, No. 2, pp. 137–60.

Carroll, William C. (2010), "'Love's Labour's Lost' in Afghanistan," *Shakespeare Bulletin*, Vol. 28, No. 4, Winter, pp. 443–58. Available online: https://www.jstor.org/stable/26348477. Last accessed March 18, 2020.

De Luce, Dan (2020), "No Guarantees for Afghan Women in Draft U.S.-Taliban Deal," *NBC News*, February 23. Available online: https://www.nbcnews.com/politics/national-security/no-guarantees-afghan-women-draft-u-s-taliban-deal-n1140471. Last accessed June 23, 2020.

Doucet, Lyse (2020), "Afghan Conflict: U.S. and Taliban Sign Deal to End 18-year War," *BBC*, February 29. Available online: https://www.bbc.com/news/world-asia-51689443. Last accessed July 17, 2020.

Faiez, Rahim (2020), "Afghan Officials Say Taliban Attacks Kill 11 Troops, Police," *ABC News*, March 30. Available online: https://abcnews.go.com/International/wireStory/afghan-officials-taliban-attacks-kill-11-troops-police-69868022. Last accessed April 7, 2020.

Friends of the American University of Afghanistan (2015), "AUAF Launches Afghanistan's First Gender Studies Program," May 18. Available online: https://friendsofauaf.org/auaf-launches-afghanistans-first-gender-studies-program/. Last accessed December 3, 2019.

German, Lindsey (2008), "Women and the War on Terror," *Feminist Review*, No. 88, pp. 140–9. Available online: www.jstor.org/stable/30140882. Last accessed April 6, 2020.

Krastev, Nikola (2005), "Afghanistan: Theatre Brings Images of Afghan Life to U.S. Audiences," *Radio Free Europe Radio Liberty*, December 6. Available online: https://www.rferl.org/a/1063578.html. Last accessed March 1, 2020.

Nordland, Rod (2018), "U.S Aid Program Vowed to Help 75,000 Afghan Women: Watchdog Says It's a Flop," *New York Times*, September 13. Available online: https://www.nytimes.com/2018/09/13/world/asia/afghanistan-women-usaid.html. Last accessed April 1, 2020.

Quinby, George H. (1960), "Theatre in Iran and Afghanistan," *Educational Theatre Journal*, Vol. 12, No. 3, pp. 200–4.

Rahman, Maseeh (2004), "Risky Revival of Afghan Theater Puts Women Center Stage," *Christian Science Monitor*, November 26. Available online: https://www.csmonitor.com/2004/1126/p01s04-almp.html. Last accessed February 15, 2020.

Tordjman, Simon (2006), *An Introduction to the Theatre Today in Central Asia and Afghanistan*, International Network for Contemporary Performing Arts (IETM). Available online: https://www.ietm.org/en/system/files/publications/theatre_in_central_asia_and_afghanistan.pdf. Last accessed March 15, 2020.

Ward, Lucy (2001), "Leaders' Wives Join Propaganda War," *The Guardian*, November 16. Available online: https://www.theguardian.com/uk/2001/nov/17/afghanistan.september11. Last accessed December 1, 2019.

Section Three

Perspectives on *Black Watch*

1

Unities, Communities, and Disunities in Gregory Burke's *Black Watch*

Kate McLoughlin

Gregory Burke's play, *Black Watch* (2007), looks straight into the eye of the storm. In the context of the chaotic British-American exit strategy from the Iraq War that began in 2003 and the absorption in 2006 of the Black Watch (the Royal Highland Regiment) into the Royal Regiment of Scotland following Ministry of Defence restructuring, a band of brothers must maintain the state of willingness to kill and die under orders. In the process, a marked sense of insiders and outsiders is created. On the inside are the men, each with a familial nickname: Cammy, Granty, Rossco, Stewarty, Macca, Nabsy, Fraz, and Kenzie. On the outside are the Writer and the embedded Reporter. The Sergeant and the Officer are sometimes in, sometimes out. Audience members must examine their own status. The power of the nucleus is such as to question who has the right to write, or speak, of war experiences.

Before exploring its aesthetic or martial consequences, it is worth considering how this deeply felt sense of belonging is created. The word "pride" is mentioned early. On the first page of the "Author's Note," Burke relates that a former Black Watch Regimental Sergeant Major put the actors through their paces in rehearsal. This was an exercise in preoccupation with detail—"The exact way to wear your tam-o'-shanter" (Burke 2007b: viii)—for, as Burke relates, the details added up: "Mostly what he taught them about was pride. To take a pride in yourself. To take a pride in what you are doing. To take a pride in your appearance. To take a pride in what you represent" (Burke 2007b: vii).

What are the grounds for all this pride? An obvious candidate is "history:" the sense of continuity with a glorious past. The Black Watch Museum website has a section inviting the viewer to "Experience our History" (https://theblackwatch.co.uk/museum/), and the regiment's past is also strongly represented in the play. Burke identifies it as "the Golden Thread" (Burke 2007b: viii), one of what the army euphemistically calls

---

This chapter began life as a paper given at the British Council-sponsored video conference *Dramas and Trauma* between the University of Glasgow and Cal State LA on October 3, 2007. I would like to thank Alison Reid of the British Council, my fellow-chairs Robert Eaglestone and Lauri Scheyer, the other panelists, and Willy Maley. The chapter has not been updated to reflect political events since 2007. The views expressed are my own.

"force-multipliers" (Burke 2007b: vii): those special attributes, like the Red Hackle, which attract a potential recruit to one regiment rather than another, or, in Cammy's words, "get the cannon fodder hammering down the recruitment office doors" (Burke 2007a: 32). Cammy rehearses the army's official line on history: "That's what a regiment is, ay? It's history. The Golden Thread. That's what the old timers go on about. It's what connects the past, the present, the future … " (Burke 2007a: 25).

Lord Elgin makes an appearance in the play, citing the resonant references of Robert the Bruce and Bannockburn and following this, Cammy narrates The Black Watch's history while the other soldiers dress him in and out of different uniforms from the regiment's past. The narration is not unproblematic. As Cammy tells the audience:

When Scotland was an independent nation we were fucking mercenaries tay half ay fuckin Europe. But it was 1739 when we really threw our lot in way the British.
Beat.
Some people thought we chose this dark tartan tay reflect our black, betraying hearts. Bollocks. Fuck all that Cullodenshite. The Highlands were fucked. (Burke 2007a: 30)

That the Black Watch was raised by the London government in the face of the Jacobite rebellions complicates its historical, and its Scottish, identity. The regiment has a strong regional attachment, with the "settled communities" (another army euphemism) of Perthshire, Fife, Dundee, and Angus at its heart (Burke 2007b: viii), and the regimental songs sung in the play feature inter-Scots rivalry (Burke 2007b: 20). But at the end, echoing the Watch's origins, Nabsy comments that they fight "No even for Scotland" (Burke 2007a: 72).

"History" and "nation" are, as ever, complicated sources of pride. A stronger adhesive is required to glue the characters together. Cammy's speech about the "Golden Thread" is immediately undermined by the following exchange:

WRITER. Is that why you think your grandad joined?
CAMMY. I dinnay ken.
ROSSCO. He was probably just a fucking idiot tay.
GRANTY. He's fay a long line ay idiots. (Burke 2007a: 25)

The scene concludes with Lord Elgin trying to persuade the young men to enlist for the First World War. As they agree, they give such reasons as "What the fuck else are we gonnay day?" and "I cannay be arsed way the pit anymair" (Burke 2007a: 29). Boredom, harsh working conditions, and lack of opportunities may be more potent "force multipliers" than the Golden Thread or the Red Hackle. And this, in turn, suggests that what may weld the men together is the fact that the regiment is, as Burke says in his "Author's Note," "overwhelmingly, a working-class institution" (Burke 2007b: viii).

Class is one possible element in the "them-and-us" outlook so important to a sense of belonging. The Officer's emails to his girlfriend in *Black Watch* are of a completely dissimilar tonal texture to the men's utterances (in the televised 2007 BBC2 production directed by John Tiffany, he speaks with an English accent [Tiffany 2007b]) and the gulf between the ranks is obvious. But the difference should not be overstated. The officer modifies his verbal register when talking to the men—there are no swear words in his emails, but he swears when he is with them—suggesting an attempt to overcome the distance created by military hierarchy. He also recommends that they leave their pictures of women and cars up when talking to the embedded reporter, an attitude also indicative of at least attempted empathy: in the televised production, the men applaud him for it (Tiffany 2007b). And, just as the officer/men divide is tempered, a "them-and-us" attitude is also lacking towards the "enemy." While there is certainly no meeting of minds with the Iraqis—the joking comment "The infidel shall be attacked at the rising ay the sun and at its setting. And when he unpacks his decadent western sunblock" (Burke 2007a: 11) is indicative of the soldiers' lack of understanding of the culture they are within—neither is there demonization. Indeed, the men regard the attacks as excessive: "This isnay fucking fighting. This is just plain old-fashioned bullying like" (Burke 2007a: 40). In the following exchange, the Writer tries to discover what makes the men kill:

> WRITER. Did you worry about having to shoot people?
> ROSSCO. No if they're firing at you.
> CAMMY. It's nothing tay day way them being Muslims or Arabs or anything.
> ROSSCO. I dinnay give a fuck who you are, if you fire a gun at me I dinnay like you. It's nothing personal. (Burke 2007a: 48)

There is no personal, racial, or ideological hatred here, no sense that the men have been indoctrinated to see the "enemy" as sub-human. A definition of self against "other," then, also fails wholly to explain the play's strong sense of belonging.

The most powerful adhesives in *Black Watch* are not, in fact, official "force-multipliers" such as pride and history, nor even the impulses of class consciousness, but the unofficial phenomena of language and humor. In a play containing a number of linguistic textures—the Officer's emails, the extracts from the *Today* BBC radio program, the songs, the pub stories—the men belong to a language community demarcated by a particular accent and vocabulary. In the following extract, their utterances are infiltrated by a line from the Writer:

> CAMMY. D'you get these young lassies tay be researchers and then shag them?
> GRANTY. I'll show you how tay be a writer.
> ROSSCO. If you chow on this.
> WRITER. I don't really know Sophie that well.
> ROSSCO. You dinnay ken her that well? (Burke 2007a: 22)

Here, the Writer's "I don't really know Sophie that well" is conspicuous for a number of reasons: his use of "know" instead of "ken": his use of the woman's name, Sophie, instead of "lassie"; his lack of swearing; his idiomatic "really" and "that well"; and, in the televised production, the fact that his accent indicates a higher social class than the troops' (Tiffany 2007b). The single line conveys an educated, politically correct attitude and constitutes a linguistic difference that is a barrier between this character and the men. The barrier's aesthetic consequences are explored later in this chapter.

The most salient feature of the men's discourse is their swearing. The word "fuck" is rife throughout the play and the men routinely refer—though not necessarily in a derogatory way—to other people as "cunts." Constant and strong swearing is rebarbative to those who are not used to it. It can offend sensibilities and provoke anger. It is anti-authority, a disruption of polite conventions. In *Black Watch*, if the Perthshire dialect fences the men in, the swear-words are the spikes on top of the fence.

The troops' humor has a similar effect. When explosions occur in the televised production, they laugh (Tiffany 2007b). The many funny moments in *Black Watch* are characterized by sophisticated wordplay and a droll attitude to events. Rossco first appears in the scenes set in Iraq carrying a piece of paper:

> CAMMY. What the fuck are you daying?
> ROSSCO. Battlefield skills.
> CAMMY. And what the fuck battlefield skill is that?
> ROSSCO. It's the importance ay having a piece ay paper in your hand.
> CAMMY. Very important.
> FRAZ. You should always carry a piece ay paper way you.
> CAMMY. It's fucking crucial tay survival in the modern theatre ay operations.
>   (Burke 2007a: 15)

What is noticeable here is that Cammy, initially baffled by the piece of paper, immediately understands, and begins to take ownership of, the joke. In a further exchange in which the spirit of *Catch-22* is not far off, Rossco further explains that having a piece of paper decreases the possibility of being checked: "Cos if you've got time tay be checking some other cunt's bit ay paper then you're obviously no fucking busy enough yourself" (Burke 2007a: 16). The pay-off to the joke occurs sometime later when the Sergeant asks Rossco what he is doing and then, on being shown the piece of paper, says "Okay. On you go then" (Burke 2007a: 19).

Two things are notable about these moments. Firstly, they occur in the deadliest of situations: this really is "gallows humor" (Burke 2007a: 12). Secondly, they relate to what Paul Fussell called "chickenshit" (Fussell 1989: 80). "Chickenshit" refers to phenomena such as being given the wrong-sized ammunition for weapons; to being ordered to carry out pointless tasks (like the flying missions in *Catch-22*); in the context of *Black Watch*, to the regiment being deployed to the lethal "triangle of death" (Burke 2007a: 8) south of Baghdad, at the same time as being downgraded to a battalion; to the fact that carrying around a blank piece of paper is accepted as official business by the army. If a "them-and-us" divide does not exist between the men and their Officer in the play, it certainly does between the men and their higher superiors and between the men and the pro-war politicians in London.

In addition to verbal humor, *Black Watch* refers to another, carnivalesque variety: the game of "toby tig" (Burke 2007a: 24). As Rossco explains, this is a game in which you go up to someone, "get your cock out and whack them on the puss [face] way it" (Burke 2007a: 24). Toby tig is part of the secret history of the regiment—what might be called the invisible Golden Thread. The Writer has no idea how to respond to it, at that moment definitively rendered an outsider. Later in the play, there is mention of other things which it is deemed unsuitable to show to outsiders: the pictures of women and cars (Burke 2007a: 34–8); even smoking (Burke 2007a: 37). Humor, indecent games, pornography, mild sedatives: these are all outlets for insiders which keep outsiders at bay.

What is created is nothing less than a "tribe" (Burke 2007b: viii). *Black Watch* presents a very masculine group; far from home; whose members (in the case of Fraz) choose to return to service ("I wasnay gonnay let these cunts go back tay war wayout me, was I?") (Burke 2007a: 19); who are sexist, racist, and homophobic; who have responded, in Burke's words, to "the seductive nature of surrendering yourself to an institution that has refined its appeal to the male psyche's yearning for a strong identity" (Burke 2007b: viii). It is, explicitly, not a "metropolitan" or "multicultural" group (Burke 2007b: viii), and in many ways it is unattractive. Ostensibly, its members spend most of their time teasing, criticizing, even fighting with each other, but there is a moment in the play when the strong bonds of feeling between them shine through. This is when Stewarty is becoming belligerent toward the Writer and his friends remove him from the pub before he can do any harm. "Today," writes Burke, "in our supposedly fractured, atomised society, the regiment exists on a different plane" (Burke 2007b: viii). This chapter has suggested some possible sources of this unity but not yet asked how and why it functions. In the final section, these questions are addressed.

It is a chilling fact that a military unit's propensity to kill is proportionate to its internal cohesion. In *An Intimate History of Killing*, Joanna Bourke notes that, in the First World War, "love for one's comrades was widely regarded as the strongest incentive for murderous aggression" (Bourke 1999: 141). After the Second World War, in the belief that "human warmth […] was essential to the offensive spirit," men were encouraged by their commandants to touch each other (Bourke 1999: 87). This outlook is quite clear in *Black Watch*, delivered explicitly at the end of the play:

CAMMY. That's what we joined the army tay day.
ROSSCO. Fight.
MACCA. No for Britain.
NABSY. No even for Scotland.
CAMMY. I fought for my regiment.
ROSSCO. I fought for my platoon.
NABSY. I fought for my section.
STEWARTY. I fought for my mates. (Burke 2007a: 72)

The "even" in "No even for Scotland" is significant—nationalism dies hard—but the steady reduction of unit size confirms that loyalty and love are the stronger the more closely they are focused. This is also the thought underlying Henry V's call-to-arms that is his St. Crispin's Day Speech:

> No, faith, my coz, wish not a man from England.
> God's peace! I would not lose so great an honour
> As one man more methinks would share from me
> For the best hope I have. (*Henry V*, 4.3.30–3)

The "happy few" are happy, or blessed, because they *are* few. Reinforcements would dilute, rather than enhance, their force as a fighting unit (or, at least, this is the pragmatic line Henry takes in the interests of maintaining morale).

Now, if unity has consequences for effective fighting, it has other consequences for the representation of that fighting. Throughout war literature—if so expansive a phrase may be used—the right to write (or speak) about conflict is tied to experience.[1] The gulf between non-combatants' expectations and "reality" is made clear at the very beginning of *Black Watch*, when triumphal bagpipe and drum music and moving saltire lights, reminiscent of the Edinburgh Tattoo, give way to the bathetic entry of Cammy "dressed in civvies": "A'right. Welcome to this story of the Black Watch" (Burke 2007a: 3). The bathos is a reminder that the war ceremonials that the public is used to—another is the annual Festival of Remembrance—are completely sanitized versions of what happens in conflict and effectively function as rituals of forgetting.

In *Black Watch*, the gap between combatant and non-combatant is even more evident in the scenes involving the Writer and the embedded Reporter. As already described, the Writer is completely differentiated, linguistically, from the troops. Bullying him, the soldiers question his masculinity: "He looks like a poof" (Burke 2007a: 5) (in the televised production, he wears a tank-top and comports himself nervously [Tiffany 2007b]). They also comment explicitly on his lack of war experience—"Go tay fucking Baghdad if you want tay ken what it's like" (Burke 2007a: 7)—and when he tries to express understanding, he is twice told, "You dinnay" (Burke 2007a: 60, 61). (At this point, members of the audience, drawn to empathize with the soldiers rather than the nervous Writer, might themselves experience feelings of awkwardness.) The Reporter, though supposedly "embedded," is equally distant from the men's experience. Not only is he shown a cleaned-up version of their quarters, but his opening gambit—"I'm sure you're probably very busy" (Burke 2007a: 37)—reveals diffidence as well as ignorance, as though he is approaching unpredictable wild animals. It is worth noting, though, that when the explosion occurs, the stage direction specifies that he does *not*, unlike Cammy, Rossco, and Granty, dive into the back of the wagon (Burke 2007a: 38)—is this bravery or naivety?

If a play emphasizes the problem of a writer's inexperience, what are the implications for that play itself? Does the fact that Gregory Burke has not served in Iraq or anywhere else somehow invalidate his authorship of *Black Watch*? The evidence from and surrounding the play is contradictory. At certain points, the value of experience is questioned. When the Writer asks the soldiers what being in Iraq taught them, Cammy simply replies, "That I didnay want tay be in the army any more" (Burke 2007a: 7), an observation that is neither particularly informative nor surprising. On the ground, the troops find it difficult to make sense of what is happening and have to resort to watching the news to "find out why the fuck we're here" (Burke 2007a: 9). The Reporter is better informed about the deployment than the men (Burke 2007a: 41). (The very fact that the characters have survived to tell the tale in the pub would, in many other conflicts, have made them atypical.) So combatants, the play hints, may not be the best tellers of war.

But this is contradicted by the fact that, as the National Theatre of Scotland director John Tiffany notes, Burke turned to "real-life" stories as the material for *Black Watch*, interviewing Iraq veterans in a Fife pub (Tiffany 2007a: xii). The play took shape in an improvisatory way (like the war, it might be said), without a script, through a process of extemporization on the basis of interviews, traditional songs, and "the dimensions of the drill hall" (Tiffany 2007a: xii). "For the most part," Tiffany reveals, "we were making it up as we went along" (Tiffany 2007a: xii). When combat is, at least for most fortunate Westerners, unlikely to be a direct personal experience, a creative approach which is communal and collaborative and which involves veterans' recollections and material like traditional war songs may be the most appropriate. (Mirroring the military, the theatrical company itself drew closer: indeed, one of the actors, whose first professional job it was, told Burke that he was considering joining the army if acting didn't work out [Burke 2007b: vii]).

Fiercely forged unity, then, is both militarily and aesthetically significant: outsiders do not—may not—fight or write. It is also one of the factors which make soldiers' re-integration into peacetime society so difficult. Fused to fight, what do veterans do with their nuclearity upon their return? How do they re-engage with outsiders? In September 2007, General Sir Richard Dannatt, then head of the British army, called upon local councils to give homecoming parades and football teams to offer free tickets to games to Iraq veterans (Norton-Taylor 2007): a clue that appreciation is key to easing soldiers' return. In *Black Watch*, the issue is almost the first thing that Cammy mentions:

CAMMY. I didnay want tay have tay explain myself tay people ay.
Beat.
See, I think people's minds are usually made up about you if you were in the
    army.
[…]
And people's minds are made up about the war that's on the now ay? (Burke 2007a: 3–4)

In the public mind, the soldiers who wage the war are associated with the propriety both of its prosecution and of the manner of its conduct. Ironically, in *Black Watch*, as the Scottish soldiers watch the explosions in Fallujah and criticize the excessive force that the Americans are deploying, they unconsciously mete out the same undiscriminating treatment that they resent receiving themselves.

As the bombs explode, there is a palpable sense that everything is disintegrating. In the last scenes of the play, Cammy informs the Officer that he is leaving the regiment. The reason is not the fighting—"I enjoyed the war fighting, sir" (Burke 2007a: 69)—nor, he tells the Writer, is it that he has seen his friends die: "people getting killed is part ay it ay" (Burke 2007a: 66). Instead, it is because "'t's fucking knackered" (Burke 2007a: 71). What Cammy seems to mean is that war is no longer "fair" when it takes such forms as suicide bombing or the use of disproportionate "shock and awe" ordnance.

He does not question the *casus belli*—it is left to the Officer to make the point about the "biggest western foreign policy disaster ever" (Burke 2007a: 71) but rather seems to invoke what now seem outdated notions of honor and fair play. In its emotive final moments, as drums and bagpipes play "The Black Bear," it is not clear whether *Black Watch* itself endorses these notions, ironizes them, or bids them farewell.

Note

1   See Campbell (1999: 203–15).

Works Cited

Bourke, Joanne (1999), *An Intimate History of Killing: Face to Face Killing in Twentieth Century Warfare*, New York: Basic Books.
Burke, Gregory (2007a), *Black Watch*, London: Faber and Faber.
Burke, Gregory (2007b), "Author's Note," in *Black Watch*, London: Faber and Faber, pp. vii–viii.
Campbell, James (Winter 1999), "Combat Gnosticism: The Ideology of First World War Poetry Criticism," *New Literary History*, Vol. 30, No. 1, pp. 203–15.
Fussell, Paul (1989), *Wartime. Understanding and Behavior in the Second World War*, Oxford: Oxford University Press.
Norton-Taylor, Richard (2007), "Embrace Returning Troops, Pleads Army Chief," *The Guardian*, September 22.
Shakespeare, William (2000), *Henry V*, ed. T. W. Craik, in *Arden Shakespeare Complete Works*, London: Arden.
Tiffany, John (2007a), "Director's Note," in Gregory Burke, *Black Watch*, London: Faber and Faber, pp. ix–vii.
Tiffany, John, dir. (2007b), *Black Watch*. BBC2, June 27.

2

Better Break It: A Case Study of *Black Watch*

Christopher Merrill

The stage direction reads: "*There is a blast outside the wagon*," and in the production of *Black Watch* that I attended, in the Freud Theater at UCLA, the wagon was a hollowed-out pool table in which five soldiers in combat gear sat side by side. When the sound of an explosion shook the auditorium, the soldiers tumbled into one another, orders were shouted out, the wagon lurched in one direction and then another until it finally came to a stop. Confusion reigned until a soldier described their predicament.

"We've been hit," he said. "We're going nowhere" (Burke 2010: 53).

This was an apt metaphor for our situation in the wake of 9/11, 3/11, and 7/11, in the seventh year of President George W. Bush's war on terror, when these notes were first assembled.[1] We had been hit—in New York and Washington, in London and Madrid, in Bali and Islamabad, in Amman and Casablanca—and we were going nowhere. The dramatic power of *Black Watch* lies in its revelation of some of the ways in which terror can induce paralysis—physical, moral, and political. Certainly our conduct of the war on terror, the most visible emblem of which was the quagmire in Iraq, had paralyzed the American body politic—and alienated people the world over. Never had so many viewed the United States in such dark terms—which made my presence at a conference on Scotland's place in the world a bit of an anomaly. The last thing anyone needed was a lecture from an American about how to win hearts and minds. It would have been equally foolhardy for me to tell the Scottish government how to devise a cultural diplomacy suitable for its strategic needs. But perhaps it would prove useful for me to discuss what I took to be a particularly successful example of cultural diplomacy—the international tour of *Black Watch*, which played to enthusiastic crowds, in the autumn of 2007, in Los Angeles and New York.

What impressed me from the opening scene of *Black Watch* was its determination to rouse us from our collective stupor. With a skilful mixture of stories and jokes collected from veterans of Scotland's famous regiment, song, dance, and video sequences, the play raises important questions that cannot be ignored about the nature and history of our involvement in Iraq—and the consequences of sending soldiers on an ill-defined mission. Kafka said that "a book should serve as the axe for the frozen sea within us" (Kafka 1904). *Black Watch* is such an axe.

It is also a fine piece of theatre diplomacy—a prestige gift, in Nicholas Cull's phrasing, which in my country helped to articulate questions about our adventure in Mesopotamia. Drama can clarify a crisis—personal and political, religious and social—and in its attention to the details and textures of daily life for soldiers in the war zone *Black Watch* brought into focus some of our uneasiness about the hell to which we had consigned hundreds of thousands of troops—and millions of Iraqis. What the National Theatre of Scotland gave us was a means of considering our collective role in this tragedy, and this was a very great gift. Our refusal to acknowledge the costs, and indeed the scale, of the debacle in Iraq not only diminished us in the world's eyes but also hindered our ability to formulate policies adequate to the situation. *Black Watch* was a corrective, an honest attempt to deal imaginatively with the damage done in our name. The invasion and occupation of Iraq and its attending crises—the prison scandals at Abu Ghraib, Bagram, and Guantánamo Bay; the "extraordinary renditions" of terrorist suspects; the "disappeared;" the Department of Justice memoranda condoning torture; the violations of the Geneva conventions; and more—will keep writers and artists busy for a long time, trying to make sense of it all.

The action alternates between battlefields and military bases in Iraq and a Scottish pub, where a writer queries members of the Black Watch regiment about their tour of duty. "So what was it?" he asks near the end of the play (Burke 2010: 66)—a question that ripples outward from the memory of one young man to include so much of what we still do not understand about this tragedy: why did we come to believe that Iraq possessed weapons of mass destruction? What made us think that we could spread democracy throughout the Middle East, at the barrel of a gun? What was Iraq? Not that the play offers answers, but the articulation of such questions can help to clear our vision—and so begin to heal our soul sickness.

In his roundup of the best plays of 2007 *The New York Times* drama critic Ben Brantley called *Black Watch* "an essential testament to the abiding relevance—and necessity—of theater." Indeed theatre is a communal activity, which delights, instructs, challenges, and explains individuals, and nations, to themselves. Thus when *Black Watch* concludes with the troops declaring that they joined the army not for the government, British or Scottish, but for their regiment, their company, their platoon, their section, and, most decisively, their mates, we not only feel the power of the bonds forged by war but may also question whether we have exploited that camaraderie for ignoble purposes.

"That's what a regiment is," a soldier says. "It's history" (Burke 2010: 25). And the history narrated in an unforgettable fashion—a soldier spirited around the stage, changing uniforms as he recites the different battles fought by his regiment—concludes, memorably, in Mesopotamia. "Here we are. Again" (Burke 2010: 33).

Alas, as an officer realizes in the last scene of the play:

> It takes three hundred years to build an army that's admired and respected around the world. But it only takes three years pissing about in the desert in the biggest western foreign policy disaster ever to fuck it up completely. (Burke 2010: 70)

The same holds for the good name that a country acquires—its brand, if you will. The American experiment in democracy has endeared it to freedom lovers everywhere.

But we have tarnished our reputation. Cultural diplomacy is one way to restore our standing in the community of nations. We need our own *Black Watch*.

What can Americans learn from this play? First, that our most important ally had the courage to ask hard questions about its role in the occupation of Iraq—which was not the central front in the war on terror but which became the terrorists' main rallying point. This was important for us to hear, because it inspired some Americans to ask crucial questions. We are an insular people by nature—we tend not to travel abroad, a fact that has become particularly salient during the novel coronavirus pandemic— and our failure in Iraq reinforced our insularity, blinding us to the costs that other nations paid for our miscalculation. *Black Watch* reminds us that decisions taken in Washington—to send a regiment of Scottish soldiers to Fallujah on the eve of our presidential election, for example—can resonate in a pub in Fife—where, as it happens, part of my family comes from. This was sobering news.

No less sobering is the view that the soldiers take of the American military. They are by turns impressed with its technological superiority and dismayed by its approach to war. "After a while it's more bullying than fighting," says one soldier. "Bullying's the job," says another. "It's no' the reason you want tay be in the army, though," says a third. The scene ends with the bitter realization that Iraq posed no threat—that in fact the invasion ruined the lives of millions of Iraqis, who hardly figure into the soldiers' thinking: an absence that with each scene carries greater and greater weight.

This play also contains important aesthetic lessons, prominently in the exquisitely choreographed sequences in which the history of the Black Watch regiment, the Golden Thread, is rehearsed and then the soldiers mime the contents of the letters they have received from home. One test of a play is how well competing truths are embodied and revealed on stage; another is the work it will generate from other artists. I saw *Black Watch* with a film maker who, like me, was taking notes. A writer has to figure out how to make exposition interesting, and the solutions discovered in *Black Watch* are inspiring. "Immature poets imitate; mature poets steal," T. S. Eliot wrote (Eliot 1920). I hope no one will notice if I steal part of this strategy for a poem or a book!

Then there is the attending drama of the writer gathering his materials from the veterans in the pub, which like so much of the play is rooted in personal experience. It is instructive that the National Theatre assigned Gregory Burke the task of paying attention to the Black Watch regiment (I hope that American theatres will adopt this as a working principle: what better way to foster a creative environment?), then to commission a play certain to raise the hackles of politicians and pundits, and finally to join forces with the British Council to perform it in the United States. In short, here was an example of courage, which is what we most need if we hope to prevail in the war on terror.

Lastly, the ensemble nature of this creative enterprise is intriguing to American artists, who are accustomed to working alone. In a culture that celebrates the lone genius it is bracing to see what can be created when talented men and women from a variety of disciplines combine energies and ideas to create something new. *Black Watch* is indeed greater than the sum of its parts and is thus a model of cooperation. The play would not succeed without its movement and music, its shifting patterns and forms of debate.

It also prompts a reconsideration of the journalist's role in ferreting out the truth, at home and abroad. When the writer asks what it felt like to be attacked, for example, Stewarty grows agitated (Burke 2010: 58). It turns out that in the tragic event around which the play revolves—a suicide car bomber detonating his payload, killing three soldiers—Stewarty broke his arm. Now he circles the writer, in a menacing dance, to reenact his response to the injury, which was to re-break his arm again and again to avoid returning to duty.

> It would get better and I would break it myself.
>   *Beat*
> Get better. Break it myself.
>   *Beat*
> Better. Break it.
>   *Beat*
> Better.
>   *Beat*
> Break it. (*Pause.*) Write that down.
> WRITER. I will.
> STEWARTY. Write it down way a broken arm though.
>   *Stewarty grabs the Writer's arm.*

This turn of phrase will remind Americans of former Secretary of State Colin Powell's "Pottery Barn" analogy: if you break it, you own it, he warned the president before the invasion. And we broke Iraq, which at the time of this writing made us responsible for its security until at least 2018—the likeliest date, according to its defense minister, of its forces being able to defend the borders.[2] What an expensive purchase.

This is reflected in the language itself. Just as the military breaks individuals down in order to meld them into a cohesive fighting unit, so the playwright breaks apart the language, laying bare its violent underpinnings. The vocabulary of *Black Watch* is at once brutal and restricted, as it is in war. In *The Things They Carried*, the definitive work of fiction about the Vietnam War, Tim O'Brien advises mothers not to send their sons to war if they do not want to hear them curse. But what poetry we hear in the timing of the soldiers' jokes, in their quick rejoinders, in the power of their cursing. There is poetry in common speech, which is all these soldiers have, and flashes of insight.

This scene raises another issue: we know that soldiers wound themselves to get out of the fray. They may experience survivor's guilt upon their return to civilian life. But we cannot really know what they went through in the war zone, and this is what sends Stewarty over the edge. He wants to break the writer's arm so that he will know, in his bones, what it was like to be attacked. What he asks is the question that only literature can answer: how to know something we have not experienced? *Black Watch* bridges the gap between what we know we know and what we do not know.

When I first arrived in Sarajevo, in 1993, to cover the siege, taking notes for my book, *Only the Nails Remain: Scenes from the Balkan Wars*, an older journalist told me that what makes the evening news is usually the worst of what occurs in the war zone but that in the Bosnian capital what appeared on television was what Sarajevans experienced every day. Nevertheless I soon learned that what might be crystallized in a dispatch from Sniper Alley, or narrated in a radio report with gunfire crackling in the background, or filmed at night with tracer rounds fired from the surrounding hills, was as nothing compared to the daily lives of men, women, and children, of soldiers and peacekeepers, of diplomats and journalists, all trying to survive and discover some meaning in the hell they found themselves in. Which means telling jokes. What an American writer may take from *Black Watch* is another way of telling a joke—a different pace and rhythm and inflection: a different sense of timing, a different way to measure time.

In my country we have grown accustomed to politicians and pundits mouthing platitudes about supporting the troops, suggesting that those who question any aspect of the war—the rationale for the invasion, the decision to disband the Iraqi Army, the wisdom of the surge, and so on—do not support those who volunteer to put themselves into harm's way. That this critique comes largely from a class conspicuous in its aversion to serving in Vietnam, Iraq, or Afghanistan—very few congressmen or media figures have children in the armed services—makes it all the more important to create a forum in which to raise questions vital to the health of a democracy. *Black Watch* portrays the men we send to war—in our name—in a space in which questions may be raised that, at least in the United States, were avoided for far too long.

I have written that cultural diplomacy, which has been defined as "the exchange of ideas, information, art, and other aspects of culture among nations and their people in order to foster mutual understanding," is the linchpin of public diplomacy; for it is in cultural activities that a nation's idea of itself is best represented. What people around the world love about American culture—the idea of America, if you will—is the sense of freedom coursing through the writings of Emerson and Thoreau, of Hemingway and Fitzgerald; the music of Duke Ellington, Charlie Parker, and John Coltrane; the paintings of Jackson Pollock, Mark Rothko, and Robert Motherwell; the choreography of Martha Graham and Merce Cunningham; the films of Orson Welles, Woody Allen, Martin Scorsese; the antics of Charlie Chaplin and Robin Williams. Culture spreads from individual to individual, often by subterranean means, and what American artists and writers offer at their best is a compelling vision of freedom.

But freedom is conditioned in part by the questions that we ask of ourselves; of our political and religious institutions; of our artists, thinkers, and writers; and by the truthfulness of the answers that emerge. The very fabric of our lives depends upon this exchange; and when we stop asking hard questions, out of fear or inertia, all bets are off.

Black Watch encourages us to renew that conversation.

When the late Susan Sontag wanted to do something for Sarajevans during the siege, she staged a production of Samuel Beckett's *Waiting for Godot*, the quintessential drama for those in the grip of terror. War is defined by waiting—long spells of boredom punctuated by moments of pure terror—and one of the glories of *Black Watch* is its unflinching look at soldiers enduring the tedium of war. Take the scene in which an embedded reporter is due to arrive to interview a soldier about his service in Iraq. The sergeant orders the soldiers to turn off the porn they are watching, afraid of how it will play in the Islamic world. Then he cracks a joke—"It's important that we have a reminder of what we're here fighting for. Porn and petrol"—that has a particular sting for an American audience. Most of the pornography on the Internet is made in America, and since we also make little effort to conserve oil the sergeant distills an uncomfortable truth about our lofty talk of bringing democracy to the Middle East. "The exceptional curse of oil" is what the American sociologist Larry Diamond attributes to the countries, twenty-three in all, whose economies are dominated by oil; none is a democracy (Diamond 2008: 74).

"Porn and petrol": that line brought down the house in Los Angeles.

A nation acquires an image through its history, geography, and culture—an image that is perforce simplified. Writers play a leading role in creating what Benedict Anderson calls an imagined community, which is central to how a nation regards itself—and how it is regarded by others. When Americans think of Scotland, they think of crags and heaths and the Loch Ness monster; of tartan and shortbread; of *Braveheart* and *Trainspotting*; of Robert Burns and Sir Walter Scott and Harry Potter. What *Black Watch* adds to the picture of Scotland is the gritty humor of men trapped in a war that in their hearts they know is lost, a war for which we bear responsibility.

The American artist Richard Serra was commissioned to create a sculpture for UCLA, a fourteen-foot-high torqued ellipse made of steel, which dominates the plaza by the Freud Theater. This was where my friends and I went after seeing the performance of *Black Watch*. It was a clear, cool evening, and walking in a circle around the interior of Serra's ellipse, which like every genuine work of art torques your view of things, I looked up at the sky and saw stars: a rare event in the City of Angels. I remembered the dead soldiers floating on wires above the stage. We had much to talk about.

Notes

1   This essay was originally delivered as a lecture at a conference in Edinburgh, in January 2008, titled "Scotland's Place in the World."
2   The Iraq-US Status of Forces Agreement, which was signed by George W. Bush in 2008, obliged the United States to withdraw its troops by the end of 2011.

Works Cited

Burke, Gregory (2010), *Black Watch*, London: Faber & Faber.
Diamond, Larry (2008), *The Spirit of Democracy: The Struggle to Build Free Societies Throughout the World*, New York: Henry Holt and Company, 2008.
Eliot, T.S. ([1920] 2015), *The Sacred Wood: Essays on Poetry and Criticism*, facsimile ed. of original, Eastford, CT: Martino Fine Books.
Kafka, Franz (1904), Letter to Oskar Pollak, January 27.
Merrill, Christopher (1999), *Only the Nails Remain: Scenes from the Balkan Wars*, Boulder: Rowman and Littlefield Publishers.

3

Gallant Forty Twa: The National Theatre of Scotland's *Black Watch* as Exemplary and Unintentional Political Theatre

Shawn Renee Lent

"See *Black Watch*! See *Black Watch*! See *Black Watch*!" This is what I read on my Facebook newsfeed the morning of April 3, 2011. I had already seen the National Theatre of Scotland's *Black Watch* in Dublin, New York, and Chicago and was looking forward to a fourth encounter with the hit production. Yet somehow, I was more thrilled to find out whether the show was also a hit amongst my friends and colleagues; *Black Watch* as a shared experience. In times when we had to be reminded of the fact that the United States and its Allies were countries at war, the focus of the play could not have been more relevant.

The National Theatre of Scotland (NTS) is not the first to endeavor into political theatre and cultural diplomacy. But the company's *Black Watch* has brought audiences on three continents to their feet and has placed the Iraqi War into the heart of dialogue amongst all whom the show reaches. The play details the controversial and tragic 2004 deployment of the titled Scottish regiment (the Gallant Forty Twa) to Camp Dogwood near Fallujah, a dangerous deployment where the Black Watch soldiers were to replace American military pulling out of the region questionably close to the timing of that year's presidential election. NTS's theatrical telling of this story has acquired an array of prominent awards including four major Laurence Olivier Awards and the New York Drama Critics' Circle Award for Best Foreign Play.

Black Watch premiered at the Edinburgh Festival Fringe in 2006 as one of the first projects for the newly launched National Theatre of Scotland based in Glasgow but producing work in alternative venues rather than a home theatre building. Along with the Scottish Opera, Scottish Ballet, Scottish Chamber Orchestra, and Royal Scottish National Orchestra, NTS receives direct funding from the Scottish Government as one of the country's five selected National Performing Companies. Following its successful premiere in Edinburgh, *Black Watch* took to the road for a Scottish Tour in 2007 (Pitlochry, Aberdeen, Glasgow, Dumfries, and Dingwall), a US Tour in 2007 (Los Angeles and New York), an International Tour in 2008 (Sydney, Perth, Coventry, Virginia, Toronto, London, Dublin, New York, and more), and a UK/US Tour in 2010–2011 (Glasgow, Aberdeen, Belfast, London, Washington, DC,

Charlotte, Austin, Coventry, Glenrothes, Chicago, and New York). *Black Watch* and its touring cast are big news. In speaking to the project's importance to its home country, lead actor Paul Higgins says, "I have to be careful here because I haven't lived in Scotland for approaching thirty years [Higgins resides in London], but I think the NTS has been a great boost to Scottish theatre at home. The diversity of work, the variety of venues, the reaching out to non-theatregoers, the redefining of what theatre is in Scotland" (Higgins 2011). Regarding the *Black Watch* project specifically, Higgins adds, "Scottish newspapers, which didn't mention theatre unless there was some sort of sex scandal, fell over themselves to cover our first trip to NYC" (Higgins 2011).

When the National Theatre of Scotland's Artistic Director, Vicky Featherstone, was challenged to build a full twelve months of programming for the pilot year of the company, she searched the newspapers for a current, contemporary story that had national relevancy. Featherstone found the story of the Black Watch deployment and attack and commissioned director John Tiffany (also Associate Director of the company) to bring it to the stage. Tiffany reached out to playwright Gregory Burke whom he had known since first collaborating in 2001. For both Tiffany and Burke, *Black Watch* was never intended to tour or to be a tool for any sort of cultural diplomacy. Burke explains,

> I wrote a script for a play that I never in a million years thought would have any of the success it has. From a writer's point of view, it's easy to make an audience sympathize with handsome, young men who are going to die tragically in a suicide bombing. Beyond that, I know very little. I think, bottom line, that theatre is show business rather than politics or diplomacy. (Tiffany 2011)

Despite the creative team having no intentions for *Black Watch* other than great theatre, NTS decided to tour the piece internationally with support from a major institution in cultural diplomacy, the British Council. The tour itself was a risk and the Los Angeles premiere were a test of the Americans' reception. To complement the performances, the British Council commissioned post-show discussions with veteran soldiers, online dialogue events, expert panels, and an essay by distinguished academic Nicholas J. Cull of the University of Southern California's Center for Public Diplomacy titled "The National Theatre of Scotland's *Black Watch*: Theatre as Cultural Diplomacy" (2007). Without meaning to do so, the play had become exemplary political theatre.

In order for any play to work as a tool for diplomacy, it must have wide appeal and relevancy. And *Black Watch* works. It has worked for most everyone: for politicians in Scotland, veterans in Australia, from those of Scottish heritage to those of hardened American pride, from the non-theatregoers to the critics. Few productions with similar goals have been able to reach the same level of impact in the contemporary political and social climate. Part of the play's fundamental success is its medium, the theatre, which Michael Rohd describes as "a practice that ... offers time and place-based tools to create space for encounter, dialogue, analysis and reflection" (2011).

During the first international tour of *Black Watch*, the run of performances at St. Ann's Warehouse in Brooklyn struck a special chord with those involved. When asked about audience reception, actor David Colvin who portrayed Macca in the 2008 touring production explains,

> New York surprised me. The reception was incredible even with the accents, the swearing and the un-glorious nature of the war depiction (something Americans do not get a lot of). To be honest [*Black Watch*] was sold out in every corner of the world. It was successful because it was honest, but it was also BRAVE and theatrical. It's easy to look at some of the production decisions (the singing, the dancing, the songs, for example) as genius, but at the time they were enormously brave and had a high probability of failure, or even ridicule! (2011)

Burke adds, "New York was special because, obviously, it was playing in DUMBO [Down Under the Manhattan Bridge Overpass] and just over the river is the site of the atrocity whose opportunistic appropriation by those in power at the time unleashed the tragedy in Iraq that led to the death of the [Black Watch] soldiers" (2011).

This chapter highlights three elements of *Black Watch* that I believe lend to its particular success. Separate interviews were conducted with Tiffany, Burke, Higgins, and Colvin. The purpose is to weave together excerpts of those interviews and to tell the story of *Black Watch* as a successful yet unintentional example of contemporary political theatre.

Likeability

Political theatre requires likeable characters. Likeability becomes critical for the theatrical audience. Although the all-male cast of *Black Watch* can be seen engaging in deplorable behavior and spouting nasty language (scripted verbatim according to interviews with Iraqi War veterans), there is something likeable about each soldier and we in the audience grow to forgive and empathize with them. They are simply boys putting up a front, both in the pub and in war.

The likeability factor is established first thing in the play, before anyone is swept into any action. As a central character and narrator, Cammy serves as the audience's guide. It is agreed that he must be played by an attractive and genuinely charming young actor with a perfect balance of vulnerability and pride. Cammy's mates are much harder to like, but Burke is clever to often provide them with likeable moments. Each of the young soldiers in this Black Watch regiment displays some of the traits of likeability that we value, as identified by Martina Boon:

- has something to fight for.
- is willing to sacrifice for something.
- has some special skill or ability.
- has some handicap or hardship that makes him an underdog.
- has a flaw that readers (audience) can relate to and forgive.

- operates from motivation the readers (audience) can see and understand.
- has wit, spunk, or a sense of humor.

Likeability is important in theatre and the first spark in cross-cultural understanding. Audiences must like a character enough to tap into empathy. They may even grow to like a character sufficiently to care about and truly "hear" them. This liking could apply to an emotional or psychological receptivity toward the actors, the producing company, or the culture they represent.

In the case of *Black Watch*, likeability was not an intention of the creative team. As Colvin explains, "We were not there to be liked as characters, nor disliked. We were just there to give a truthful representation of these boys, something I think we achieved" (2011). Perhaps for *Black Watch*, likeability results from the common sympathy felt for boy soldiers, despite their rough demeanors and language which can be attributed to a combination of culture and trauma. The play is a splendid example of verbatim theatre, and Burke's mastery of the soldiers' vernacular and spirit derives partly from the fact that he came from the same place and socio-economic class as many of the Black Watch soldiers. Several others in the cast also shared this lineage. Tiffany explains, "The actors became passionate about the project because we very rarely hear soldiers' stories. It was important to show them [the soldiers] as they really are, shocking and swearing, not presented as moral angels" (2011). Burke adds, "They are young lads acting as young lads do. Everybody, deep down, even the most politically correct person on earth, loves a gang of unapologetic lads" (2011).

Liveness

Black Watch has an unmistakable level of immersiveness for both the performers and the audience, plunged together into a highly sensory and blaring experience. The play has the contemporary feel of a rock concert. Prior to performance, *Black Watch* ticket-buyers are sent no less than three e-mail messages warning them of the strong language and profanity, loud explosions, and strobe lighting used in the show. No intermission, no late seating, no reentry. There is no escape. Anyone needing to leave the show for any reason must be escorted by an usher. Audiences must navigate Scottish linguistic features and the rattling loud volume of the drum and fife. Public dialogue is a key component in cultural diplomacy, but *Black Watch* achieves this by giving its audience no space for reflection during the play. Only after the final bows is the audience given a chance to process. Post-show dialogue has an almost explosive, unleashed quality, critiquing both the specific production and the broader themes of the ethics of war. In seeing the play alongside three US Army Iraq War veterans, journalist David Pratt was surprised to find, "all three admitted having come expecting an antiwar play. What they got, they said, was a rollercoaster tale of *esprit de corps* that any soldier, anywhere, could identify with" (2007).

With talented collaborators such as Davey Anderson (music), Laura Hopkins (set design), Gareth Fry (sound design), Colin Grenfeld (lighting design), and Steven

Hoggett (choreography), Tiffany says, "I sought to create a mini Edinburgh Tattoo, with all its exhibitionism It's a fucked-up version of the Tattoo" (2011). Higgins says of the work:

> John Tiffany wanted to assault the audience's five senses and let them know they weren't in for a typical night at the theatre. In the original, we staged the play in a Drill Hall which has become a car park—decades of oil on the floor, no toilets, no bar, no returning to your seat if you left, queueing outside regardless of weather, no interval. The unconventional traverse seating meant that the audience were confronted with each other. The sound was overwhelmingly loud, often accompanied by video and/or movement so that the audience didn't have many moments in which to relax or settle. It's a lot to ask of audience— it demands they put themselves in your hands—so you better do something interesting. (2011)

Along with the music and surprising stagecraft, movement has a strong role in the success of the show. Dance is an international language and for a war story such as *Black Watch*, dance is a pivotal medium. Tiffany explains, "The soldiers aren't particularly articulate, the choreography needs to get inside them. We had to find a way to convey the story not through text without manipulating the story" (2011). Hoggett helped with the telling of the narrative and explored what it means to move like a soldier in a boy's body. His genius is a physicality that is powerful both with collective bravado and faltering stoicism. Paired with intensely intimate moments and gestures, Hoggett's choreography asks the actors to engage in slow-motion combat, marching, throws, lifts, full-out running, somersaults, and assaults. Colvin reflects, "From my point of view, the commitment of the company was always absolute, nothing but 100 percent was accepted. It was in the training we received from the [actual] Black Watch drill sergeant" (2011).

Black Watch, with its new blend of highly intense theatrical elements, is a contemporary piece. The play appeals to the audience of its times. It addresses our need for action, offline storytelling, and a shared cultural experience. It demands presence. Tiffany sums up this idea beautifully: "It is becoming more and more important that live performance find its liveness" (2011).

Ensemble

The third element that is crucial to the success of *Black Watch* is ensemble. Higgins suggests, "Likeability and ensemble might be linked in *Black Watch*. Good teamwork is very attractive. We actors developed into a very good team and we were playing a team. The [characters] looked out for each other" (2011). Colvin adds, "*Black Watch* as a whole was the perfect example of a company working as an ensemble. We put our well-being in each other's hands in the physical moments and for a group of ten actors there was no stand-out role. We worked as a company of soldiers; what affected one, affected all" (2011).

While engrossed in *Black Watch*, I could not help being moved by the physical volume of ten men moving together. The strong ensemble engages in synchronized marching drills, sharing of weights, and brotherly banter. Higgins says,

> The key moment, for me, in *Black Watch* is the parade at the end when some of us fell and were picked up and brought back into line by the others. I suppose, in terms of ensemble, "Fashion" (when we picked Cammy up and changed his uniform while he recited the history of the regiment) was the ultimate for us non-Cammies; the spotlight was on him while we did all the hard work as efficiently as we could. (2011)

In the case of *Black Watch*, the emphasis on brotherhood stems directly from the soldiers' stories. As Tiffany explains, "They are not fighting for their country, or even their regiment; they are there for their mates" (2011). *Black Watch* is the story of a regiment, not an individual soldier. In finding empathy for this group of lads, we in the audience are brought to a new level of understanding of their shared experience. We are asked to engage with a group perspective, rather than an individual character's narrative.

Black Watch became a star (although an unintentional one) in British cultural diplomacy. For most of the creative team, the project was an exciting and high-profile opportunity with no broader agenda. As Colvin says, "To put it simply it was a job and nothing more. In fact, it was only [to be] a summer job! The National Theatre of Scotland was new and I knew nothing about them. I was excited about a project set where I was brought up, but my main feeling was that of excitement about being employed for the summer!" (2011). In 2011, looking toward the future of the company, Colvin continued, "The NTS will continue to represent Scotland's culture and history both here and abroad. I believe it will tell the stories of Scotland and the stories that the Scottish cultural community wish to be told. If those stories have an international audience, then that's a bonus" (2011). Higgins added, "Abroad, NTS has made Scottish theatre an international player, but the *Black Watch* effect must wear off. It's hard to follow, what next?" (2011).

Tiffany explained that although *Black Watch* was created for a Western audience, NTS discussed touring the piece to the Middle East, including Iraq and Eastern Europe. If that were to have happened, Tiffany had no intention of adapting the show whatsoever. The piece was built on the true stories of soldiers and is meant to honor them, not to tailor to audiences. On tour, *Black Watch* would maintain its constant use of the word "fuck," stage decoration including a poster featuring female genitalia, and the comment that this is a war for "porn and petrol" (Burke 2010: 34). For Tiffany and the project, the telling of the stories of these Black Watch soldiers trumps any notion of cultural sensitivity or cultural translation.

As policy, the National Theatre of Scotland does not directly do political work. The NTS may be a child of the Scottish Government, but it is not a tool for it. In the company's manifesto posted online, the following can be found "[National Theatre of Scotland] is not, and should not be, a jingoistic, patriotic stab at defining a nation's identity through theatre. In fact, it should not be an opportunity to try to define anything. Instead, it is the chance to throw open the doors of possibility, to encourage boldness" (Reinelt 2008: 236). This point was particularly relevant during the 2011–13 political climate in Scotland, with the Scottish National Party (SNP) working toward its 2014 referendum for independence which was tied to an argument against UK participation in the Iraq War. Alex Salmond, who was Scotland's First Minister (2007–2014), stated "there's no way on Earth that Scotland would ever have participated as an independent country in the illegal war in Iraq" (Currie 2011). The Black Watch soldiers were killed in 2004 and the play was created as a response, premiering in 2006. Despite this history, the creative team is adamant that the work is neither antiwar nor nationalist.

Although the British Council and numerous critics have embraced *Black Watch* as effective political theatre, the creative team focuses on the theatre, not the politics. When asked about the role of theatre in our interview, Burke shared his views passionately:

> When you construct a piece of entertainment you apply certain techniques to that piece of entertainment, be it a film, play, documentary, etc., in order that the audience response is the one you seek. That's show business, isn't it? Also, in show business, we as an audience seek out the product that we enjoy, or that confirms our view of the world. Now, when some form of entertainment's subject matter relates to the politics of the day, you still use the same cynical, show business techniques to manipulate the response you seek from the audience. I suppose what I really mean is that I am a cynic. I do believe that creation—art, writing, puppetry, bungee jumping—fills the gap that constitutes the horror of existence. I just don't believe that it changes anything or has any influence on everybody. People who earn their living creating things, and I include myself in this, just tell themselves that what they do makes a difference in order to give their life meaning. (Tiffany 2011)

Both Burke and Higgins speak to theatrical quality being more important than political intentions. For them, engaging or entertaining an audience is the focus, rather than educating or challenging an audience. Higgins says, "*Black Watch* became a tool of cultural diplomacy because of its impact on the audience as a piece of entertainment, not because of any particular agenda. Good political intentions won't usually produce good theatre" (2011). That said, looking closer at Burke's notion of "applying techniques" in order to create the desired audience response, could we consider likeability, liveness, and ensemble as excellent techniques for political theatre? Could these be the theatrical techniques to best change hearts and minds?

Works Cited

Boon, Martina (2011), "Crafting Character Likeability," *Adventures in Children's Publishing*, February 15, Weblog entry June 1.
Burke, Gregory (2010), *Black Watch*, London: Faber and Faber.
Burke, Gregory (2011), Personal Interview, June 6.
Colvin, David (2011), Personal Interview, June 18.

Cull, Nicholas J. (2007), "The National Theatre of Scotland's *Black Watch*: Theatre as Cultural Diplomacy," Los Angeles: USC Center on Public Diplomacy, pp. 1–25. Available online:https://www.uscpublicdiplomacy.org/sites/uscpublicdiplomacy.org/files/legacy/pdfs/273656-TBC-R1_LoRes_(2)_-_BW_. Last accessed July 20, 2020.

Currie, Bryan (2011), "Salmond: Scotland Would Have Said No to Iraq War," *The Herald Scotland*, May 15.

Higgins, Paul (2011), Personal Interview, June 6.

Pratt, David (2007), "A Vet's Eye View," *Herald Scotland*, September 22.

Reinelt, Janelle (2008), "The Role of National Theatres in an Age of Globalization," in S. E. Wilmer, ed., *National Theatres in a Changing Europe*, New York: Palgrave Macmillan, p. 236.

Rohd, Michael (2011), "Civic Theater by Michael Rohd," *Howl Round*, May 29. Available online: howlround.com/civic-theater. Last accessed July 18, 2020.

The Scottish Government (2010), *National Performing Companies—Report on Activity 2007/08 and 2008/09*, March. Available online: webarchive.org.uk/wayback/archive/20180521002252mp_/; http://www.gov.scot/Resource/Doc/310051/0097836.pdf. Last accessed July 18, 2020.

Tiffany, John (2011), Personal Interview, June 20.

4

Black Watch: Revising Scotland's Militarized Identity

Lynn Ramert

In 1947, a small presentation of Highland piping and dancing appeared in front of Edinburgh Castle. By 1950, the first official Edinburgh Military Tattoo played nineteen performances to over 100,000 audience members (Martine 2001: 27). Today, it attracts an annual international television viewership "of over 100 million" ("Royal" 2018). The Tattoo is thus a sizable and impactful example of the lasting manifestations of a Scotland identified through Highland signifiers that reify the martial image of Scotland. It is a spectacle of almost overwhelming sight and sound, a circus of tartan and bagpipes, and hardly a place that invites contemplation of the messages conveyed about Scottish identity and its deeply embedded ties to the military.

In 2006, from underneath the shadow of the massive Tattoo high atop Castle Rock, the National Theatre of Scotland staged its first landmark production at the Edinburgh Festival Fringe. *Black Watch*, written by Gregory Burke and directed by John Tiffany, positioned itself as an alternative kind of entertainment to the Tattoo, as well as a critical foil to the massive event. The Fringe, with its roots in defying the establishment of the official Edinburgh International Festival, was an ideal place to premier a piece that challenges mainstream notions of Scottish identity. It is somewhat ironic, then, that it was produced by a national theatre, an institution that is often associated with conservative, traditional, state-sanctioned notions of national identity. On the other hand, national theatres, such as those in Ireland and Finland, have served as cultural agitators for political change or, at the very least, the recognition of the value of marginalized cultures. The very fact that Scotland has a national theatre is indicative of the Scots' desire to explore both their cultural identity as distinct from British identity and Scotland's role within British culture.

Scotland's deep involvement with war and empire has significantly inflected Scottish identity. Scots were involved in imperial atrocities, including during the Indian Rebellion of 1857; many individual Scots benefitted from the Empire, and many perpetuated the missionary goal of "civilizing" the native peoples of colonized lands. Is, then, Scotland colonizer or colonized? What does it mean to be both? Can Scotland have participated in and even benefitted from the Empire and yet still claim to be an exploited nation?

Unlike the Tattoo, *Black Watch* scrutinizes this Scottish intimacy with war and empire. The result is somewhat ambiguous, a sort of "support the soldier, but not the war" kind of message. It is, after all, difficult to dislike the men we get to know over the course of the play and to not find them impressive or to fault them for being cogs in the wheels of the military machine (which they deny being in their efforts to establish personal agency). But *Black Watch* shows that oftentimes Scots soldiers did not benefit from, and were in fact exploited by, the imperial machine, and encourages critical reflection on Scotland's role within Great Britain and the British Empire and its legacy. The result is a nuanced depiction of a Scotland seeking a new identity and independence in a new century.

Black Watch in some ways replicates the representation of Scottish identity in the Tattoo, from the tartan and bagpipes to the projections of the waving saltire and marching in formation, but it also offers significant revisions. Most importantly, *Black Watch* invites the audience to consider the issues it exposes. Based on the "concept of a self-reflexive military parade," the play both provides a "pointed critique of [Scotland's] tendency to mythologize the glory of the Scottish military" (Griffin 2008: 470) and takes a critical stance toward its intimacy with the British Empire and the many wars fought in its name. More than a play about war, *Black Watch* signals a cultural shift in Scotland in which culture producers are willing to critically examine the foundations of Scottish cultural identity, and most importantly, its deeply entrenched identification with the military.[1] Unlike the Tattoo, which displays Scotland's military past as only a celebration of tradition, *Black Watch* takes a critical look at the history of the military in Scotland and individual soldiers' experiences of it. The highly ambivalent and complex representation of masculinity in the play challenges popular notions of the military, martial entertainment, and mainstream Scottish identity.

Black Watch tells the story of the famous Scottish regiment of the same name. Widely acclaimed inside and outside of Scotland, the play received many awards, including four Oliviers. It was the National Theatre of Scotland's first major success as well as the first play that it toured internationally. It is based on interviews with former Black Watch soldiers and their experiences during their controversial deployment for Operation TELIC in Iraq in 2004, including the deaths of three soldiers and an interpreter in a car bomb explosion. A character called the Writer meets with former soldier Cammy and his Black Watch friends in a pub in Fife, and the action of the play cycles between the pub and Camp Dogwood in the Iraqi desert.

Black Watch reveals a history of the shifting dynamics of imperial power. The Black Watch was itself formed as a kind of imbedded informant group; they were meant to "watch" over their own people and keep order for the government. Even though a British colonization of Scotland is alluded to in the play, Cammy insists that he, his fellow soldiers, and Scotland have agency; it just happens to be that the choice the earliest Black Watch soldiers made was to recognize that "the Highlands were fucked" and use their warrior skills to their advantage and support first the Scottish government and then the union (Burke 2007: 30). Part of the deal was that Scottish soldiers would agree to be "bullies" for Britain. "We'll need to get fucking used tay it," Cammy proclaims, "Bullying's the fucking job. That's what you have a fucking army for" (Burke 2007: 4). In a scene called "Allies," the Scots marvel at the American fire power, and Rossco comments that "it's good to be the bully" (Burke 2007: 40), taking up Cammy's earlier line of thinking that it is better to be the aggressor than the victim. Coming from a nation that has often considered itself a victim of English exploitation and bullying, the Scots soldiers might feel a sense of empowerment in bullying others, even if it is in the name of the British army.

Black Watch manages to balance a depiction of the exploitation perpetrated both by and upon the Scottish soldiers whose tale it tells. Although the soldiers deny that the history of the Black Watch interests them—they claim it is "drum[med]" into them "non-fucking-stop" and is what the "old timers go on about" (Burke 2007: 25)—the play insists that the regimental history is important. A scene called "Fashion" demonstrates this, as Cammy strolls a red carpet and has his picture taken in each of a series of "significant and distinct uniforms from the regiment's history" (Burke 2007: 30). The use of traditional Black Watch songs also emphasizes the regimental history. One of the activities in which the men engage in the desert to pass time is to "have a sing-song," they tell the Writer (Burke 2007: 46). They demonstrate by belting out the chorus of a traditional Black Watch song, "Twa Recruiting Sergeants":

And it's over the mountains and over the main
Through Gibraltar, tae France and tae Spain
Wi' a feather in our bonnet, and a kilt aboon your knee
Sae list my bonnie laddie and come awa wi' me. (Burke 2007: 46)

At other times in the play, traditional regimental songs are used to make poignant statements about the soldiers, and their arrangements noticeably shift from tradition. Rather than fast and rousing, like drinking songs, the songs are presented as slow and deliberate, highlighting the stories in the lyrics and the beauty of the male voices in harmony. When "Twa Recruiting Sergeants" is presented this way, the unscrupulous methods of recruitment and the historical reasons men joined the army come to the fore. The song begins, "There was twa recruiting sergeants came frae the Black Watch / Through markets and fairs, some recruits for tae catch" (Burke 2007: 49). Other verses express that the young men who join "dinna ken the danger that [they're] in" and that some were forced to join because "This greedy ole farmer, he wouldna pay yer fee" (Burke 2007: 49). This last line may refer to the practice of paying for a replacement to be sent to war in place of any young recruit, and the unwillingness of a (likely Anglo) landlord to pay the fee for their tenant, possibly because sending him off to die in war was an easy way to reduce the surplus population on their land, which was the main goal of the Highland Clearances.

The Black Watch regiment's history was marked early by manipulation and broken promises, if not outright fraud. In 1743, after being ordered to England and feeling that the terms of their recruitment for service in Scotland only had been broken, the Black Watch mutinied and attempted to march back to Scotland against orders (Adam 1965: 445). Three members of the regiment were executed (Adam 1965: 446). Within ten months, the entire regiment had been sent abroad, to places such as Gibraltar, Jamaica, Georgia, and Flanders, where it began to distinguish itself in battles such as Fontenoy (Adam 1965: 446). Cammy recognizes this duplicity as typical for the army, stating, "they told us that we'd never have to serve abroad. (*Laughs.*) But that's the fucking army for you" (Burke 2007: 31). *Black Watch*, through its candid central character, does not shy away from telling unpleasant truths about the history of the storied regiment, shifting the focus from the celebratory mode of the Tattoo to critique.

Perhaps the most daring revision that *Black Watch* attempts is to rewrite the masculinism that comes with the martial Scottish identity. The play makes it clear that a major motivation for joining the military is to fulfill a hyper-masculine fantasy, which the military exploits as a recruitment tactic. In addition to football, guns, and drink, Lord Elgin advertises "exotic poontang and that" (Burke 2007: 28). The men who fought in Kosovo claim that "the fanny's fantastic over there" (Burke 2007: 24). For the young men, soldiering translates into a sort of sexual prowess, as their motivation to come to the pub to talk about their experiences demonstrates. When the soldiers first meet the Writer at the pub, they are disappointed because Cammy told them that a "bird" named Sophie would be conducting the interview. Granty explains, "[f]rom what he fucking told us, we were all getting our cocks sucked by this posh lassie," and Rossco adds, "[s]he was gagging for a line up from some battle-hardened Black Watch toby" (Burke 2007: 5).

Of course, the military is a historically masculine institution, but masculinism is deeply entrenched in Scotland's overall culture, as well, making the sexism in the play comment doubly on both institutions. The importance of the military and Highland warrior identity in Scotland is just part of a larger patriarchal culture. From military heroes William Wallace and Robert the Bruce, to literary icons Walter Scott and Robert Burns, to popular culture figure Sean Connery (whose James Bond is the pinnacle of masculine power and allure), to football culture, Scottish culture is dominated by masculine motifs.[2] No women are physically present in *Black Watch* (aside from the pornographic images posted on the outside of the army vehicle); the cast consists of ten men who play multiple roles. Most references to women are highly and disturbingly sexualized, as indicated above by the soldiers' belief that Sophie would be desperate to perform oral sex on all of them in "a line up." The soldiers' superiors largely support this exploitation of women, as a kind of morale booster. The Sergeant tells one of the new soldiers "how much fucking fanny he's going to get when he returns home" (Burke 2007: 18). And although the Sergeant worries about how the porn on the army vehicle will read to "the Muslim world tuning intay the BBC" and orders the men to take it down before an interview, his superior Officer states that there is nothing "wrong with a healthy young woman taking a bit of pride in her appearance." He tells the men to leave up the pictures of naked women and cars, stating, "It's important that we have a reminder of what we're here fighting for. Porn and petrol" (Burke 2007: 35).

Despite the problematic aspects of a single-sex culture driven by testosterone and characterized by the demeaning of those who do not belong to this culture, namely women and homosexual men, *Black Watch* also conveys the beauty of embodied masculinity and male camaraderie, through both the stark arrangement of the songs mentioned previously and choreographed movement. When the tension and testosterone-filled atmosphere nearly explodes, the Sergeant allows the soldiers to play another sort of game where each man fights with each of the other soldiers for ten seconds each. As they fight, the lights change to a violet-blue, the music rises, and the soldier's movements become slow and deliberate. The scene then transforms into a carefully choreographed ballet highlighting the beauty, skill, and physicality of hand-to-hand combat, even featuring the synchronized movements of a fencing match. One man lifts another into the air as another rolls on the ground, and a third spins with a missed punch. The scene draws attention to the beauty in the movements of a physical fight, collapsing the distinctions between traditionally "masculine" fighting and war and "feminine" beauty and graceful movement.

The "Ten Seconds" scene seems to purge something inexpressible through language, a physical release of anxiety and even boredom. In another scene that starkly contrasts the loudly expressed, patriarchal, and sexist masculinity so prevalent throughout the play, the men receive letters from home and perform another ballet of choreographed interpretations of them. This time, it is private and deep emotion that is expressible only through physical movement, not language. These unspoken moments of intimacy reveal an entirely different side of the soldiers, one that could be considered a feminine counterpoint. The men are rendered silent, speechless, as if they are unable or not allowed to express this tender, emotional side of themselves in the theatre of war or in a masculine society. The letters arrive after Stewarty appears alone on stage, covering his head in terror as gunshots and explosions surround him. Stewarty begins to read his own, but then he drops it and begins to gesture. More men enter the stage and begin to repeat this process until all of the letters have been distributed. Each man repeats his own series of gestures, revealing what is in his letter. Some of the stories are hard to follow, but some are more obvious, as when one man gestures a growing pregnant belly and another traces a heart over his chest. Perhaps this scene emphasizes that soldiers must compartmentalize portions of their lives—they must know how to turn off the emotions linked with loved ones at home in order to survive life in a war zone—but it also may criticize the hyper-masculine Scottish soldier identity that does not typically provide a space for verbal expression of emotions such as love and fear. What is allowed instead are strings of profanity and misogynistic language.

The beginning of the letter scene, when Stewarty is seen on the ground, huddled in fear during a mortar attack, is quickly overshadowed by the emotion of the interpretation of the letters, yet it is of great importance, for another unspoken aspect of military service is Post-Traumatic Stress Disorder (PTSD). The phrase is never spoken, but audiences suspect that Stewarty suffers from the disorder. He explains to the Writer that his arm was broken during his time in Iraq, and that as it healed, he kept breaking it himself: "Get better. Break it myself ... Better. Break it ... Better. Break it. Better ... Break it" (Burke 2007: 64). "Write that down," he demands, "Write it down with a broken arm though" (Burke 2007: 65). He grabs the writer's arm and nearly breaks it. "If he wants tay ken about Iraq, he has tay feel some pain," he proclaims. The other soldiers tell the writer that Stewarty had been "signed off with depression after we got back from Iraq the first time," but that "they lost his paperwork" when they needed to send men back. And "no just his. Everycunt who'd tried to leave. Stewarty shouldn't have been there the second time" (Burke 2007: 65). Although military culture fosters a sense of hyper-masculinity and an image of a healthy, virile nation, Stewarty's case is an example of how the real results of military combat may in fact be a kind of hypo-masculinity, a disordered way of thinking that leads to a sense of powerlessness, the waste of healthy life, and even violence turned inward against oneself. The lives of the soldiers, as well as Iraqi and Afghan citizens, are being lost, destroyed, and wasted.

The Highlandized, martial image of Scotland has been repeated so often, from King George's royal visit in 1822, to filmic depictions in movies like *Braveheart* and *The Last King of Scotland*, to the annual Royal Edinburgh Military Tattoo, that it has become an integral part of Scottish identity, perhaps even the dominant aspect of the culture. Repetition helps identity become permanent, and *Black Watch* recognizes the importance of repetition by taking up circularity and repetition as key features of the play, from Stewarty's arm-breaking and the motions of the soldiers as they read the letters from home, to repeated lines and the cycling of the scenes between the pub and the desert. The theme of repetition starts before the play even begins with the loop of blaring bagpipe music played over speakers as the audience members find their seats. The phrase, "That's the fucking army for you" is uttered multiple times, and the men reenlist or are redeployed, even if they are not ready. During the Fashion scene, when Cammy is repeatedly dressed and undressed in the various historical Black Watch uniforms as he recites the places of their many deployments, he underscores that they are back in Mesopotamia, "Again" (Burke 2007: 33). This scene especially shows the automatized manner in which the martial values are inculcated. The other men "manoeuvre him around" and "resemble a squad assembling and disassembling a military cannon" (Burke 2007: 30). Although Cammy's speech reveals some skepticism of Scotland's military values, all he can do is smile for the camera that flashes at him in each uniform, and then continue to be moved around like a mannequin in a tartan shop window. The play ends with the soldiers marching in parade formation, and as they begin to fall, their fellow soldiers lift them to their feet, they reform, and the march starts again, over and over until "a thunderous drumbeat stops" them and they freeze in a tableau, the hall silent except for the heavy breathing of the actors (Burke 2007: 73). All of the behaviors represented in the play have been performed by many soldiers before and will continue to be performed after them. The soldiers speak of "the Golden Thread," the history of the regiment that "connects the past, the present, the future" (Burke 2007: 25). Challenging the persistent tradition of military identity in Scotland, the play seems to ask, is this an endless cycle?

Although *Black Watch* ends with this scene of repetition, which also could be interpreted as echoing the Tattoo's veneration of the military (if one disregards the stumbling and falling of the soldiers), the penultimate scene of the play provides a counter and the possibility for change and a new way for Scotland to move forward. In the scene called "The Future" in the script, Cammy, granted permission to speak candidly, asks the Officer, "What the fuck are you doing here?" and the Officer responds, "Well, I'm … I'm … what's the word … Cursed" (Burke 2007: 70). He explains that his father and grandfather served before him: "Some of us … It's in the blood." The Officer's word choice—cursed—might very well express the fate of Scottish identity as well as Scotland itself if it cannot disentangle itself from the legacy of its martial history. Although Scottish identity will always be haunted with the specters of imperialism and militarism, "cursed" like the nameless Black Watch Officer, Cammy demonstrates that change is possible and can be made on the basis of sound reasoning, agency, and choice. During this scene, Cammy is "*mopping up blood*" after his friends are killed by the suicide bomber, and he tells the Officer that he plans on leaving the army. Michael Mooney proposes that this "symbolic, cleansing finish" is a gesture of being "unafraid of appearing feminine before the authority of the English Officer" ("Backpages" 2008: 279). With his resignation, Cammy "becomes responsible, a Scottish working-class subject Burke sees fit to represent the new Parliament in Edinburgh, and better assess the history between that Parliament and its *predecessor*" ("Backpages" 2008: 279, emphasis in original). Cammy's "feminine" action at the end of the play also suggests that a strong, self-possessed Scottish identity does not have to be a martial or masculine one and leaves the door open for alternative Scottish identities.

Notes

1 *Black Watch* is not the first production to critique Scottish identity. Another example is Isabel and Murray Grigor's 1981 Edinburgh International Festival exhibition called "Scotch Myths" that aimed to critically analyze popular depictions of Scots and Scotland, but instead seemed to simply deride them. Another celebrated play that critiques Scotland's relationship with England is John McGrath's 1973 *The Cheviot, the Stag, and the Black, Black Oil*.
2 There are elements of Scottish culture that challenge the dominant masculine discourse. Maureen M. Martin suggests that the "Glasgow style" of architect and designer Charles Rennie Macintosh and the tea culture of 1920s Glasgow, along with female authors such as Margaret Oliphant, offer alternatives. Mike Goode's book on *Sentimental Masculinity* and Walter Scott serves as a reminder that "masculinity" is culturally constructed and that what constitutes it changes over time. Mary Queen of Scots has also been an enduring and important female figure in Scottish culture.

Works Cited

Adam, Frank (1965), *The Clans, Septs, and Regiments of the Scottish Highlands*, 7th edn, Edinburgh: Johnston & Bacon.
"Backpages 18.2" (2008), *Contemporary Theatre Review*, Vol. 18, No. 2, pp. 269–86, doi: 10.1080/10486800802067228.
Burke, Gregory (2007), *Black Watch*, London: Faber & Faber.
Goode, Mike (2009), *Sentimental Masculinity and the Rise of History, 1790–1890*, Cambridge: Cambridge University Press.
Griffin, Bradley W. (2008), Review of *Black Watch*, *Theatre Journal*, Vol. 60, No. 3, pp. 469–71, doi: 10.1353/tj.0.0048.
Martin, Maureen M. (2009), *The Mighty Scot: Nation, Gender and the Nineteenth-Century Mystique of Scottish Masculinity*, Albany: State University of New York Press.
Martine, Roddy (2001), *Edinburgh Military Tattoo*, London: Robert Hale.
"The Royal Edinburgh Military Tattoo Supports Global Ambition with Enhanced Web Presence" (2018), *The Royal Edinburgh Military Tattoo*, November 9. Available online: www.edintattoo.co.uk/news/the-royal-edinburgh-military-tattoo-supports-global-ambition-with-enhanced-web-presence. Last accessed July 12, 2020.

5

Bringing War Home: Staging the Stories of Soldiers and Refugees

Eva Aldea

When the audience enters the performance space of Joe Murphy and Joe Robertson's play *The Jungle* they enter the notorious refugee encampment that existed outside Calais, France, from January 2015 until the residents were evicted by the French authorities in October 2016. The shanty town sprung up when official reception centers proved insufficient during the large influx of migrants to Europe in 2015, many of whom were aiming to gain asylum in the UK. A majority of these migrants were refugees from Syria, Afghanistan, and Iraq, fleeing wars directly or indirectly waged by Western powers. International treaties allow the UK to carry out border checks on French soil, meaning that migrants without adequate documentation to enter the UK become stuck in Calais, where they are unable to formally seek asylum in the UK. Their only chance to do so is by gaining entry to the UK clandestinely.

During a performance of *The Jungle* the theatre space becomes the camp's Afghan restaurant. The audience is seated at tables with condiments and menu cards, the stage is a central runway that feels like an extension of these, and the performance often spills over into the spaces between audience members. Before the play starts there is already activity: conversations, exchanges, wiping of tables, other tasks of everyday life in the restaurant and the camp. Looking around, the newly arrived audience realize that their seats seem to be in one of the several designated zones: Afghanistan, Syria, Iraq, Eritrea, and so on.

The staging of *The Jungle* deliberately makes the audience enter the world of those who have not been able to enter theirs. While the play is only minimally immersive, this set-up is palpably poignant: on any night of its West End run in the center of London, the comfortably cosmopolitan audience is being taken to the *outside* by being placed on the *inside*. The refugee is a symbol of that which the cosmopolitan center wants to keep out, to protect itself from, and by doing so inevitably perpetuates: insecurity, violence, war. The refugee turns up at our doorstep reminding us that there is no such thing as a safe world, that the wars our governments wage have human victims, and that bombing a country "back to the stone-age" means that its people need to find somewhere else to live.

While the staging of *The Jungle* attempts to put us *in the midst of* the life of the refugee, it also raises the question as to whether it is possible to represent that experience at all. It shares this dilemma with a play that over a decade earlier attempted to place the audience inside the soldier's experience. Theatregoers entering the performance space of Gregory Burke's *Black Watch* which "reveals what it means to be part of that legendary Scottish regiment, and what it means to be a part of the war on terror," (Burke 2007: back cover) also find themselves engaged in the play before it actually begins. Scaffolding towers and seating banks flank the main stage esplanade, echoing a parade ground setting, and loud bagpipes and drum Tattoo music blare onto the as yet empty space.

Both *The Jungle* and *Black Watch* use a range of quasi-immersive staging techniques: unconventional stage construction allows the performance to overlap with the "safe" space of the audience. Special effects are employed to amplify this sense of immersion: music, noise, smoke, and lighting invading the space of the spectator. These techniques go some way to shift the audience outside of their comfort zone and to convey some of the experiences they are trying to represent, but the plays share a certain self-conscious insight into the fact that they cannot engage their audiences fully in what they are depicting, that trying to communicate the experience of the soldier or the refugee is bound to fail. Ultimately, neither play can claim it has made the audience feel what it is "really like" to be a soldier or refugee. In the last analysis, these are fairly traditional pieces of theatre that reach a fairly traditional section of the theatre audience. However, this is key to how we can read these plays, in particular *The Jungle*, as interventions in a discussion about war and its effects.

In a way that is different to *Black Watch*, where while immersed by noise and light spectators are essentially on the sidelines, *The Jungle* audience finds itself inside the refugee camp, part of that which is watched, under scrutiny. The play works on giving a voice to the voiceless and bringing to our attention the misery on our doorstep, but the venture is ultimately more about how the European subject reconstitutes itself in relation to the migrant.

The question of authenticity and representation is a shadow cast by both plays. The sense that what we are seeing as an audience is somehow "real," or even "factual" is key to both works, while both also eschew the verbatim model. *Black Watch* dramatizes its own inception in the opening scene, pitting the Writer against a bunch of soldiers on leave, whose stories we become privy to. The scene immediately articulates the play's self-awareness that representing the soldier's experience is difficult, even impossible. Being a soldier is categorically not what you *think* it is.

> CAMMY. It wasnay like I thought it was gonnay be. I don't know what the fuck I thought it was gonnay be like, but it wasnay like what it was. (Burke 2007: 5)

In one of the most commented on scenes in the play, soldiering "reality" literally erupts into the pub interior, the green baize of the pool table splitting open reveal men in uniform. Discordant, the voice-over in this scene is an extract from a radio news show, extending the sense that there is irreconcilable distance between the life of the soldier and of those watching: the audience and the commentator. The climax of the play is the moving, highly stylized performance of an armored vehicle hitting an improvised explosive device, the consequences performed in slow motion with the aid of winch cables. This is nothing like being blown up, but it is all about commenting on soldiers being blown up.

It is, after all, impossible to put war itself on the stage, impossible to fully convey its horrors. All we can do is balk at the senseless bloodshed, feel torn at the noble indoctrination of young men, ponder the legality or otherwise of the military action, all at a remove. The question is, then, does the figure of the refugee—the human being affected by war—allow a possibility of staging war that is more accessible to an audience that has no experience of war?

The Jungle faces the same issues of authenticity and of representation as *Black Watch*. The first scene, after establishing the setting through an informal census, hits us with the most emotionally and viscerally resonant of events: the burial of a young boy, accompanied by rites and songs, and then the invasion of the camp by French police with smoke and explosions and chaos.

The next scene cuts to a lone narrator, breaking the fourth wall. Thus, while less explicitly than *Black Watch*, *The Jungle* also comments on its own coming into being: these are the stories of real people. The approach in developing the production, like *Black Watch*, was a workshopping process where elements of factual events and real stories were woven into a fictional performance that includes multiple voices, and that "honors" the humanity the playwrights encountered in the camp (Marcoina 2018).

An arresting aspect of the performance of *The Jungle* is that some of the actors are "real" refugees. It is not clear, of course, from the performance itself who is an erstwhile Jungle resident and who is a professional actor, although the details are available by reading the program carefully (Ambassador Theatre Group 2018). This fact inevitably adds something to the experience of the audience: the refugee has made it across the channel and is standing here in the cultural heartland of the UK. The person, whoever they may be, is now not merely hosted by us, accepted and integrated, but is extending their hospitality to us that night.

Thus, while *The Jungle* cannot immerse the audience fully in the experience of the refugee, it positions the audience in a manner that has potential to make them reconsider not only the experience of those that flee but their own place. Rather than simply allowing the spectator to pretend they are experiencing something they do not have the capacity to fully comprehend, the play attempts to question the privileged position of the audience member. This chimes with Rosi Braidotti's notion of a nomadic subjectivity that "addresses the need to destabilize and activate the centre" and through which "mainstream subject positions [are] challenged in relation to and interaction with the marginal subjects" (Braidotti 2011: 5).

Braidotti, building on the work of Gilles Deleuze and Felix Guattari, develops the idea of a nomadic subject as a framework for rethinking identity, self, and consciousness. The nomadic subject is not predicated on the place it occupies or the miles it travels, but the way it relates to these. The idea of the nomad stands in opposition both to the sedentary occupant and the traditional migrant: for these, place and identity are intertwined and determined, while for the nomad they are always contingent and temporary. Nomadic consciousness does not reject place or stability, community or belonging, but "rather consists in not taking any kind of identity as permanent: the nomad is only passing through; he only makes those necessarily situated connections that can help him to survive, but he never takes on fully the limits of one national, fixed identity" (Braidotti 2011: 64).

What is key to practicing a nomadic subjectivity in art, to Braidotti, is awareness and accountability of one's location and the configuration of its contingency. Through memory and narrative, she states, we can bring into symbolic representation aspects of our subjective location that usually escape our awareness. It makes us aware that such a "location" is, "in fact, not a self-appointed and self-designated subject position, but rather a collectively shared and constructed, *jointly occupied spatiotemporal territory*" (Braidotti 2011: 16, my emphasis).

It is this raising of consciousness of location that is the potential effect of *The Jungle*, whereas it is less possible in the case of *Black Watch*. The issue lies not so much in the staging techniques but in the way the plays situate characters and audience, or rather, the demands that this situation places on the audience in terms of awareness of their own position. The challenge to become aware comes both from the physical and symbolic placement of the audience and the representation of subjectivity on stage. It is the combination of these two elements that allows for Braidotti's jointly occupied territory: a sharing of space that is uncomfortable and therefore consciousness-raising.

Black Watch is a play that takes the audience to war. It displaces the spectator and tries its hardest to represent the experience of the soldiers. However, the audience will always remain on the sidelines, literally and figuratively, in the face of events onstage. This is not to say that what it tries to achieve is not worthwhile, but rather that it has a limited capacity to change the sense of subject position of either lay audience member or soldier character.

Black Watch is a play about war from the perspective of the Western soldier, of course, and as such encounters with the enemy are minimal. Take the scene where the characters tell the tale of a donkey and cart being "taken out" by a high-tech missile "at the bargain-basement price ay seventeen thousand, nine hundred and fifty-four quid to the British taxpayer" (Burke 2007: 19). This is typical of how the other is represented in the play, obliquely, through dark humor highlighting the asymmetry of the warfare: "This isnay fucking fighting. This is just plain old-fashioned bullying" (Burke 2007: 40). The play is aware of the fact that it offers little or no engagement with experience on the other side:

WRITER. Did you have much contact with Iraqis?
STEWARTY. I thought you were interested in us? I thought it was about our story?
WRITER. You didn't know any Iraqis?
STEWARTY. What the fuck have the Iraqis got tay fucking day way anything?
   (Burke 2007: 46)

Thus *Black Watch* struggles with the possibility of representing the experience of either side in war. We cannot ever understand how it is to be a soldier on "our" side, let alone to even consider the life and death of the other. This is perhaps inevitable for a play that takes us *to* war. We simply cannot share this territory, however, immersive the staging is.

The Jungle, on the other hand, brings war home. It does this in two ways; partly by representing the stories of those who have come to our shores but also by inviting us into *their* home. The narratives of the refugees' lived experience of war are important, but key is the representation of their current need as a result of war to find those "situated connections" and "community" necessary for survival. The staging of the play, the way that the audience is invited inside the place that is by its definition on the outside, allows the play to "bring home" how the connections and community that the refugees build in the camp are the same as those we all want and need and have, and how theirs are perilously temporary, excluded from permanence and privilege whilst just at the edge of our home nation.

Watching *The Jungle* becomes that uncomfortable sharing of territory, represented by us sitting on benches in the Afghan restaurant in the refugee camp, that impacts on how we perceive both the other as subject and our own situated subjectivity, and which therefore allows the possibility for a "becoming-minoritarian" of the audience member. Braidotti refers to Deleuze and Guattari's idea of "becoming" in her description of nomadic subjectivity. Crucially, becoming is not an imitation but a precisely "empathic proximity." It is not that the audience becomes or acts being the minority, rather "nomadic shifts enact ... a creative sort of becoming; they are a performative metaphor that allows for otherwise unlikely encounters and unsuspected sources of interaction, experience and knowledge" (Braidotti 2011: 27).

The initial knowledge that we gain in this "unlikely encounter" between metropolitan elite and refugee is what Judith Butler refers to as the relative "grievability" of human lives. War operates within an epistemological frame that sees some lives as valuable and, in Butler's analysis, "grievable," and others as devalued and ungrievable. It is the frame for the common reporting of war where enemy casualties are anonymous numbers. It is the frame for the asymmetry of grief represented in *Black Watch*, which deals directly with the grievability of the soldier, but spends little time considering lives and deaths of the Iraqis. "Only under conditions in which the loss would matter does the value of life appear. Thus, grievability is a presupposition for the life that matters" (Butler 2009: 14). Butler's analysis highlights how in *Black Watch*, the lives of our soldiers matter, Iraqi lives do not.

The opening of *The Jungle* is thus key. It starts with a census, but one that is more than a tally, one that implies that these people actually *count*. The burial scene that follows immediately establishes the grievability of the characters we are about to get to know. Just before the funeral the news that the French authorities are to destroy the camp reaches the restaurant. Sam is translating the verdict of the judge in Lille to the gathered crowd:

> SAM. Has not been convinced that this evidence is sufficient to change her first verdict ... Consequently ... she upholds the notice and gives legal authorization for the eviction to begin.
> PAULA. Yeah, knock it down. Knock it down and never let it happen again. But not like this. Not when they have nowhere to go. Kids will disappear. Mark my

word. Hundreds of them. They'll run, or be taken, and we'll never see them again. Mark my word.
Numbed silence
The body of a boy is carried on, shrouded in white, raised into the air, bathed in light, then buried. A song is sung in Arabic. (Murphy and Robertson 2017: 21)

The Jungle Camp, then, is the space where the refugee from war temporarily finds the community necessary to become recognized as grievable. It is, however, always under threat of eviction and erasure. The boy is buried in "Angels Corner" which after the camp is razed will return to the anonymous mud of Calais. Its people will disappear, their numbers unknown, the dead ungrieved again.

The chaos of explosions and gas that marks the invasion of the camp—and stage—by police abruptly ends when the character Safi exclaims "Stop. Let's stop for a moment" (Murphy and Robertson 2017: 25). This narrator-character addresses the audience on his own, taking us back to the origins of the camp. We witness the division of land according to nationality, the building of dwellings, hear accounts of the "game": attempting to reach the UK by clandestinely climbing onto lorries. Most importantly we witness the setting up of Salar's restaurant, a symbol of the camp becoming a community, for better and worse:

SAFI. A restaurant. Mosques, churches, shops. And people from many countries living together in peace—
Norullah spots Okot [rifling through bags of food destined for the restaurant] *and sprints towards him. A fight breaks out.* (Murphy and Robertson 2017: 32)

Life in the camp is by no means friction free, but the restaurant becomes the place where the inhabitants meet, discuss, and argue. It becomes the symbolic space where differences are heard. It literally becomes the stage where the community of the camp is played out, and it is as such that it is significant as the space that we, the audience, are invited into. It is here, in Salar's restaurant in the Jungle Camp, that we are given an opportunity to become aware of our own position in relation to the stories that we share a space with for an evening.

Despite the similarities in staging, *Black Watch* holds us at an arm's length whereas *The Jungle* invites us in. The beginning of the two plays demonstrates this through the characters of the Writer and Safi: the first signals the distance between the lay person and the subject of the play, the latter directly connects with the audience. The endings are similarly representative. The Writer's last line invites the climactic scene in *Black Watch*, the IED explosion, asking the soldiers in the pub what happened: "So what was it?" (Burke 2007: 66). The play ends with a tableau of "exhausted, breathless soldiers left in silhouette" after a stylized parade (Burke 2007: 73). In contrast, Safi's last monologue addresses the audience with poignant words: "Thank you for your hospitality. I hope one day to return to Aleppo. When I do, you are all very welcome" (Murphy and Robertson 2017: 121).

Works Cited

Braidotti, Rosi (2011), *Nomadic Subjects: Embodiment and Sexual Difference in Contemporary Feminist Theory*, 2nd edn, New York: Columbia University Press.
Brown, Ian (2019), "Performance, Theatrical Engagement and Ambivalence in Two Stage Representations of Scottish Soldiering," *Scottish Literary Review*, Vol. 11, No. 1, pp. 125–43.
Brown, Mark (2007), "Tales from the Front Line," *The New Statesman*, Vol. 26, March, pp. 44–5.
Burke, Gregory (2007), *Black Watch*, London: Faber & Faber.
Butler, Judith (2009), *Frames of War: When Is Life Grievable?* London: Verso.
Cox, Emma (2014), *Theatre and Migration*, Basingstoke: Palgrave Macmillan.
Gener, Randy (2008), "Oh, What A Glorious War," *American Theatre*, October 23.
Haydon, A. (2013), "Theatre in the 2000s," in D. Rebellato, ed., *Modern British Playwriting, 2000–2009*, London: Methuen Drama, pp. 40–98.
Jeffers, Alison (2012), *Refugees, Theatre and Crisis: Performing Global Identities*, Basingstoke: Palgrave Macmillan.
King, Robert L. (2009), "Stage Effects and Staged Effects," *The North American Review*, Vol. 294, No. 3/4, pp. 71–4.
Lukowski, Andrzej (2017),"The Journey from the Calais Jungle to the London Stage," *International New York Times*, December 11. Available online: https://www.nytimes.com/2017/12/06/theater/the-journey-from-the-calais-jungle-to-the-london-stage.html. Last accessed March 31, 2020.
Marcolina, Cindy (2018), "BWW Interview: Joe Murphy and Joe Robertson Talk THE JUNGLE at Playhouse Theatre." Available online: https://www.broadwayworld.com/westend/article/BWW-Interview-Joe-Murphy-And-Joe-Robertson-Talk-THE-JUNGLE-at-Playhouse-Theatre-20180625. Last accessed March 31, 2020.
Martin, Carol (2018), "Our Reflection Talks Back." Available online: https://www.americantheatre.org/2017/08/22/our-reflection-talks-back/. Last accessed March 31, 2020.
Mason, Paul (2018), "The Jungle Gives Refugees a Voice," *The New Statesman*, July 5, 2018.
Murphy, Joe and Joe Robertson (2017), *The Jungle*, London: Faber & Faber.
Shekel, Liron (2018), "Why Does It Feel Radical Listening to Someone Speak?: Interview with Joe Murphy and Joe Robertson." Available online: https://alondon.net/interview-with-joe-joe/. Last accessed March 31, 2020.
Soloski, Alexis (2018), "The Jungle," *The New Yorker*, December 25, pp. 18–19.
Thompson, James, Jenny Hughes, and Michael Balfour (2008), *Performance in a Place of War*, Chicago: The University of Chicago Press.

Section Four

Perspectives on *The Great Game: Afghanistan*

1

"My Country Has Been Imagined Enough": *The Great Game*, Neo-Imperialism, and Gender

Emer O'Toole and Daniel O'Gorman

Ten years on from the premiere of *The Great Game: Afghanistan* at the Tricycle Theatre, this chapter appraises the production's engagement with the moral complexities surrounding gender that arose from the 2001 invasion and continue to underscore discussion of the region in the West today. When taken as a whole, this multiauthored collection of plays offers nuance to questions that a single play or journalistic source might simplify or proselytize upon. Even while we critique some of these gender representations, we aim to show the value of an undertaking where the plays, in dialogue, build arguments and offer rebuttals to each other. The chapter follows three main strands of enquiry. First, it examines the production's critique of the human rights justification for the intervention in Afghanistan. Second, it analyzes the plays' wrangling with questions of international duty to women's rights in the region, exploring what forms of internationalist solidarity—if any—the collection might champion. Finally, it considers how the collection both challenges and reinforces postcolonial constructions of gender, with a particular focus on contemporary "peacekeeper masculinity."

Human Rights and Imperialism

Colin Teevan's "The Lion of Kabul" centers upon a dilemma that a UN Director of Operations, Rabia, faces when two of her Afghan aid workers go missing in 1998. Namely, in the legal no-man's-land of late 1990s Afghanistan, where the UN and the Taliban refuse to recognize each other, it is unclear what rights the men hold, and whose responsibility it is to ensure that justice is served. The fiercely misogynistic and anti-Western mullah, Khan, has been summoned to negotiate a way forward, but, via multiple frustrating exchanges, it becomes apparent that it is not just Rabia's demands, but also the values underpinning the language of her demands, that make any deal impossible:

> KHAN. It is people of the West who have no principles, who are godless, who are unjust.

RABIA. We respect human rights, we respect freedom.
KHAN. Is it not our human right to reject your freedom? That is one human right you do not recognize. You will not recognize it until we look like you and act like you and are slaves to your economic system. (Teevan 2009: 164–5)

That Khan is an avowedly patriarchal mullah and Rabia a Western woman—specified in the stage directions to be "*of Pakistani/Indian origin but born and raised in Britain*" (Teevan 2009: 153)—lends complexity to the intersecting power structures underlying the exchange. Teevan does not mean for his audience to endorse the extremist worldview of the mullah. Rather, he uses this confrontation to foreground the ways in which their own deeply held values fall short of universality and might be contingent upon a culturally and historically bounded consensus logic. The play poses the difficult question of how far the imperative of universal human rights can be enforced before it comes to resemble a form of imperialist oppression.

The question of women's rights was central to the justification for the 2001 invasion. The liberation of women from the Taliban was a keystone of pro-intervention rhetoric, despite the fact that, as Joseph Slaughter has argued, the West long knew "that the Taliban were a violent and repressive regime, especially toward women" (2007: 11–12). The US-led military coalition positioned itself in the well-established colonial position of what Gayatri Chakravorty Spivak described as "white men … saving brown women from brown men" (Spivak 1993: 93). In *Precarious Life*, Judith Butler observes: "The sudden feminist conversion on the part of the Bush administration, which retroactively transformed the liberation of women into a rationale for its military actions against Afghanistan, is a sign of the extent to which feminism, as a trope, is deployed in the service of restoring the presumption of First World impermeability" (2004: 41).

As global development scholar Deniz Kandiyoti has pointed out, there is not just a clash of values at play in the case of the Afghanistan invasion, but also one of geopolitical and economic interests. She situates "the politics of gender—defined as a process of appropriation, contestation and reinterpretation of discourses on socially sanctioned gender relations and women's rights—in the context of evolving institutional frameworks and the nexus of global and local factors that shape the policy agenda in post-Taliban Afghanistan" (Kandiyoti 2009). Kandiyoti reminds us that there is a complex history of colonial actors implicating women's rights in Afghanistan with vastly differing agendas. David Edgar's "Black Tulips" performs historicization by drawing its readers' attention to an earlier but less commonly discussed invocation of women's rights as justification for military action in Afghanistan: the 1979 Soviet invasion. Indeed, multiple plays emphasize the limitations and hypocrisies underlying a feminist justification for the invasion. Naomi Wallace's "No Such Cold Thing" subverts realism to show how a young Afghan girl is killed by an American marine, while Simon Stephens's "Canopy of Stars" depicts a British soldier using a superficial desire to protect women's rights to aggressively vent his frustrations at the disappointments of family life under late capitalism.

Perhaps the play that conveys the ironies of the invasion's self-proclaimed feminism most sharply is Richard Bean's bitingly sardonic "On the Side of the

Angels," which follows the misadventures of a New Labour-style marketing team for a human rights NGO, who are tasked with "selling" Afghanistan to the charity's fundraisers. It ends on a note of brutal sincerity, when an aid worker barters a deal between two warring Afghan families, on the condition that a ten-year-old girl marries a fifty-year-old man. This leaves the marketing team horrified, including the earnest, *keffiyah*-wearing Graham who cannot help but intervene, disappearing from the security of the compound in an attempt to rescue the girl. Although we are never shown the outcome of his actions, we are left with the understanding that he is making matters worse, allowing his noble yet arguably narcissistic compulsion to help the girl take precedence over the Afghan lives at stake, and forcing his colleagues into danger. The play foregrounds some harsh realities of gender oppression in post-invasion Afghanistan, while implying that the attempt to hastily impose a human rights framework on complex and heterogenous local contexts is shortsighted and reductive.

Feminist Solidarities

In a critique of the Asia Foundation, whose mobile theatre practice in Afghanistan aims to create positivity toward elections, Maurya Wickstrom professes skepticism toward the discourse of "social change" that undergirds Theatre for Development work in the global South. She argues that such language often fails to distinguish between "collective, structural change made in the interests of those who wish to free themselves from domination by specifically exploitative, capitalist, neoliberal regimes" and "a generic change in the behaviors of targeted communities," useful to the economic goals of neoliberalism (2012: 91).

The plays of *The Great Game* are perceptive about pursuit of social change that ultimately serves hegemonic agendas, consistently addressing cynical uses of women's rights by global powers to justify imperialism. Michael Vicente Perez reminds us that "treating the feminist role in the Afghan invasion as an instance of feminism fails to address the fact that feminism also challenges that very role …. [D]efining feminism by what some feminists did runs the same risk as claiming Islam is what Muslims do in its name" (Perez n.d.). With some exceptions, the plays are less surefooted in lauding pursuit of social change that genuinely challenges oppression or articulating a politics of solidarity with Afghan women's rights advocates.

Amit Gupta's "Campaign" and Joy Wilkinson's "Now is the Time" acknowledge the internally motivated anti-imperial and feminist reforms that defined the rule of King Amanullah in the early twentieth century. However, enthusiasm for the radical potential of this history is muted. In "Campaign," Professor Kahn, an Oxford scholar specializing in early twentieth-century Afghan history, explains to Kite, a predatory British foreign office "spook," that Amanullah was foolhardy in his reforms, allowing the British to use women's rights to incite Tribal chieftains in revolt. Now, the Foreign Office wants to remind the Afghan people of this history to manufacture a popular "Afghan nationalist campaign fueled by the desire for a secular democracy" (Gupta

2009: 64). This would give the British and American administrations an excuse to withdraw troops and invest military resources in Pakistan.

In Wilkinson's play, Amanullah poignantly insists that "Now is the time" (Wilkinson 2009: 82) for women's rights, even as Queen Soraya veils herself and the visionary couple flees the country. Read through the lens of history provided by Gupta's play, Amanullah's worthy, wrongheaded mistake is legible. In both plays, Amanullah's gender reforms are represented as incompatible with the contemporaneous culture of Afghanistan and a political weak spot to be exploited by foreign powers and internal enemies. Now is not the time. Women's rights are ammunition for the enemy's campaign.

In David Grieg's "Miniskirts of Kabul," our Western protagonist, a female writer, envisions an interview with former communist president Mohammed Najibullah, who, in 1996, is sheltering in the UN guesthouse, under Taliban fire. In the erotically charged meeting, the writer is rebuffed when she asks if it's true that, under communist rule, there were miniskirts on the streets of Kabul. "Have you come all this way—imagined yourself all this way—imagined yourself sitting with me in a city under siege—to ask me about women's fashion?" (Greig 2009: 141). Najib asks scornfully. While a Western feminist tendency to reduce Afghan gender politics to burqas and veils merits critique, there is also a misrecognition here of the politics of modesty norms. The writer's question is not mere frivolity and fetishization—it implies, as she explains, an interest in "how it felt to be a woman in Kabul in the 1980s" (Greig 2009: 141). Ultimately, the conversation glosses genuine gendered inquiry, when Najib answers the question "Do you like women?" with "Too much" (Greig 2009: 141). The possibility of communist commitment to women's rights as a driving force of many Afghan actors is foreclosed.

The play shows self-reflexivity in its depiction of this meeting: its most memorable line is when Najib says to the writer: "My country has been imagined enough. My country is the creation of foreign imaginings" (Greig 2009: 134). Despite this, Greig's apparent reluctance to identify indigenous drive for "social change" rooted in anti-hegemonic commitments, and express solidarity with these efforts, echoes a similar reticence in Western feminist discourse.[1] As Kandiyoti explains, post-invasion debates by Northern feminist and public intellectuals, "centered less on the plight of Afghan women per se than on the transformation of their own state and society in the aftermath of the 9/11 events." She notes further: "A common reaction to the 'othering' of women in Afghanistan was, paradoxically, a fulsome recognition of their radical alterity" (Kandiyoti 2009).

There is something unsatisfying about a suspicion of human rights that runs so deep as to consign all Afghan women, feminists, and gender justice workers to the role of unknowable subalterns. As Spivak argues, human rights, though often deployed to hegemonic ends, are not inherently Western. She gestures to the power of new diasporas in shaping human rights discourses and observes, "in the global South, the domestic human rights workers are, by and large, the descendants of the colonial subject, often culturally positioned against Eurocentrism" (Spivak 2003: 16). Mona Eltahawy has pilloried liberal Westerners who stay silent on women's rights issues out of alleged respect for Middle Eastern cultures. She says, "I implore allies of the countries in this part of the world to pay more attention to women's rights and to refuse to allow cultural relativism to justify horrendous violations of women's rights" (Eltahawy 2015: 28).

While Afghan women, feminists, and gender justice workers are heterogenous, they are not unknowable others. They speak and can be heard—they are members of the Afghan parliament, workers with RAWA (the Revolutionary Association of the Women of Afghanistan), writers, and activists. One means of avoiding neocolonial imposition is to listen to women articulating their own politics and critiquing Western feminisms and economic systems that try to erase or instrumentalize them. Jasbir Puar writes of RAWA's response to the US-based non-profit the Feminist Majority Foundation:

> A letter written on April 20, 2002 condemns the foundation's representation of its handiwork as having "a foremost role in 'freeing' Afghan women" while failing to mention RAWA's twenty-five-year presence in Afghanistan (indeed, failing to mention RAWA at all), as if it had "single-handedly freed the women of Afghanistan from an oppression that started and ended with the Taliban." (2017: 6)

RAWA critiques the Feminist Majority's "hegemonic, U.S.-centric, ego driven, corporate feminism" and decries the fact that it ignores abuses of Afghan women's rights perpetrated by US allies. In her memoir, *Raising My Voice*, Afghan politician Malalai Joya observes that "Most international agencies attach conditions to their grants in order to control their recipients. And they won't fund projects run by critics of warlords [as Joya calls the Northern Alliance], the Afghan government and foreign occupation" (2010: 137). A decade later, women's rights activists such as the founder of the Voice of Women Organization, Suraya Pakzad, warn that Afghanistan could "return to chaos" with the wrong kind of peace deal: "Women [are] very clear that they do not want a deal to be at the expense of women's rights. They do not want a trade-off. They want peace with women's rights" (qtd in Lamble 2019: n. pg.).

That the support of women's rights in situations representing complex intersections of neocolonialism, neoliberalism, and patriarchy requires work to understand multilayered histories and political perspectives should not provide an excuse to locate all such solidarity as inherently corrupted. Perhaps the play that goes furthest toward addressing the complexities of supporting Afghan feminism is Abi Morgan's "The Night is Darkest Before Dawn." Stereotypes of Afghan gender roles are complicated when a widowed female teacher asks her brother-in-law to allow her to educate his daughter, Behrukh, in a US-funded school. He initially declines the offer, prompting the frustrated US aid worker Alex to reflect: "we offer them free education and they just laugh at us" (Morgan 2009: 203). However, in this play, being a good father can mean not educating your daughter; and the moral cost of risking lives— particularly the lives of others—for women's rights is writ large. Yet when the teenage Behrukh, who grew illiterate under the Taliban, tells an allegorical story about a man who finally accepts money on recognizing that it is a reward from God, the play champions the need to support Afghan women on their own terms, including improving access to an education that gives them control of their own stories.

Peacekeeper Masculinity

Underlying any debate about feminist solidarity with Afghan women is the question of gender construction: not just of femininity but also masculinity. Gender played a role in all the "Great Game" interventions in Afghanistan over the years, whether in the form of masculine colonial rationality or the chauvinism of "white savior" narratives. As Pierre Bourdieu puts it in *Masculine Domination*: "We have embodied the historical structures of the masculine order in the form of unconscious schemes of perception and appreciation. When we try to understand masculine domination we are therefore likely to resort to modes of thought that are the product of domination" (1998: 5).

A shift in representations of "masculine domination" takes place between the collection's historical plays and plays set in the post-2001 present. The historical plays display a clear critique of traditional British colonial masculinity. The contemporary-set plays offer less clear-cut attitudes in the face of twenty-first-century colonial masculinities. Critics such as Laleh Khalili have identified "a new form of masculinity" that emerged through US counterinsurgency policy and doctrine. This new form of masculinity, Khalili argues, is "authorised by consumerism and neo-liberal feminism, in which 'manliness' is softened, and the sensitive masculinity of the humanitarian soldier-scholar (white, literate, articulate, and doctorate-festooned) overshadows the hyper-masculinity of warrior kings" (2011: 5). Claire Duncanson succinctly termed this phenomenon "peacekeeper masculinity" (Duncanson 2009: 63), while Julia Welland called its central figure the "liberal warrior" (Welland 2017: 530).

Ron Hutchinson's "Durand's Line" and Gupta's "Campaign" encourage critical thought on the topic of masculinities, including through their deliberate consecutive positioning in the production. In both, the impulse for imperial mapping in the leading British characters fits into a traditional conceptualization of colonial manliness. There are clear parallels between the stories each play tells: the first is set during the colonial mapping of Afghanistan in 1893, and the latter is a contemporary–set play, its action occurring in London in 2009. Hutchinson dramatizes the fateful meeting between British diplomat Mortimer Durand and the ruling Afghan emir Abdur Rahman, in which the two tensely negotiate the mapping of the country's borders, with Durand hoping for an outcome that helps keep Russia at bay. "A thing has to be defined—Good God," Durand naively exclaims in response to Rahman's warnings about imposing borders where they are not wanted, "progress flows from the act of it" (Hutchinson 2009: 46). Later on, he reveals his true colors: "The world's been mapped, all of it … This is the biggest odd and end left" (Hutchinson 2009: 48). Rahman beseeches Durand to consider what will happen if such mapping "leads to greater problems than it pretends to cure?" (Hutchinson 2009: 46). In "Campaign," the dynamic between the two main characters—Kite and Professor Khan—is similarly tense, and Kite's lack of sincerity in support of Afghan people is apparent when he says "Our governments would prefer an exit strategy that doesn't appear to be an outright abandonment of the Afghan people," to which Khan incredulously replies: "Doesn't appear to be …." (Gupta 2009: 64).

However, there is another, more contemporary colonial masculinity present in "Campaign," making it one of the more perceptive of the collection's contemporary-set plays in identifying and critiquing the figure of the "liberal warrior." The seemingly unassuming American policy advisor Martin Speed plays a quiet role in the background. Speed spends much of the play scribbling notes as Kite makes his pitch to Khan, offering an occasional bumbling "don't mind me," and claiming to be present just "to observe" (Gupta 2009: 54). At the play's denouement he reveals his hand, as well as the underlying purpose of the meeting itself, which turns out to have less to do with Afghanistan and more with expanding the mission into Pakistan: "Pakistan's our theatre now," he exclaims excitedly, "it's where we build our stage!" (Gupta 2009: 64). Through this Shakespearean evocation, Western theatre culture is shown to overlap with the colonial, in much the way that Edward Said describes when he writes: "We are all taught to venerate our nations and admire our traditions: we are taught to pursue their interests with toughness and in disregard for other societies" (1994: 20). The justification that Speed gives for the expansion into Pakistan reinforces this overlap between culture and imperialism, couching the mission in the language of both a contemporary-style "peacekeeping" alliance and an old-fashioned imperative to "civilize": "The Pakistani government need us—it's a delicate, delicate situation, paranoia about India, nuclear weapons—it may be our last chance to keep them in the civilized fold" (Gupta 2009: 64). In Speed, the "hard" masculinity of Durand and Kite merges with a softer, twenty-first-century masculinity in tune with the language of human rights.

Other contemporary-set plays in the collection, such as Simon Stephens's "Canopy of Stars" and Naomi Wallace's "No Such Cold Thing" (performed separately but included as a bonus play in the printed collection), tend to be less clear-sighted than "Campaign" in their critique of the discourse of "peacekeeper masculinity" and the "liberal warrior" figure (despite the insights they show in alternative ways). Their depictions of disillusioned working class soldiers—British (Stephens) and American (Wallace)—who have developed forms of hyper-masculinized psychosis, offer important insights into the way military personnel can be let down by their military and national welfare systems. Both plays rely on the trope of the "face-to-face encounter," in which, as Khalili points out, "the foot-soldiers of the US military ... directly and repeatedly encounter the conquered": a binary that is already "very conspicuous" in reportage on the War on Terror (2011: 4). Omitted from these plays is a discussion of the "peacekeeper masculinity" that necessitates the soldiers' presence in Afghanistan in the first place. However, their positioning at the end of the collection, with historical plays like "Durand's Line" and "Campaign" still fresh in mind, mean that these absences become hauntingly apparent.

Note

1   Afraid, perhaps, of reinscribing modes of representation that resemble Oprah Winfrey and Eve Ensler's infamous *Beyond the Burqa* Broadway show, too easily legible as cultural propaganda for the "War on Terror," Northern feminists have engaged in necessary criticisms of their own cultural contexts.

Works Cited

Bourdieu, Pierre (1998), *Masculine Domination*, tr. Richard Nice, Stanford: Stanford University Press.
Butler, Judith (2004), *Precarious Life: The Powers of Mourning and Violence*, London: Vintage.
Duncanson, Claire (2009), "Forces for Good? Narratives of Military Masculinity in Peacekeeping Operations," *International Feminist Journal of Politics*, Vol. 11, No. 1, pp. 63–80.
Eltahawy, Mona (2015), *Headscarves and Hymens: Why the Middle East Needs a Sexual Revolution*, London: Weidenfeld and Nicolson.
Greig, David (2009), *The Great Game: Afghanistan*, London: Oberon Modern Plays.
Gupta, Amit (2009), *The Great Game: Afghanistan*, London: Oberon Modern Plays.
Hutchinson, Ron (2009), *The Great Game: Afghanistan*, London: Oberon Modern Plays.
Joya, Malalai (2010), *Raising My Voice*, London: Rider.
Kandiyoti, Deniz (2009), "Gender in Afghanistan: Pragmatic Activism," *Open Democracy*. Available online: https://www.opendemocracy.net/en/5050/gender-in-afghanistan-pragmatic-activism/. Last accessed July 7, 2020.
Khalili, Laleh (2011), "Gendered Practices of Counterinsurgency," *Review of International Studies*, Vol. 37, No. 4, pp. 1471–91.
Lamble, Lucy (2019), "Wrong Peace Deal Could Mean 'Return to Chaos' for Afghanistan," *Guardian*, August 20. Available online: https://www.theguardian.com/global-development/2019/aug/20/wrong-peace-deal-could-mean-return-to-chaos-for-afghanistan. Last accessed July 10, 2020.
Morgan, Abi (2009), *The Great Game: Afghanistan*, London: Oberon Modern Plays.
Perez, Michael Vicente (n.d.), "Feminism is for Everybody," *Critical Muslim*, Vol. 21, No. 20. Available online: https://www.criticalmuslim.io/feminism-is-for-everybody/. Last accessed July 9, 2020.
Puar, Jasbir (2017), *Terrorist Assemblages: Homonationalism in Queer Times*, 2nd Edn., Durham and London: Duke University Press.
Said, Edward (1994), *Culture and Imperialism*, New York: Vintage.
Slaughter, Joseph (2007), *Human Rights, Inc.: The World Novel, Narrative Form, and International Law*, New York: Fordham University Press.
Spivak, Gayatri Chakravorty (1993), "Can the Subaltern Speak?" in Patrick Williams and Laura Chrisman, eds., *Colonial Discourse and Post-Colonial Theory: A Reader*, Hemel Hempstead: Harvester, pp. 90–105.
Spivak, Gayatri Chakravorty (2003), *Other Asias*, Malden, Oxford and Carlton: Blackwell.
Teevan, Colin (2009), *The Great Game: Afghanistan*, London: Oberon Modern Plays.
Welland, Julia (2017), "Violence and the Contemporary Soldiering Body," *Security Dialogue*, Vol. 48, No. 6, pp. 524–40.
Wickstrom, Maurya (2012), *Performance in the Blockades of Neoliberalism: Thinking the Political Anew*, London: Palgrave Macmillan.
Wilkinson, Joy (2009), *The Great Game: Afghanistan*, London: Oberon Modern Plays.

2

The Geography of Identity

Reza Aslan

"Men are not tied to one another by papers and seals [but] by resemblances, by conformities, by sympathies."

Edmund Burke wrote those words nearly two centuries ago, at a time in which the concept of nationalism was about to transform Europe and lay the groundwork for modernity. Nationalism is a political philosophy that places the nation-state at the center of collective identity. At the heart of the idea lies the belief that human beings must put aside the multiple markers of identity that have for centuries defined society and instead define themselves principally in terms of their national boundaries. In other words, a community of likeminded individuals sharing a common geography should be bound together not by race, religion, tribe, or ethnicity but by citizenship, or, as Burke put it, by "papers and seals."

When the nation-state was an autonomous, territorially bounded entity governing a community of people who shared some measure of cultural homogeneity—as was the case throughout much of the nineteenth and twentieth centuries—the concept of nationalism thrived. But as the age of modernity slowly gave way to the age of globalization, and the territorial boundaries that divide human societies into separate and distinct nation-states began to dissipate, societies all around the globe began to reassemble around older, more primal forms of identity, like religion and ethnicity. Indeed, the continent where the concept of nationalism first arose and from which it was imported to the rest of the world through conquest and colonialism is now the continent in which that concept—and, in fact, the very notion of the nation-state—has been most fiercely challenged by the most obvious exemplar of the age of globalization: The European Union. Twenty-seven sovereign nation-states (and counting), twenty-three languages, dozens of ethnicities, half a billion members, all bound together by a single currency, a single parliament, a single birth certificate, a single citizenship. A continent without borders. *That* is the new modernity.

All of this brings us to Afghanistan and the current debate over the pros and cons of "nation-building" in the Middle East. It is ironic that the very same people who have so utterly absorbed the ideals of globalization and so thoroughly welcomed the unprecedented geopolitical realignments that have followed are the same people who seem bent on making nationalism the key to stability and security in areas of the world in which the very idea of the nation-state has always been a wholly foreign concept. The map of the Middle East is a palimpsest, with arbitrary borders, made-up names, and fabricated nationalities often aggressively imposed by foreigners. This is a region of the world in which nationalism was never the primary marker of collective identity. Tribe, clan, religion, ethnicity—these are the things that form identity. Citizenship? Well, that is just a piece of paper.

This is particularly true among the dusty villages of and mountainous provinces of Afghanistan, where collective identity has been shaped not by allegiance to any federal government but rather through centuries of alliances and tribal affiliations. And yet, the globalized nations of the world that have breached this mosaic land continue to cling to the outmoded idea that the path toward modernity must go through a strong centralized government with the power to define the values and mores—the very identity—of everyone who happens to fall within the bureaucratic boundaries of the state. That is a path toward modernity, no doubt, if by modernity one means the early twentieth century.

For more than twenty years now Western powers have been struggling to build a strong, centralized government in Afghanistan with the power to exercise authority over all the different provinces in the country. The belief is that unity comes from centralization, and that the key to stability is to empower Kabul to define identity (read: citizenship) for all Afghans. This approach is neither appropriate to Afghanistan's history and culture, nor does it mesh with the globalization trends that these same Western powers have so eagerly adopted for themselves.

We should be taking the exact opposite approach in Afghanistan. Decentralization and a system whereby Afghans can maintain semi-independence over their own provinces—over their own identities—is the only way to maintain peace and security in this infinitely diverse part of the world. Allow Afghans to be Afghans—however they understand that designation. Then, perhaps, the country can more legitimately join the global—and globalized—community.

3

The Legacy of an Empire

Farid Younos

The Great Game: Afghanistan arrived at the Berkeley Repertory Theatre in Fall 2010 when Afghans around the world were debating the validity of the Durand Line. The play addressed the wounds of occupation, manipulation, and double standards by foreign powers, and asserts a historical fact: Afghanistan has always been sandwiched between hostile superpowers for regional supremacy.

"Durand's Line" by Ron Hutchinson addresses a major tribe of the region, the Pashtuns, who were cut in half by the "Divide and Rule" policy of the British Empire. The implication of this policy caused acute animosity later between Pakistan and Afghanistan and drained the financial resources of Afghanistan in defending the rights of the Pashtuns on the other side of the border. The Durand Line policy cemented the Great Game to continue between superpowers for another century to come. Fall 2010 witnessed a major divide between Afghans who supported the return of the lost territories, and those who believed the Durand Line did not have a political or economic advantage for Afghanistan and Afghans needed to focus on their country's reconstruction.

The play on the Durand Line is significant not only because some Afghans desired the return of the lost territories, but some non-Afghan political commentators saw that as a solution for Afghan peace and stability. Daniel Serwer, Director of Conflict Management and American Foreign Policy Programs at Johns Hopkins University, wrote in *The Atlantic*:

> Afghan recognition of the Durand line as part of a broader deal with the Taliban would provide Pakistan with an important benefit, without depriving it of "strategic depth" inside Afghanistan. This would have to be done in a way that allows a good deal of free movement across the border, since otherwise the Taliban and other locals, who have enjoyed relatively free movement for decades, would object. But agreeing to and demarcating the Durand line would markedly improve relations between Kabul and Islamabad, enabling them to collaborate on what really counts for the United States: ensuring that their border area does not become a haven for international terrorists. (2011)

Very important issues were highlighted in this play. One is that the name of Afghanistan was established by colonial policy. Before the reign of Amir Abdul Rahman Khan (1880-1901), Afghanistan was Khorasan. Afghanistan as we know it today emerged as a result of British policy in the region. This historical fact was enacted during the conversation between the Amir and Sir Henry Mortimer Durand, Indian Foreign Secretary of Her Majesty, Queen of Great Britain. The character of Durand commented to Thomas Salter Pyne, Engineer to the Amir, about the book written by the Amir:

> DURAND. It's about the Silk Road and Samarkand and peculiar goings-on that make you wonder if that actually happened or the fella wasn't just—well, *dreaming*—like in his head he was making up a place that wasn't really there—
> RAHMAN. As with your—(*Mocking*.) Afghanistan—
> DURAND. If that's a dream, let's dream it together.
> *Durand holds out the map and continues:*
> There it is. A thing few men have been given. A moment that comes once in five hundred, a thousand years. To birth a country. To call a nation into being at the very center of the world. In the end this isn't about Delhi or London or Moscow and their endless scraps and intrigues. It's about the reach of a man's imagination and how wide is his soul.
> *Beat*
> And the monopoly of the opium trade, too.
> *He indicates the map again*
> See where you sit—astride the route which the Russians must take to threaten India; the path whereby East could hurl itself on West; where North and South collide; you play a role in the fortunes of a dozen of nations and two entire continents and you will not sign? Sign and have this new thing spring from the brow of History? With your name forever on it?
> RAHMAN. The Rahman Line? Or the Durand? (Hutchinson 2010: 41–2)

The legacy of the Indian-British Empire to the region was two-fold: it created a new country called Afghanistan out of the old Mughal Empire and Persian Empire, and a division with a main regional tribe, the Pashtuns. Until the present, the issue of the Durand Line is a concern for Afghanistan and Pakistan and also a regional matter politically. The Amir was right when he said to Durand, "But these are only imaginary lines on paper, after all." Durand responded, "Not when backed by the actions of the finest army in the world." The Amir shot back with alarm, "You will fight for these imaginary lines?" (Hutchinson 2010: 34).

The border crossing of the militants, the insurgency, and Al Qaeda into Afghanistan's mainland has become a major security issue for Pakistan and Afghanistan. The current "finest army in the world" is not capable of stopping the insurgency. The matter has been solved from the Pakistani point of view by recognizing the Durand Line as a legitimate border between Afghanistan and Pakistan, but the majority of Afghan Pashtuns did not accept this perspective. Pakistani Pashtuns were uninterested in joining Afghanistan or creating an independent Pashtunistan. The result is an insurgency pouring into

Afghanistan because, to them, the line—as the Amir had said—is an "imaginary line," not a de facto border. The conversation about the Pashtuns and creation of Afghanistan as a sovereign country is a significant aspect of this play:

> DURAND. You don't want the Russians here any more than we do, Amir. They're a threat to you as well as to us.
> RAHMAN. And you would rather fight them here than across the mountains. On our territory instead of yours.
> DURAND. We won't have to fight them if we can establish you as a sovereign and stable country between them and us.
> RAHMAN. Which makes me what? An ear of grain between two millstones?
> DURAND. Waziristan and the Pashtuns are in the wrong place, and we all see that. In some ways, your entire country is.
> RAHMAN. How thoughtless of Providence to put us in the wrong place.
> DURAND. The narrative of the pacification of the Waziris, who are the key to Afghanistan and thus to the region is to be read here—here—here—and here—
> RAHMAN. Regardless of the Waziris themselves?
> DURAND. They are a piece with their land. They have been regarded as wild ungovernable as it. We will change that.
> RAHMAN. With ink?
> DURAND. It's easy to mock and look for flaws in a scheme—far easier than to do but we're about doing.
> We will be defining the Western border of India for the first time, which means we will be, in effect, creating a new country on the other side of it. (Hutchinson 2010: 35)

This conversation is a little different from what we read in Amir Abdul Rahman Khan's autobiography, *Tajul Tawarikh*:

> Since Sir Henry Mortimer Durand was a shrewd and clever politician and spoke Persian fluently, all the discussions went well. In order to have a record of my talk with Sir Henry Mortimer Durand and other members of the embassy, I arranged that my secretary, Sultan Mohammad Khan, would be seated behind the curtain, about whom no one knew except me, so that he may record our talk in a short-hand form. The record of the entire discussion has been preserved in the government secretariat … The agreement that was determined with regard to the boundaries was signed and sealed by me and by the members of the embassy. (1373: 420–21)

Two paragraphs later, the Amir continues:

> On 13 November 1893, I held a public Darbar (court) in the Salam Khana hall [a hall where the king receives the visitors ostentatiously] which was also attended by my two eldest sons and the leading chiefs of various tribes and both the civil and military

officers of Kabul. I presented, before the audience, an outline of the understanding agreed upon and the terms signed by the two sides, for the information of those present and also the nation. I praised Allah SWT for the existence of friendly relations .... I also thanked Sir Mortimer Durand and other members of the Mission for their wise way of settling the disputes. (Khan 1373: 420–21)

This narration of the event by the Amir is presented in much more in detail than in the play. We also discover that the Amir's secretary was sitting behind a curtain recording the proceedings while we saw a servant standing in the corner of the room in the play. The Amir indicated he was alone with Durand during this casual, amicable, and friendly conversation.

From this scene in the Amir's autobiography, and friendly conversation between the Amir and Durand, we learn another important political fact: the Durand Line was not imposed by the British, but Amir Abdul Rahman Khan accepted it wholeheartedly. The scene of the play and autobiography show that the Amir was not manipulated. During this conversation or negotiation, Durand was "irritated," "looks stung," "perplexed," and was even "controlling himself." Many Afghans, particularly the Pashtuns of Afghanistan, are under the impression that the Durand Line was imposed on Afghans. At the end of this historical negotiation and friendly conversation, the Amir says, "I sign because I must, Sir Mortimer, but I think you make me sign because you must, too—and may your God and mine forgive us both" (Hutchinson 2010: 48). The issue of the Durand Line is not as complicated as one might think. It is a lost territory for Afghans and will never come back based upon the following historical and political analysis.

During the nineteenth century, colonial Britain feared that Czarist Russia might invade India. At that time, India was under the domination of the British and not independent. Pakistan did not yet exist. Today, the Colonial British and Czarist Russian Empires no longer exist. The Durand Line agreement was signed on November 12, 1893. After more than a century, the Durand Line can be studied and analyzed under two categories: first, political relations with colonial India prior to the partition of the Indian subcontinent; and second, political relations after the partition of the Indian subcontinent and the creation of independent India and independent Pakistan. The key point in the history of Afghanistan is its political status as a buffer state, sandwiched between two great powers, namely, Britain and Russia in the nineteenth century, and the Soviet Union and the United States in the twentieth century. The similarity of conditions before and after the partition of the Indian subcontinent result because Afghanistan was politically sandwiched, which caused the country to confront various calamities and miseries.

Political relations between Afghanistan and British India until the independence of Afghanistan in 1919 had been colonial. Even though Afghanistan has never been directly under colonial rule, it was under the political sphere of influence of the British Empire. In order to meet the interests of the colonial British, the kings of Afghanistan received annual subsidies from the government of British India. In order to possess and occupy some regions of Afghanistan, the colonial policy of the British was based on the motto "divide and rule." Since the Amirs of Afghanistan were indulged more in their own interests than the needs of the whole nation, no plan existed for solidification, preservation, and advancement in the regions within their jurisdiction. Due to the absence of such a policy, Afghanistan lost the regions under its occupation, and the country became a protectorate. Next, I will explain step by step the regression instead of advancement of Afghanistan.

In 1799, resulting from a civil war within the Sadozai dynasty, Afghanistan lost Punjab, which was then possessed by Sikhs. In 1819, a hundred years before the Treaty of Rawalpindi (when His Majesty Amanullah officially recognized the Durand Line treaty), Kashmir was lost and handed over to the Sikhs (Ghobar 1346: 120). Before the Treaty of the Durand Line, Afghans lost the main region of Peshawar. In order to gain power, advised by Sir William Hay Macnaghten, Shah Shuja joined Ranjit Singh so he would defeat Amir Dost Mohammad Khan whom Ranjit Singh hated. Shah Shuja gave up much control of Peshawar. In June 1838, fifty-five years before the Durand Line Treaty, a secret treaty was signed between Ranjit Singh, Shah Shuja, and British India. Hence, Peshawar was lost. Amir Dost Mohammad Khan was the first Amir of the Mohammadzai dynasty who signed a treaty with the British, the Treaty of Jamrud. By signing this treaty, he suffered the hardest blow during the Great Game in the nineteenth century, which resulted in the loss of the regions inhabited by the Pashtuns. In January 1857, when he was watching British officers walking on the streets of Peshawar, he realized he had lost possession of the region to the advantage of British India and the Punjabis. He never attempted to repossess the lost region. Indeed, none of the kings who ruled the country after Shah Shuja asked for Peshawar to be repossessed. Amir Dost Mohammad Khan was the first Mohammadzai ruler who passively accepted the loss of the region. Additionally, he paved the way for the intervention of the colonial British. During the reign of Amir Sher Ali Khan in 1876, the British army occupied the city of Quetta. Quetta was inhabited by the Pashtuns and part of Afghanistan (Ghobar 1346: 120).

On May 26, 1879, Amir Mohammad Yaqub Khan handed over Kurram, Pishin, Sibi, and the Khyber Pass to the British by signing the Treaty of Gandomak, exactly one hundred years before the Soviet occupation of Afghanistan in 1979. The Treaty of Gandomak was the first scheme leading to the drawing of the Durand Line, which materialized in 1893. The Durand agreement, based on the policy of "divide and rule," laid the foundations for future disunion, separation, and unrest in the region.

The Durand agreement was signed in 1893 by Sir Henry Mortimer Durand, who represented the British Empire, while the British Parliament had no information about the treaty, and by Abdul Rahman Khan, the Amir of Afghanistan, without the involvement of the Grand Council. Basically, this treaty was made between these two persons. For this reason, after the death of Amir Abdul Raman, this agreement was considered unlawful; however, in practice, it was observed by both sides. In fact, by signing this agreement, Amir Abdul Rahman Khan officially surrendered to British India the lost regions of Peshawar and its surroundings and other regions inhabited by the Pashtuns. This happened with the explicit consent of the Amir; it was not "imposed" or "forced." The word "imposed" was used to refer to the Durand Line Treaty during and after the reign of Sardar Mohammad Daoud. However, there is no evidence of such words being used in history books.

This presentation of historical evidence can be safely interpreted as the confessions of the Amir. The Amir, through his own authority, surrendered the regions and codified it by signing and sealing it. Later, he threw a pompous party in its honor. It is to be noted that the English representative, Sir Mortimer Durand, spoke fluent Persian, and difficulties associated with mutual understanding of each other or the negotiations, which might have been considered incorrectly translated by a third party, did not exist.

From the point of view of international law, after the death of the Amir, the agreement was considered as valid. However, from the practical point of view, it was seen as a matter of fact. Since 1901 (the year of the death of Amir Abdul Rahman Khan), all the kings of Afghanistan and its presidents have accepted this line as a de facto line and forfeited any future claim over the Durand Line. The Taliban, who are mostly Pashtuns, also ignored the Durand Line while in power from 1996 to the time of their fall by the Americans.

The Durand agreement did not have formal validity during the reign of Sarajyia, Amir Habibullah Khan (1901–19). However, due to its acceptance by the Amir of Afghanistan and the desires of British India, the validity of this line continued as de facto and both sides observed the line as is. The British proposed a renewal of the agreement to Amir Habibullah Khan. In fact, the Amir endorsed and signed the previous agreement in 1905. Also, during the reign of Amir Habibullah Khan, Afghanistan had a Postal Agent and a Commercial Agent in Peshawar. In 1919, Afghanistan obtained independence. On August 8, 1919, by signing the treaty of Rawalpindi, all previous agreements were annulled except the Durand Line. This time, Afghanistan acted as an independent state, and the fifth article of this agreement mentioned that it officially recognized the Durand Line as an international boundary between Afghanistan and British India. Also, the peace treaty between Afghanistan and British India was signed on November 21, 1921 by Mahmood Tarzi, the Foreign Minister of independent Afghanistan, and Sir Henry Dobbs. In the second article of the treaty, the Durand Line was recognized as an international boundary between Afghanistan and British India.

In his book *Afghanistan in the Path of History*, Afghan historian Mir Ghulam Mohammad Ghobar related that His Majesty Amanullah not only recognized the Durand Line but based on the advice of his advisers, he refused to meet with the tribal leaders so political relations between the two countries would not be jeopardized. During the reign of Mohammad Nadir Shah, from October 1929 to November 8, 1933, the practical and lawful validity of the Durand Line was observed and fortified by both sides. It is noteworthy that with the backing of the British and religious leaders, Mohammad Nadir Shah was enthroned. Since Mohammad Nadir Shah and his brothers obtained power with the support of the British, his family was grateful to the UK. From the start of the rule of Mohammad Zahir Shah in 1933 until Indian independence and the creation of Pakistan in 1947, the two brothers of King Nadir Shah, Sardar Mohammad Hashim Khan and Sardar Shah Mahmood Khan, did not issue an official declaration about the Durand Line.

In 1950, after the creation of Pakistan, the Durand Line was officially declared as the international boundary by Britain. The political conditions and circumstances of the region are such that there is no possibility either of annexation of the region or of creating Pashtunistan by the division of both Afghanistan and Pakistan, although some commentators such as Serwer see the political solution of Afghanistan in the recognition of the Durand Line. On March 31, 2010, Pakistan's Constitutional Reform

Committee agreed that the Northwestern Frontiers be named and officially recognized as Pakhtunkhwa. That means the lost territories are now officially part of Pakistani territory.

The historical value of Hutchinson's play in relation to contemporary Afghanistan is to show that more than 125 years after the Treaty of Durand's Line, Afghanistan is still sandwiched between major superpowers. With the presence of American forces in the country, the legacy of the Great Game continues. As Durand said to the Amir, "We don't have to fight them [Russians] if we can establish you as a sovereign and stable country between them and us" (Hutchinson 2010: 34). As performed and written, "Durand's Line" illustrates both the historical events and national significance of this political moment. It does so by drawing on recorded documentation where politics is juxtaposed with human-scale ramifications. Hutchinson successfully depicts the personalities of the historical characters as fully fleshed human beings who are performing as individuals, not merely in roles as political figures. For example, in a poignant exchange, the audience discovers that the Amir has sent some precious cucumbers and apricots to Durand. During their conversation, the Amir solicitously asks Durand "Did you receive them?" Durand replies with a somewhat distracted and perfunctory, "Yes." The Amir inquires further with authentic personal care and curiosity: "How did you find them?" Durand more politely, but still briefly, responds "Excellent!" (Hutchinson 2010: 33). The Amir now rests for a moment before negotiations continue, pleased and satisfied that his gesture—diplomatic but also as personal as such gestures are—was well received. In the performance at the Berkeley Repertory Theatre, this scene was truly absorbing to the audience in its social civilities in a seemingly contrastive function from the larger matters at hand during an important political discussion. This moment reveals that individuals turn to simple needs and conversations in times of greatest crisis and tension. It is the power of theatre that made the play so engaging in encompassing a pivotal point in world events presented from an intimate angle. For Afghans and non-Afghans alike, it is revelatory to learn how the British carved and tailored the geography and cultures of Afghanistan, and how Afghanistan's leadership willingly participated. We see it in the moment when Durand says to the Amir, "If that's a dream, let's dream it together" (Hutchinson 2010: 41). Again, we see this coinciding of personal desires and emotions as they play out on a global stage when Durand holds the map and repeats, "There it is. A thing few men have been given. A moment that comes once in five hundred, a thousand years. To birth a country. To call a nation into being at the very centre of the world" (Hutchinson 2010: 42). The most valuable part of this play is its ability to educate the public about historical circumstances and show how major political events are often driven by personal motives with lasting human impacts.

Works Cited

Ghobar, Mir Ghulam Mohammad (1346 [Islamic solar calendar]), *Afghanistan in the Path of History*, trans. Farid Younos, Kabul: Kabul Press.

Hutchinson, Ron (2010), "Durand's Line," in *The Great Game: Afghanistan*, London: Oberon Books, pp. 33–48.

Khan, Amir Abdul Rahman (1373 [Islamic solar calendar]), *Tajul Tawarikh: An Autobiography*, trans. Farid Younos, Peshawar: Saba Books.
Serwer, Daniel (2011), "A Political Solution to the Afghanistan War," *The Atlantic,* July 11. Available online: https://www.theatlantic.com/international/archive/2011/07/a-political-solution-to-the-afghan-war/241376/. Last accessed July 7, 2020.

4

Imagining the Great Game

Christopher Merrill

Why would anyone choose to spend an entire day in the theatre watching a cycle of plays about Afghanistan? The physical prospect is daunting—how to sit for the length of a transoceanic flight to travel only in one's imagination?—and the subject is one that many of us prefer not to think about. Nevertheless crowds lined up for performances of *The Great Game: Afghanistan* at the Tricycle Theatre in London, testifying to a hunger in the human soul for large-scale dramas that tackle difficult subjects. The success of these twelve commissioned plays on the history of British, Russian, and American involvement in Afghanistan suggests that we may not always choose to avert our gaze from the most significant foreign policy challenge of our time. "Life in the theatre is more readable and intense because it is more concentrated," Peter Brook notes. What *The Great Game* offers is a chance not only to experience the full range of human emotions, in plays and monologues and verbatim pieces, but to be instructed in the complexities of a land that for over a century and a half has bedeviled policy makers, buried dreams, spilled blood.

"My country has been imagined enough," says Mohammad Najibullah, the last president of the Soviet-backed regime in Afghanistan, whose imaginary dialogue with a British writer furnishes the action in David Greig's "Miniskirts of Kabul." September 1996: Kabul is about to fall to the Taliban, and the writer, who has read all the books about the doomed leader, wants to understand his point of view before the UN compound in which he has taken refuge is overrun. "My country is the creation of foreign imaginings," Najibullah says above the sound of shelling in the distance; the consequences of this doomed enterprise are everywhere on display:

> The border between Pakistan and Afghanistan is an imaginary line—Pakistan is a dreamed up country—Pakistan—which—by the way—is paying for those Taliban peasants to right now throw rockets at my city—Every blood conflict in the world today has its origins in the imagination of British surveyors. You come here imagining. You expect me to co-operate?

All quotations from Nicolas Kent and General Sir David Richards are taken from the author's personal interviews with them.

In fact Najibullah helps the writer to imagine his perspective—his desire "to invent a new way of being Afghan" and a new society, his view that his countrymen are not ready for democracy, his fear of the Islamists. And yet because this Afghan leader cannot imagine a different fate for himself other than a glorious return to power, the play points to the limits of imagination. History records that he spurned the chance to flee, that the Taliban tortured and executed him, and that in the new order the opportunities granted to women under the Communists vanished.

This, then, is a cautionary tale about the imagination—its uses and abuses, its centrality to public and private discourse, its role in the unfolding drama of history—which may stand for the whole of *The Great Game*. The director, Nicolas Kent, commissioned twelve playwrights to find points of contact—correspondences—with a faraway place, imagining the human costs and consequences of invasions and independence movements and occupation; what they discovered working independently of one another, in plays of thirty minutes or less, was, in the words of David Edgar, "a central, coherent theme: that western interventions in Afghanistan have almost always produced the opposite effect from that which was intended." His "Black Tulips" thus traces the Soviet debacle back to its idealistic origins, when a commanding officer asks, "What happens if we fail?"—the same question that American policy makers are asking decades later.

Kent cites three sources of inspiration for his Afghanistan epic: Shakespeare's *Henry VI*, Ariane Mnouchkine's theatre spectacles, and his decision to challenge a workshop of younger writers to produce ten-minute plays on the tragedy in Darfur. "Bloody Shakespeare": this is how he describes his reaction to a performance of the trilogy of plays that one critic called "a fantasia on historical themes"—an apt description of *The Great Game*. Mnouchkine, founder of the Parisian avant-garde stage ensemble Théâtre du Soleil, reminded Kent of the power of a long immersive work. And the success of the Darfur plays made him think there might be an audience for a subject about which he himself knew very little at the outset of the project, though he was convinced it would become the story of our time.

"I just kept on being told about the first, the second, and the third Anglo-Afghan Wars," he said one afternoon in his office at the Tricycle Theatre, "and in my ignorance I knew there had been a first Anglo-Afghan War, I didn't know there had been a second, and I certainly didn't know there had been a third. I thought I had better find out more."

Thus began his education in what has been called "a tournament of shadows," a detailed history of which he supplied to the playwrights; from these darkened corners emerged stories illuminating a world in which, for example, an Afghan working for the UN cannot believe that men have walked on the moon, while a UN official cannot fathom the grisliness of a certain Taliban form of justice. This disjunction between world views is a key feature of the plays. Insofar as they render different perspectives of self and other, they can extend a viewer's range of sympathy and cultivate his or her powers of empathy, which in the rush of daily life are routinely blunted (to say nothing of what happens in the midst of war). The breakup of any colonial order is often presaged by its failure to understand its subjects—to win hearts and minds, in common parlance—which is why theatre is an ideal vehicle for the exchange of information and ideas essential to cultural diplomacy and cultural relations. It is a forum for discovering common ground between different peoples.

For theatre is a communal exercise (like war), and *The Great Game* explores the conflicts and tensions arising from decisions taken, for good or ill, by men and women whose knowledge of Afghanistan was inevitably partial. Over the course of the performance—standing in line, sharing a table for lunch or dinner, drinking tea or coffee—members of the audience develop bonds with one another, and by the end of the night they may feel as if they have gone on a long journey, during which they witnessed unimaginable things. The gruesome action takes place off stage, for war is what happens over there, and if we do not necessarily experience the purging of emotions—the clarification that Aristotle identified in his *Poetics* as integral to drama—the force and complexity of the conflict are brought home to us.

It turns out that immersion in the subject has its pleasures. Like Wagner's *Ring* cycle, Fassbinder's *Berlin Alexanderplatz*, or the novels of Dostoevsky and Tolstoy, *The Great Game* illustrates that more is more. "I'm asking people to take part in a seminar on Afghanistan, for a day," Kent told me, "where they will be entertained, they'll learn, they'll laugh, hopefully they'll cry, they'll think—and they'll be thinking about the biggest problem for American and British foreign policy for the decade to come. That can only be good to come to."

Which is why General Sir David Richards, former commander of NATO forces in southern Afghanistan, argues that policy makers and military officers should devote a day to *The Great Game*. For the plays offer the kinds of vivid impressions that, he believes, would have made him a better commander, because they would have allowed him "to see things from a more Afghan perspective than a Western perspective." We cannot act in concert with the Afghans until we have some idea about who they are. *The Great Game* should be part of the education not only of those deployed to Afghanistan, he says, but of modern soldiering.

"There are so many nuances to our presence there," he notes, "that unless you have a deep nuanced understanding of its history, and the different views and approaches to the problem, you cannot begin to hope to solve it."

Not that a day in the theatre will bring peace to the region. "Are we in our ninth year in Afghanistan or are we on our first year for the ninth time?" an American officer asks. Think of the plays in *The Great Game* as twelve provisional answers to that question, none of which is conclusive. For, as Kent argues, "Theatre is the greatest instrument of debate."

5

The Great Game as Diplomacy: From London to the Pentagon

Nicholas J. Cull

A few moments into the first play of the cycle *The Great Game: Afghanistan* a character in Victorian costume remarks, "It is easy to argue on the wisdom or folly of conduct after the catastrophe has taken place" (Jeffreys 2010: 17). The plays, however, are more than an example of this. They were created at mid-point of the catastrophe of Afghan intervention with an eye to shaping its outcome. The cycle's creator, Nicolas Kent (working with co-director Indhu Rubasingham of London's Tricycle Theatre),[1] had a track of engaging pressing political issues from Northern Ireland and Apartheid South Africa to work on the War on Terror and the so-called "Tribunal Plays" depicting controversial legal cases. *The Great Game* went beyond this, not merely raising consciousness around NATO's war in Afghanistan but seeking to influence with its architects. In Fall 2010 and Winter 2011, Kent brought the play on tour to the United States. Despite many elements of the play plainly criticizing Anglo-America foreign policy, the British government assisted in this effort through its cultural relations arm, the British Council. Once in the United States the British Embassy intervened to ensure that the play reached one American audience in particular: the policy makers of the Department of Defense. An unprecedented case of theatre in the service of diplomacy emerged.

Background

During the twentieth century national governments awoke to a problem. The cherished mechanisms of traditional government to government diplomacy no longer matched a world in which the people had a direct influence on foreign policy. Diplomacy changed. Institutions sprang up to carry the necessary messages: international radio stations, embassy press offices, publications aimed at foreign

---

The author is grateful to Kanta Kochhar-Lindgren and the editors associated with the journal *Theatre Topics* whose insights shaped an earlier version of this essay.

readers, international exchanges. From the mid-1960s on, US officials dubbed such activity "public diplomacy." The term caught on. One sub-branch of public diplomacy deployed the tools of culture to engage their audience. Hence, scholars and practitioners came to speak of a distinct practice of cultural diplomacy within or parallel to public diplomacy. Many governments had agencies dedicated to this work, such as the British Council, founded in 1934.[2]

Given the historic role of theatre in helping nations understand who they are in the first place, it was only to be expected that the dramatic arts would be pressed into the service of cultural diplomacy. Theatre operates within cultural diplomacy in four main ways, each with a varying expectation of interactivity with the target public.

Theatre Diplomacy as Prestige Gift

As every anthropologist knows, when people seek to build relationships they typically begin with a gift. Notable diplomatic gifts have ranged from France's gift of the Statue of Liberty to the United States. In the case of theatre, the donor country takes an art form that is acknowledged to be the best that the country has to offer and makes it available to a foreign public. This was how the British Council's theatrical diplomacy began, with gambits like the 1938 tour of Egypt and Italy by the Old Vic which included Anthony Quayle in *Henry V* and Alec Guinness in *Hamlet*.[3] The prestige gift is still a part of diplomatic practice.

Theatre Diplomacy as Cultural Information

A second more sophisticated from of theatrical diplomacy uses drama to counter stereotypes of the sponsoring country and develop understanding of life as it is really lived. The US government funded a Mediterranean tour of George Gershwin's *Porgy and Bess* in 1954 and 1955 to live down the country's reputation for racism.[4] A self-confident state will even share works that are explicitly critical of its life. The British Council has become especially identified with a willingness to tell the uncomfortable truths about life as seen from Britain through its drama. In sharing such work internationally, the British Council is acting as a credible conduit for British culture. It is helping to build a reputation for itself and for Britain as honest and trustworthy, as a resource for future contact with publics around the world.

Theatre Diplomacy as Capacity Building

The third aspect to theatre diplomacy is capacity building. Accepting that a healthy arts scene is an important part of a democratic public sphere, a number of Western countries have sought to encourage and/or ingratiate themselves with rising generations of writers and performers around the world. Several major cultural relations agencies bring the next generation of theatre professionals on study trips to be mentored by their arts establishment, including The Kennedy Center in Washington D.C. and the British Council.

Theatre Diplomacy as Dialogue

At its most complex theatre can be a diplomatic device to open a two-way conversation and exchange. This ranges from facilitating the exhibition of the work of others in one's own country to engagement of foreign producers and directors for mutual development to the selection of plays with an agenda to create new discussions and even to challenge taboos. The US Department of State has launched projects of this type. Arts festivals are a long-standing venue for the best intercultural cross-fertilization. The connection between festivals and cultural diplomacy was explicit in the creation of the Edinburgh International Festival in 1947. The British Council's Scottish representative Henry Harvey Wood co-founded the festival with the Austrian-born opera impresario Rudolf Bing.[5]

On occasion the dialogue stimulated by the performance is internal to the overseas audience. In 2003, the British Council took an acclaimed work called *L.O.V.E.*—based on Shakespeare's sonnets and created by the Swansea-based company Volcano—to the Caucasus. In Georgia a male-to-male kiss in the first act triggered a walkout by sections of the audience on opening night. The show closed immediately. In Azerbaijan the kiss was greeted with wild applause. In both cases the performance prompted debate and was seen by the British Council as a success.[6]

Theatre diplomacy is not always oriented overseas. Sometimes the audience to be challenged has been domestic, as when the British Council has taken classic British work overseas, transformed it by working with foreign artists, and then reintroduced the re-imagined work to the UK. A well-known example was director Tim Supple's work in India with Shakespeare's *A Midsummer Night's Dream*. A hybrid treatment of the play with a cast of Indian artists, street children, and in seven languages, it first toured India and then played in the UK where critics found a new dimension in the familiar work.

Cultural Diplomacy and the State

Cultural Diplomacy has historically required the brokering of a working relationship between the source of diplomacy and foreign policy—usually the nation state—and the source of art and culture, usually an artist or group of artists within the nation. The relationship presents both pitfalls as well at the obvious mutual opportunities. Artists have accidentally embarrassed diplomats by clashing with policy; diplomats have offended the artists by pressing too hard for political compliance. The British Council has been well placed to minimize these tensions by insisting on its own arm's-length relationship from the British government.

The Question of "Actors" in Cultural Diplomacy

In recent years it has been possible to observe an alternative to the partnership of the state and the artist in cultural diplomacy. Other entities have emerged as the "actors" deploying cultural diplomacy, including but not limited to international organizations, NGOs, sub-national geographical regions, and cities. There are even small groups and individuals who seek and manage to influence foreign publics according to their own personal foreign policy that may or may not overlap with that of a nation state. This burgeoning cast of international actors has been part of theatre diplomacy. The Devolution of the UK has seen the government of Scotland subsidizing international tours of National Theatre of Scotland productions such at the Iraq war drama *Black Watch*.[7]

As government funds budgets have tightened it is increasingly common for a major piece of cultural diplomacy to be a joint project. We may see a national body like the British Council collaborating with regional or non-governmental institutions to export a particular piece of culture where doing so lends credibility to the work as it emerges, a product of multiple agencies and agendas, and is all the more impressive to encounter. This is the case with the US tour of *The Great Game: Afghanistan*.

The Creation of *The Great Game*: Afghanistan

It all began with an accident. In Fall 2001, Nicolas Kent slipped a disk and found himself confined to his couch and suffering sleepless nights with the BBC World Service for company. He became a captive audience for Operation Enduring Freedom—the NATO invasion and occupation of Afghanistan. Having been saturated with Afghan War coverage, Kent was keenly aware of the disappearance of Afghanistan from the news as the media attention switched to Iraq. A suicide bombing in June 2003, previously unknown in Afghanistan, roused Kent to action. He realized that "the golden moment" of late 2001 had passed. The media did not seem to notice. *The Great Game* began as Kent's project to kick-start a debate over NATO's approach to Afghanistan.[8]

In April 2008, Kent began to actively research. He read the best authors on the region like Steve Coll and Ahmed Rashid and spent hours in conversation with American diplomat Michael Macy, then US-cultural attaché in London but with recent experience of Afghanistan. Kent decided to mount not just a cycle of plays but an entire festival including film and ceramics to open London to Afghan history and culture. He took his title "The Great Game" from the historic rivalry between Russia and Britain for control of the Northwest Frontier. His appropriation implied that the imperial meddling at local expense was still going on. With the project underway, he visited Afghanistan in November 2008 with a cameraman to see for himself and commission four short films from Afghan filmmakers for Channel 4 television in the UK. Back in London Kent's core problem was to find his playwrights. He approached well-established writers such as David Edgar and Stephen Jeffreys but took pains to bring in new and dynamic voices such as Joy Wilkinson and Ben Ockrent. Some of the writers were already identified with the region: Ron Hutchinson had scripted the British television drama *Traffic* about the drug trade out of Afghanistan and Colin

Teevan had written the play *How Many Miles to Basra?* Some had been involved in writing about race relations in Britain including Richard Bean, Amit Gupta, and Abi Morgan. Some, like Simon Stephens, had a knack of courting controversy and capturing regional voices within the UK.

Kent sketched a timeline of events in Afghanistan and commissioned writers to fill particular gaps. Some stories came easily. David Greig had found a photograph of Afghan women in miniskirts from the 1970s and knew he wanted to address life in communist Kabul. Hutchinson was initially keen to examine late-nineteenth-century Afghanistan through the prism of its most famous fictional veteran, Sherlock Holmes's Doctor Watson, but was persuaded to focus on the diplomatic shenanigans around the creation of boundaries. Kent's co-director Indhu Rubasingham compared the business of managing the writers sometimes to air traffic control, but somehow it all came together for the premiere in April 2009.

The Plays

The *Great Game* is divided into three parts: Part One: Invasions and Independence, 1842–1930; Part Two: Communism, the Mujahedeen, and the Taliban, 1979–1996; and Part Three: Enduring Freedom, 1996–2010. Each part is built around four plays. Invasions and Independence opens with Jeffreys's "Bugles at the Gates of Jalalabad," an exploration of the Anglo-Afghan War of 1839–42 centering on the ignominious British retreat with 16,000 casualties. "Durand's Line" by Hutchinson dealt with the negotiations between Sir Mortimer Durand, the British Foreign Minister for India, and the Afghan Amir Abdur Rahman that set the arbitrary boundary between Afghanistan and Pakistan and guaranteed further conflict. "Campaign" by Gupta told the story of early-twentieth-century reform in Afghanistan through an encounter between a contemporary British spin-doctor and a Pakistani-British academic where the official outlines a plan to use the great reformer Mahmud Tarzi as propaganda theme. The final play, Wilkinson's "Now is the Time," tells the story of the end of the reform era through a desperate discussion between King Amanullah Khan, his Queen, and his Minister and father-in-law Mahmud Tarzi on what they come to realize is their road to exile.

The second and perhaps most viscerally impactful part of the cycle Communism, the Mujahedeen, and the Taliban, opens with a powerful piece on the Russian war in Afghanistan by Edgar titled "Black Tulips" after the nickname for the Soviet helicopters. The piece is performed as a series of briefings, with the audience positioned as the latest wave of Russian arrivals in the combat zone. They learn of tactics, morale, and get a lesson on anti-personnel mines, and the once-demonic Russian incursion becomes understandable, especially as the briefings are delivered in the accents associated with equivalent characters in the British armed forces. The briefings run chronologically backwards so the play ends with the optimistic beginnings of the Soviet adventure.

The second play in the middle part during the first run was "Blood and Gifts" by American writer J. T. Rogers dealing with CIA aid to the Mujahedeen. This was replaced in 2010 by Lee Blessing's "Wood for the Fire," which responded to the emerging centrality of Pakistan in President Barack Obama's policy by focusing on the early days of Pakistani support for the most ideologically extreme of the anti-Soviet fighters.

The third play is an imagined encounter between the Soviet client Najibullah and a female British writer, "Miniskirts of Kabul" by Greig. The writer summons Najibullah as he was in final hours hiding in the UN compound before his assassination at the hands of the Taliban in 1996. He explains his hopes for his country. They drink whiskey, spar verbally, watch a Spice Girls video, and in the process, the cipher of anti-Soviet propaganda emerges as a human being. "My country has been imagined enough. My country is the creation of foreign imaginings," he tells the writer in a phrase that resonates with the message of the entire cycle.

The final play in this section, "The Lion of Kabul" by Teevan, is set in the Kabul Zoo in the 1990s. The audience is positioned where the animals would be, looking out at a negotiation between Taliban and a UN representative who has come to learn the fate of two of his colleagues. The one-eyed lion seems to be a metaphor for the wounded country, but as the play develops, he becomes more. We realize that the aid workers have been killed and their bodies thrown to the lion, and that the Taliban have decided the perpetrators are to be thrown live to the lion in punishment. The play ends as the two perpetrators are manhandled screaming towards the audience and their grisly end.

The third installment brings the story to the then-present of 2010. Ockrent's "Honey" is the tale of the relationship between the United States and Afghan defense minister Ahmed Shah Masoud, a prominent leader of the anti-Soviet war and an ally who, as allusions in preceding plays have suggested, had the potential to be a true leader for modern Afghanistan. At the last moment he is denied the resources needed to prevail against the Taliban. He dies on September 9, 2001. Television images of the 9/11 attacks erupt onto a screen. The audience feels a yawning void as the set opens into a deep stage. The doubling of the stage space seems to open uncomfortable possibilities at the moment the West ties its political destiny to that of Afghanistan. Morgan's "The Night is Darkest Before the Dawn" sketches life in an Afghan village and the attempts of an artless Western aid worker to open a girls' school following the initial defeat of the Taliban. The horrific repressions of the Taliban are once again revealed. Bean's "On the Side of the Angels" tells of two more aid workers and an abortive attempt to settle a land dispute and remain respectful of local culture. The play ends in shocking compromise, tragedy, and futility.

The final set and cycle as a whole ends with "Canopy of Stars" by Stephen Simons, an account of a British soldier in the NATO force in Afghanistan, his thoughts under fire, and his inability to communicate with his wife on his return home. There is little hope for the marriage or, by implication, the combatant nations.

The overall effect of the plays is to present multiple perspectives on a complex issue. Using multiple viewpoints and styles, the picture of Afghanistan that emerged is all the more vivid. Individual characters are subsumed by the greater circumstance of Afghanistan, but that was the point. The individuals and their rights are the focus of Western attention, and as Bean put it in the play "On the Side of the Angels," "The one thing that Afghanistan doesn't have and has never had is any individuals."

Conclusion: *The Great Game: Afghanistan* as Diplomacy

Many foreign plays win plaudits overseas in any season but few have the explicit goals of a work like *The Great Game: Afghanistan*. How did it rate as diplomacy? Did it justify the investment of the British Council? To return to my earlier typology:

Prestige Gift. The plays were certainly seen as an example of the sort of exciting work generated within Britain. Reviewers commented on the track record of the writers commissioned and particular cast members.

Cultural Information. The plays were received in the United States as imparting authentic cultural information about Afghanistan with the writers and performers standing in as a welcome proxy for the otherwise "un-knowable" nation. The plays presented the culpability of the British Empire in creating many of contemporary Afghanistan's problems and showed how contemporaneous diplomats and well-meaning NGOs alike were repeating the same errors. The diversity of the cast and writers spoke to the vibrancy and diversity of modern Britain. The country seemed plainly to have moved beyond its Imperial past.

Capacity Building. Both Kent and the British Council intended *The Great Game* to deepen knowledge of Afghanistan in the United States. They felt the plays had accomplished this goal among the audiences and had a spillover impact more widely. All the American reviewers—and the audience members encountered and polled by this writer—acknowledged the value of learning more about Afghanistan. Many felt themselves more equipped to discuss and vote on issues of the war as a result. However, the most remarkable example of capacity building is the way in which the play was sought by the US military as a resource.

Dialogue. The British Council intervened to ensure that the plays were part of a dialogue and maximize their impact among thinking Americans. The Council's strategy was two-fold. It began with a forty-eight-page anthology of essays edited by Christopher Merrill, *Trust Me, I'm an Expert: Talking Culture from Inside and Out*.

Contributors included the Iranian American writer Reza Aslan. The thrust of the volume was to question how culture can inform policy and how cultural advice is mediated. Sharon Memis, the Council's director in the United States, flagged the production and its themes with an op-ed on the *Foreign Policy* blog.[9] The Council also organized a program of events at each venue beginning in Washington, D.C. with a one-day conference with contributors including Georgetown Professor and former Ambassador Cynthia Schneider, and Mariam Atash Nawabi of America Abroad Media. Events in New York included a panel featuring Afghan-born economics professor Ishaq Nadiri of NYU and journalist Nushin Arbabzadah. In San Francisco there was a digital videoconference linking faculty, students, and scholars from several campuses of California State University, multiple British universities, and the American University of Afghanistan to discuss themes of the plays. The British Council also took pains to reach out to the substantial California Afghan-American community. As in the UK, Afghans took the plays to their hearts. Events included a panel with then-Cal State University East Bay President Mohammad Qayoumi, the first Afghan American to lead a US university.[10]

Implications

What, the reader may ask, is the wider relevance of this British play's unusual career? Why should a student or scholar of theatre care? Are there lessons in the original structure of the show which are applicable elsewhere? First, its multiauthor format and integration of verbatim elements—the actual statements of real protagonists in the issue—serve as an ideal mechanism for opening debate around a complex subject rather than shutting debate down as might happen with a massive text created by the heavy hand of a single omniscient author. Second, the case shows how it is possible for theatre to reach wider audiences by being open to unconventional partnerships. Today, in public diplomacy and other fields, coalitions of convenience emerge around issues rather than through fixed and administrative-heavy institutional deals. The Tricycle Theatre, British Council, British Embassy in Washington, Bob Woodruff Foundation, and the Pentagon are unlikely bedfellows, but their cooperation makes sense given the subject matter. Third, the production shows the value of collateral work, including panel discussions, to frame a production, stimulate discussion, and multiply its impact. In this case, it was especially important to bring on board an Afghan-American audience who might conceivably have resented foreign depiction of their country and challenged the credibility of the performance. However, the fourth and final lesson to come from the play is that writers and directors should not shy away from addressing the great issues of the moment, and contributing to discussions in the public sphere, especially when other media are silent. *The Great Game: Afghanistan* underlines the message that theatre has a role to play in international relations, and that in a world in which the role of the diplomat is no longer a monopoly of a nation state, a theatre company can become a relevant international actor in its own right. In a world still plagued by mutual ignorance and a lack of international understanding, theatre diplomacy has the potential to make a difference. In a world in which reputation is part of a country's security, well-crafted and honest theatre can even be seen as contributing to a nation's reputational security whether or not it supports the foreign policy of the day.

Notes

1   Formerly the Tricycle Theatre from 1980 to 2018, it became the Kiln Theatre in 2018.
2   For a succinct introduction to public diplomacy and cultural diplomacy, see Cull (2019). For historical background, see Arndt (2006). The British Council now prefers to be considered parallel to British Public Diplomacy rather than an agency of it and calls its work Cultural Relations rather than Cultural Diplomacy. Several scholars including César Villanueva Rivas argue for the same distinction between Cultural Diplomacy and Public Diplomacy. See Villanueva (2007).
3   Howard (2000: 155–6) argues that more than this "gift" aspects of the Old Vic *Hamlet* in Italy were designed to transmit an anti-appeasement warning of how a peaceful prince (read nation state) might react when roused by injustice.
4   See Monod (2003: 300–12).

5   Bruce (1975: 17–24).
6   Aspden (2003).
7   For a treatment of this play by the author, see Cull (2007).
8   This account of the creation of *The Great Game: Afghanistan* is based on the author's interview with Nicolas Kent conducted in Los Angeles on November 11, 2010.
9   Merrill (2010).
10 http://www.britishcouncil.org/usa-arts-theater-the-great-game-afghanistan.htm and Simon Gammell, British Council Los Angeles, to author, December 26, 2010.

Works Cited

Arndt, Richard T. (2006), *The First Resort of Kings: American Cultural Diplomacy in the Twentieth Century,* Washington, DC: Potomac Books.

Aspden, Peter (2003), "Does this Look Like the Best Way to Sell Britain?" *Financial Times*, July 25.

Bruce, George (1975), *Festival in the North: The Story of the Edinburgh Festival,* London: Robert Hale & Co.

Cull, Nicholas John (2007), "The National Theatre of Scotland's *Black Watch*," British Council/Centre on Public Diplomacy, Los Angeles. Available online https://uscpublicdiplomacy.org/sites/uscpublicdiplomacy.org/files/legacy/pdfs/273656-TBC-R1_LoRes_(2)_-_BW_WP_FINAL.pdf.

Cull, Nicholas John (2019), *Public Diplomacy: Foundations for Global Engagement in the Digital Age*, Cambridge: Polity.

Howard, Tony (2000), "Blood on the Bright Young Things: Shakespeare in the 1930s," in Clive Barker and Maggie B. Gale, eds., *British Theatre between the Wars*, Cambridge: Cambridge University Press, pp. 155–6.

Jeffreys, Stephen (2010), "Bugles at the Gates of Jalalabad," in *The Great Game: Afghanistan*, London: Oberon Books.

Merrill, Christopher, ed. (2010), *Trust Me I'm an Expert: Talking Culture from Inside and Out*, London: British Council.

Monod, David (2003), "He is a Cripple an He 'Need My Love', *Porgy and Bess* as Cold War Propaganda," in Giles Scott-Smith and Hans Krabbendam, eds., *The Cultural Cold War in Western Europe: 1945–1960*, London: Frank Cass, pp. 300–12.

Rivas, César Villanueva (2007), *Representing Cultural Diplomacy*, Sweden: Växjö University Press.

6

The Freedom of Boredom

Shane Belvin

Every word is like an unnecessary stain on silence and nothingness
—Samuel Beckett

On April 8, 2003, I crossed into Iraq as a staff officer, responsible for advising my commander on personnel related issues. When my artillery battalion passed through Baghdad, my duties changed drastically. Our battalion was trained to fire cannons at far-off enemies, yet we found ourselves in a guerilla war, fighting insurgents through the streets and alleys. To help my battalion adapt to fight against the ever-changing insurgency, I volunteered to train and lead a team of cooks and mail clerks for a new role that was well outside of their skill set: securing the streets of Iraq. As the leader of my newly formed platoon, I led my soldiers on countless patrols and raids through the towns of Tikrit, Taji, and Ad Dawr.

One night in December, on a routine patrol, I mistakenly led my team into an ambush. A roadside bomb made of a steel barrel, explosives, and automotive gears detonated next to my vehicle. The explosion severely damaged my vehicle and the soldier standing in the hatch was injured ... and it was my fault. As I rushed Private Fletcher to the field hospital a medic was removing numerous pieces of metal from his face. He was enraged, swearing vengeance on our enemy, and any attempt I made to calm him was in vain. When I finally got him to take a break, I exhaustedly stumbled back to the building where I had been sleeping at roughly 4 a.m. and picked up a book from a dusty stack. This one was *Ethics for the New Millennium*. In the pile were *Seabiscuit*, *Mystic River*, *Sick Puppy*, and *Adventure Capitalist*. That doesn't include the dozen or so others in circulation throughout the bombed-out factory we called home. Rather than payment in some barter system, they were simply given away as part of the never-ending rotation in the library of "nothing else to do."

Of course, books weren't the only real way to pass the time. My friends and I also took the time to answer such questions as, "If I shaved my head, how long can I go without someone telling me I need another haircut?" and "How often do I need to work out and how much government issued chicken and pork chops do I need to eat before I can bench 315 pounds?" (If you are playing at home, the answers are one month, non-stop, and enough to give you gout.)

That one night in December is my personal snapshot at the conflict inside many soldiers fighting for their country, religion, family, or tribe throughout the globe for centuries. The emotions affecting soldiers are difficult, but it is the range of emotions that tear at you, slowly, with each day you stay in combat. How can you be bored and fighting for your life at the same time? How can you be looking for something to do, mere hours after watching a friend die? While the film industry has been trying for years to capture the reality of war in pictures like *Paths of Glory*, *Platoon*, and *The Hurt Locker*, it is consistently hamstrung with financial obligations. Books, both fiction and non-fiction, may be free of the financial obligations of Hollywood, but have difficulty depicting the human interactions and dialogue at the heart of combat experience. Conversely, theatre's use of ensemble casts rather than stars, limited reliance on costly action sequences, and use of emotion as a surrogate for visual imagery lends it the luxury of portraying the complexities at the heart of military conflict.

Hollywood's depiction of war and other contemporary issues has different requirements than those of theatre. The dominant obligation when creating a large-scale blockbuster is the ability to recoup the production's costs, which can be done in one of two ways: by creating a movie with very little costs or appealing to the broadest audience possible. Ensuring broad acceptance gives the filmmaker the best chance of generating revenue through ticket and DVD sales.

Unfortunately, there is a pretty formulaic recipe to attracting audiences. This is done by having one clear protagonist, usually a movie star, and action sequences delivered at consistent intervals. The movie star/protagonist dynamic is contradictory to an accurate depiction of the everyday experience of combat. The feeling on the ground is one of teamwork, brotherhood, and mission before self. It is unlikely that a major motion picture star would sign to a film unless he or she is the central story line, in the majority of the scenes, and the "hero." Of course, it is dangerous to speak in absolutes and ultimatums. There are exceptions to every rule, and it would be remiss to not acknowledge outliers such as Steven Spielberg. A long track record of financial success has given him the freedom to take risks with his work and the ability to self-finance some productions if necessary.

John Tiffany, the director of the National Theatre of Scotland's *Black Watch*, relayed the struggles of his peers in the movie industry. His counterparts' casting process is driven primarily by funding, not how suited the cast is for the subject material. Tiffany chooses to relay Hollywood casting as, "If you want any budget, you begin with a list of 30 actors that will be bankable, start from the top, and work your way down. The top tier will get you a certain amount of funding, and as you work your way toward the bottom, the studio money available to your production becomes less and less."[1] He revels in the freedom that theatre provides in the creative process. Without it, *Black Watch* would certainly not have turned out to be the brilliant work that it is.

An "ensemble cast" is a much more accepted dynamic in theatre when compared to film. If a major motion picture is advertised as having an ensemble cast, it simply means there are a number of top box office stars. In *Black Watch*, the viewer may be uncertain who the star actually is until two thirds of the way through the production. The story is about the soldiers, not a soldier. It is about the experience of war, not about the war. It is about what it takes to volunteer to go into harm's way, and act bravely when there. *Black Watch* is able to depict the conflict in Iraq, not through the thoughtless violence and actions of a larger than life superman, but with a team of comrades in which no one person is above the mission or the soldier next to him. The creators of *Black* Watch had the courage to ask soldiers why they did it, why they fight, and why they would possibly run toward gunshots when every instinct should tell them to run away. John Tiffany and Gregory Burke found out that they did not do it for freedom, or country. Rather, they did it for the fellow soldier that may need their help. Casting a group of young unknowns as the soldiers in the Black Watch Regiment accurately represented this dynamic, and solidified the theatre as an inspired medium to address the sensitive subject of war in the twenty-first century.

As an admitted novice in the appreciation of theatre, and veteran of war, I admired *Black Watch*'s depiction of each soldier's fight against boredom. Although I thought this was strictly the accurate portrayal of soldiers' accounts of what transpired in Iraq, I later learned that is was somewhat of an homage to the Irish poet and playwright Samuel Beckett. The play's creators admitted to being strongly influenced by the works of Samuel Beckett, namely *Waiting for Godot* which is famous for being a play in which nothing really happens. Mr. Tiffany stated that he wanted to depict, "the aburdisms of being so close to death, yet so bored." This dynamic is a beautiful illustration of the value theatre brings to contemporary issues, not just war. While *Black Watch* captures the wartime experiences of a one particular unit in Iraq, John was fascinated with how this dynamic could also be translated to the medical profession, firefighters, and police officers. Unfortunately, there are countless films and television dramas that fail to ask themselves, "Why is the daily life of an emergency room surgeon only exciting if she falls in love with the extremely handsome paramedic?"

By successfully portraying this "absurdism" in *Black Watch*, the stage performance illustrates its ability to address the extreme swings between intense, life or death actions and crippling boredom. As a leader in war, I was constantly struggling with the tangential effects that this boredom provokes. It is true that idle hands are the devil's playground, and idle thoughts can be even more dangerous. How do you keep someone focused when they are bored? This phenomenon was portrayed accurately in *Black Watch* during the choreographed series of fights amongst the soldiers. I can recollect countless instances of close friends coming to blows over the slightest disagreement. A physical altercation centered on a porn magazine or a "which actress is hotter" discussion may seem absurd to the viewer, but believe me, that sequence was all too familiar. This accurate depiction of the depth of human emotion inside the world's soldiers was made possible by the freedom that *Black Watch*'s creators enjoyed when developing the production.

While costly action sequences and large, epic set pieces may help visualize the events surrounding many contemporary issues, a well crafted theatre production can spotlight the issues, the human beings, and the emotions involved in these soon-to-be historic events. The economic freedom given to playwrights comes with certain undeniable constraints. While these constraints, or considerations, in theatre can dictate certain decisions in the creative process, it can also act as an inspiration. John Tiffany acknowledges the impact that the original venue had on the performance. Much of the feel of the *Black Watch* performance was influenced by the fact that it would open at the University of Edinburgh Officer Training Corps Drill Hall. This is evident in some of the vaudeville-influenced characteristics of the performance such as direct address, music and song, and why John chose to place the audience on each side of the stage. While this affects the production, it allows the realistic depiction of war to be more entertaining, rather than overtly influencing the actual content of the piece.

One of the greatest examples of a stage production diverging from the established mores of film as a direct attempt to tackle contemporary subject matter is *The Great Game*. *The Great Game* aims to address the cyclicality of international influence in Afghanistan between 1842 and 2009. It would be nearly impossible to tackle such a broad subject matter with honesty and emotion in the routine two hour time limit. Some topics are too grand for such a tidy conclusion. *The Great Game* chooses to portray this dialogue over eight hours, either shown on consecutive nights, or in one impassioned marathon. I doubt a major motion picture studio would fund an eight hour movie, and have greater doubts that a broad audience would attend such a movie.

The length of *The Great Game* itself is critical to the production, acting as a lynchpin to the central theme, holding together the separate stories that make up this courageous work of art. The story is the duration. The length is a character in the production, possibly even more so than the characters in the individual plays. Because of the sheer volume of content, there is a limit to the depth to each character, representative of all the different stakeholders and opinions of such a conflict between two warring nations.

It would be almost irresponsible to address such a vast issue as the war in Afghanistan without acknowledging all of the previous Western failures within the region throughout time. Cinema would never allow such reflection within its commonly accepted format. By extending the runtime of the play to eight hours, the theme of repetitive futility is felt throughout the play, across each story line. Rather than blatantly dragging these themes across the audience's face, the creators are given the time to let it seep into one's heart until you feel the hopelessness that such a situation truly possesses.

The Great Game, like *Black Watch,* is given certain freedoms that allow playwrights and directors to address contemporary issues with a breadth not available to cinema. These are just two examples of a play's ability to exploit the autonomy that the theatrical medium provides it to explore some of the more profound contemporary issues of our time. This is made possible by many factors, namely the freedom from economic demands, the freedom in casting, and the freedom of boredom.

Note

1   All quotations from John Tiffany are taken from a telephone interview conducted in February 2012 by the author.

7

Narrating Peace and Healing in Multinational Theatres of War: From Ancient Greece to Afghanistan to DARPA

Tyler D. Reeb

Aeschylus, the father of ancient Greek tragedy and a soldier himself, crafted narratives addressing tragedies on the battlefield and at home—about humanity lost and regained. Like his heir apparent, Sophocles, who served as a general, Aeschylus understood that war brought tragedy to soldiers on the battlefield and families at home. And, like Homer during an earlier epoch, both playwrights used the emotional landscape of the ten-year Trojan War to explore their tragic themes. Those themes, thousands of years later, are eerily similar to the realities of soldiers and families depicted in the Tricycle Theatre's production of *The Great Game: Afghanistan*. Using modern cognitive and psychological approaches, researchers are exploring ways that political theatre can provide contexts for soldiers and their families to address the tragedies of war and develop new narratives for peace and healing.

Research on the power of narrative has been conducted at the US Department of Defense (DoD)—inquiries normally reserved for panels at the Modern Language Association. Consider the opening lines of a notice from the DoD's Defense Advanced Research Projects Agency (DARPA) promoting its workshop, "Stories, Neuroscience and Experimental Technologies: Analysis and Decomposition of Narratives in Security Contexts":

> Stories exert a powerful influence on human thoughts and behavior. They consolidate memory, shape emotions, cue heuristics and biases in judgment, influence in-group/out-group distinctions, and may affect the fundamental contents of personal identity. It comes as no surprise that these influences make stories highly relevant to vexing security challenges such as radicalization, violent social mobilization, insurgency and terrorism, and conflict prevention and resolution (STORyNET).

Humans have always used stories to determine future actions and past memories. But it is only now in the twenty-first century with breakthroughs in narrative studies that researchers from across the disciplines can study what exemplary writers from every age have known intuitively.

It seems storytelling is state of the art … again.

Counterplotting the Grim Ironies of War

In his 1901 novel, *Kim,* Rudyard Kipling popularized the term "great game," which characterized how Russian and British war games in Afghanistan had turned the country into a bloody chessboard. Afghanistan, like Vietnam and so many other exploited nations, has been used as a theatre for other empires to wage their wars via proxy.

Wars are waged using the logic that violence will end violence, that young men and women should be sacrificed on the front lines to preserve peace in the future. But what if war sacrifices the very home it seeks to save? It is a theme that Aeschylus addresses throughout *Oresteia.* Perpetrators of violence view their killings as sacrifices that will ultimately bring about peace. But each act begets more violence. From a game theoretical standpoint, each agent views their narratives as one-act, zero-sum games, when the reality is that there is always another act. The same holds true with the Taliban's barbaric stonings—there seems to always be another stoning.

Early in *Oresteia,* Aeschylus establishes the heavy hand that Zeus and other Olympians play in the fates of mortals; but that reality does not absolve the characters from judgments, which are often conveyed via the choruses in the three plays. Indeed, Agamemnon, who initiates the cycles of revenge and violence by sacrificing his daughter, Iphigeneia, is not free from such judgment. An early chorus relates Agamemnon's ruminations over the damned-if-I-do-damned-if-I-don't scenario he faces:

> My fate is angry if I disobey these,
> but angry if I slaughter
> this child, the beauty of my house,
> with maiden blood shed staining
> these father's hands beside the altar.
> What of these things goes now without disaster?
> How shall I fail my ships
> and lose my faith of battle?
> For them to urge such sacrifice of innocent blood
> angrily, for their wrath is great—it is right. May all be well yet. (Lattimore 1953: 211–16)

Although Agamemnon may agonize over his decision to kill his daughter so the gods would allow his fleet of ships the winds required to sail to Troy, his above deliberations make clear he has agency, therefore making him culpable. The chorus lines that follow describe his actions as "sacrilegious [and] utterly infidel" (Lattimore 1953: 218–19). Iphigeneia's sacrifice symbolizes Agamemnon's abandonment of his daughter with lines describing her "supplications and her cries of father" amounting to "nothing" because she is effectively muzzled "prone above the altar" like a "goat for sacrifice" (Lattimore 1953: 233-4).

Agamemnon sacrifices his daughter for military reasons that result in a domestic tragedy, setting a precedent for future sacrifices in the play that also raise military, political, and domestic considerations. In each instance, the sacrifices—whether they are political, military, or domestic—rely upon destruction of human life. The same holds true in *The Great Game: Afghanistan*. In both trilogies, human lives are destroyed to bring forth new orders of control in the play.

Beyond the obvious revenge motive, Clytemnaestra's murder of Agamemnon with an ax also serves a political end, enabling her to establish a new order and rule the kingdom with Aegisthus. But the killing is also carried out on sacrificial grounds and there is textual evidence to support this. "Now hear you this," she states, "the right behind my sacrament; / By my child's Justice driven to fulfillment, by / Her Wrath and Fury, to whom I sacrificed this man" (Lattimore 1953: 1431-3).

In composing the *Oresteia* trilogy, Aeschylus gave humanity a compelling narrative for restraint and legal deliberation as an alternative to modes of violence and revenge. But no *deus ex machina* occurs in any part of *The Great Game: Afghanistan* to reconcile cycles of violence. Throughout the trilogy, playwrights and performers remind the audience that there has never been an easy solution in Afghanistan. Rather than grope for contrived solutions, *The Great Game: Afghanistan* playwrights synthesize the sources of conflict that impede solutions into their theatrical narratives. Those sources of conflict are depicted not only on the battlefields of Afghanistan but also on embattled home fronts and in embattled minds, which is in keeping with the genuine realities of soldiers from the United States, Britain, and other countries. Soldiers, who serve their tours of duty, return home physically and emotionally wounded—different men and women than their families remember. Trauma has a way of changing people. All too often the battlefield returns home with the soldier, or the soldier simply cannot return. That reality is depicted pitch perfectly in "Canopy of Stars" by Simon Stephens, one of the concluding plays in *The Great Game: Afghanistan*.

Jay, a British soldier, has just returned home from another tour of duty in Afghanistan. He sits on a couch in his South Manchester home. It is the middle of the night and he drinks a cup of tea, watching soccer on a television. His girlfriend, Cheryl, enters the room and asks why he has not come to bed with her on his first night home and why he was unable to look his young son in the eyes or even talk directly to him. "I watched you giving him a kiss," she says, "you didn't even look at him when you were doing that. I tried to give you a hug and it felt like I was hugging a bit of just wood, Jay" (Stephens 2010: 250). Cheryl's fictional account mirrors news coverage of soldiers returning home with post-traumatic stress disorders, hugging "awkwardly" at the airport and feeling estranged from what used to be home (Dao 2011). Aeschylus understood that war permeates all national and familial boundaries, a reality as true in his day as in ours. Jay and Cheryl, like Agamemnon and Clytemnaestra, represent the tensions between war and peace in domestic spheres.

In a general sense, Cheryl presents a contemporary version of Clytemnaestra. Both seek to *kill* their soldier husbands, one in the career sense, the other in the literal sense.

Both saw how war sacrificed family. In ancient times as now, it seems the warrior's return is not always peaceful. That Jay and Cheryl debate in a theatre of war is clear. What is also clear is that soldiers are often more at home on the battlefield:

> CHERYL. I had this idea. You could not go back. You could stay here. You could hand in your notice. You could come back home and you could live with me and with Billy and it could just be normal again.
> JAY. Are you being serious?
> CHERYL. Doesn't it look like I'm being serious? (Stephens 2010: 250)

In stating "normal again," Cheryl raises the reality of the *new normal*, which means different things to her and to Jay. Each has been psychologically conditioned by their experiences on the home front and the battlefield. Jay returns home only to feel like a stranger to his own family. The battlefield has become Jay's *new normal* and he cannot imagine not going back to Afghanistan.

Like so many military couples, Cheryl and Jay embrace different narratives about Afghanistan. Cheryl tells Jay that Afghanistan will always "be a mess," that he is "making it a thousand times worse" being there, that "Billy wants his dad back." She follows her plea with a recurring question:

> CHERYL. Can we have him back now please?
> JAY. There's a school in the village, which in itself is frankly amazing. I spent a few days on patrol there. You take your helmet off. You wander round a bit. Take the shades off. Hand out a few sweets. Got to know, actually, we got to know some of the kids.
> CHERYL. Can we have him back now please?
> JAY. One of the kids that I met there was a girl called Delaram. She was ten.
> CHERYL. Don't. (Stephens 2010: 251)

With one word, Cheryl breaks her questioning, signaling the poignancy in Jay's forthcoming narrative. In ceasing her questioning, Cheryl abandons her attempt to stall Jay's narrative and instead engages him.

> JAY. On our last afternoon there she was coming home from school when a forty-year-old man stepped from out of one of the houses in the west of the town near where the school was with a water pistol in his hand and he sprayed it at Delaram. Laughed a bit. Giggled a bit. Sprayed the water pistol in her face. And it might have looked a bit strange because here was this forty-year-old giggling and spraying a water pistol at a ten year-old kid. Only what was in his water pistol, of course, wasn't water, was it Chez, it was acid. He burnt her eyes out because she was ten and she was going to school. Don't you dare tell me that I'm making that a thousand times worse.
> *Beat.*
> CHERYL. Do you think that doesn't happen here? Seriously Jay, do you mate? You want to go up Moss Side Jay it's an initiation rite for thirteen year-old girls that up there.

> JAY. If we leave now then that'll be everything fucked.
> CHERYL. Everything's already fucked. There's nothing you can do about that.
> JAY. There are people in that country who are vicious bastard monsters and they're full of just hate and they need to be stopped.
> CHERYL. There are people on our street like that.
> JAY. And the ones over here are creaming a fortune selling smack from a Helmand Poppy farm that we can burn down.
> CHERYL. It won't change anything. (Stephens 2010: 252)

Jay and Cheryl's exchange demonstrates how theatre can synthesize competing narratives into stories that represent the nature of a conflict. Aeschylus made such synthesized narratives possible with one of his greatest theatrical innovations: bringing a second actor onstage, which made dialogue and debate possible. With two actors onstage, Aeschylus could present scenes of conflict as never before. Instead of rendering the nature of conflict with single actors *telling* choruses and audiences about their conflicts, Aeschylus could *show* the conflict. Aeschylus's innovation made it possible to depict the tensions between Agamemnon's battlefield and Clytemnaestra's embattled home front. Rather than present separate monologues, Aeschylus created debate between two actors, resulting in a synthesis of two competing narratives into one charged depiction of conflict.

Aeschylus's innovation is equally effective in presenting the conflict between Jay and Cheryl. Jay sees hope in the war in Afghanistan; he envisions narratives of nation building—opening "up the power supply," protecting "the water supply," and overseeing the nation's infrastructure. But where Jay sees hope in his efforts in Afghanistan, Cheryl sees futility. She chides him for wandering off thousands of miles away to play "action hero," when he can't look his own son in the eyes.

> CHERYL. You're a coward Jay. You think you're being a hero. You're not. We're so way beyond that now. It's gone on for too long. We're not helping. We're just smashing it all up. And every time you try to make it better you do the absolute opposite. (Stephens 2010: 253)

Whether it's killing off hateful Islamic radicals, rebuilding infrastructure, or burning poppy fields in Afghanistan, Jay sees such efforts as hopeful. But, however noble the intent, Cheryl views any future efforts in Afghanistan as sinking deeper into a bottomless quagmire. What sets the Tricycle Theatre's politically charged productions apart from agitprop (and what likely explains the Pentagon's embrace of *The Great Game: Afghanistan*) is its ability to present both sides of heated political issues without contrived moralizing or offering oversimplified solutions.

Heated arguments like Jay and Cheryl's are taking place in living rooms throughout the United States, Britain, and other countries. Soldiers around the world, dealing with post-traumatic stress disorders, are struggling to reenter society and reconnect with family. In this way, as in Aeschylus's time, the familial hearth is a transnational theatre of war. War and peace are not tidy binaries, but rather part of a yin-yang continuum. Each bleeds into the other.

Claiming Narratives of Peace and Healing

The sacred role of theatre during the annual Dionysian festivals in Athens was to explore the phenomenology of tragedy and joy, which explains the clear distinctions the ancient Greeks made between tragic and comic theatrical forms. Comedies rendered experiences of laughter and joy, whereas tragedies enabled ancient Greeks to delve into the phenomenology of suffering in a communal setting.

This is the rationale for the DoD's support of Theatre of War, a production company that has presented readings of ancient Greek plays at US military bases around the world. The readings are intended to serve "as a catalyst for town hall discussions with service members, veterans and their caregivers and families about the invisible wounds of war," wrote Theatre of War Founder Bryan Doerries in a *Washington Post* editorial (Doerries 2010). The production company, which is funded by the federal Defense Centers of Excellence for Psychological Health and Traumatic Brain Injury, "aims to destigmatize psychological injury by placing it in an ancient warrior context" (Doerries 2010).

Theatre is particularly useful in giving attendees a safe haven that promotes the trust and empathy necessary for them to engage their trauma—to decode destructive aspects of their personal narratives so that they can counterplot with new stories of healing. Such thinking is informed by Dan P. McAdams's Narrative Psychological notion that humans live and embody their life stories. In his *The Redemptive Self: Stories Americans Live By*, McAdams (2005: 222) credits Silvan Tomkins for developing "script theory," a personality theory that interprets humans as "playwrights who create scripts in which they play the leading role." If a person is plagued by a victim narrative, McAdams and Tomkins both contend, it is possible for that person to restructure a life narrative into one that is redemptive.

After a production of *The Great Game: Afghanistan* in Berkeley, California, Tricycle Theatre Creative Director Nicolas Kent granted an interview to discuss how modern political theatre creates a "sacred quality" of contemplation akin to what ancient Greeks sought in their plays. Kent stressed the importance of theatre in creating a context where people can immerse themselves in narratives they experience in communal settings. "I think the great quality that theatre [offers] more than anything else is empathy," Kent said, adding that theatre teaches "emotional lessons" and compels audiences to question the ostensible "certainties of things" (Kent 2010).

When asked how he ensures that Tricycle Theatre productions never become agitprop, Kent (2010) explained that his team of writers and actors seek "to give a balanced, objective, report within the work we do." Guided by that ethos, Kent and his team use journalistic fundamentals to research their plays. For *The Great Game: Afghanistan*, playwrights interviewed leading scholars, journalists, and military and political figures, including US General David H. Petraeus, the former director of the CIA, and General Sir David Richards, then Chief of Staff for the British Ministry of Defence. But while the Tricycle Theatre playwrights use their methods to research and write their plays, Kent noted that the final theatrical production accesses aspects of human consciousness that journalism cannot. Theatre gives audiences access to the emotional contexts, and multiple perspectives that are so often missing from contemporary media coverage. "I think the theatre has a great advantage over the news media today," Kent said (2010). Beyond fact-based inquiries asking *who?, what?, where?,* and *when?, The Great Game: Afghanistan* playwrights use theatrical narratives to ask *why?* Asking why means delving into the heart of conflict.

"The problem with theatre is that it thrives on conflict. That's when theatre works best," Kent said. "So, inevitably, when we're doing public inquiry we do take the scenes that have the most conflict in them to a build a picture." Focusing on conflict in this manner creates "a distortion," Kent (2010) acknowledged, noting that an abiding goal in all productions is to "try to stay as unbiased as possible."

Kent's insights on the role of conflict in storytelling call to mind Kate McLoughlin's insights in *Authoring War* regarding how "impossible or very difficult" a subject war is to depict. She notes that "even as [war] resists representation, conflict demands it" (2011: 7). *The Great Game: Afghanistan* succeeds in narrating war because its modern chorus of twelve playwrights each built their thirty-minute plays around a central conflict. Rather than solely depicting soldiers on the battlefield, the playwrights explore sources of conflict in a transnational sense—expanding theatres of war to include familial, communal, and political spheres. Kent is correct that focusing on conflict creates a distortion, whereby playwrights increase agonistic drama to give their scripts pathos and suspense. But such distortions are necessary, just as they were in Aeschylus's time. In this regard, McLoughlin's appraisal of Tim O'Brien's story "How to Tell a True War Story" is appropriate. She notes that O'Brien "suggests that the truest account of war may actually be fictional: 'a thing may happen and be a total lie; another thing may not happen and be truer than the truth'" (McLoughlin 2011: 4).

In a time when cultural, religious, commercial, military, political, and other narratives are more seductive and confusing than ever in history, theatre offers a refuge for attendees to question their realities, to claim agency, to confront trauma, and to embrace personal narratives of healing and humanity. In ancient Greece and today, theatres of war offer places for attendees to claim personal truths, to access the phenomenology of psychological wounds, and to better understand the transnational nature of war—that deployed soldiers and families at home are all linked to the same struggle.

Theatre offers a haven for attendees to recalibrate their moral compasses. This is the timeless and sacred role of political theatre. In the future, attendees may grow to trust theatrical narratives produced by actors and playwrights more than the politicians and speechwriters. Without the empathy and sacred communalism that political theatre like *The Great Game: Afghanistan* and *Oresteia* promotes, politics would be reduced to the brutal ethos of real politick.

Works Cited

Dao, James (2011), "After Combat, the Unexpected Perils of Coming Home," *The New York Times*, May 28. Available online: https://www.nytimes.com/2011/05/29/us/29soldiers.html. Last accessed July 17.

DARPA (Defense Advanced Research Projects Agency) (2010), "Stories, Neuroscience and Experimental Technologies(STORyNET): Analysis and Decomposition of Narratives in Security Contexts," Solicitation Number: DARPA-SN-11-20, February 28, U.S. Department of Defense Agencies. Location: Contracts Management Office.

Doerries, Bryan (2010), "Answering the Call to Help Our Soldiers Heal," *Washington Post*, May 30. Available online: http://www.washingtonpost.com/wpdyn/content/article/2010/5/30/AR2010053003297.html. Last accessed November 8, 2011.

Kent, Nicolas (2010), Personal interview at the Berkeley Repertory Theatre, November 7.

Lattimore, Richard (1953), *Aeschylus 1: Oresteia*, Chicago: University of Chicago Press.

McAdams, Dan P. (2005), *The Redemptive Self: Stories Americans Live By*, New York: Oxford University Press.

McLoughlin, Kate (2011), *Authoring War: The Literary Representation of War from the Iliad to Iraq*, New York: Cambridge University Press.

Moyers, Bill (1995), *Healing and the Mind*, New York: Broadway Books.

Stephens, Simon (2010), "Canopy of Stars," in *The Great Game: Afghanistan*, London: Oberon Books, pp. 250–3.

Contributor Biographies

Eva Aldea is a writer and lecturer based in London, exploring migration in her creative and academic work. She published her essay "The Lost European Nomad" in *Brexit and Literature: Critical and Cultural Responses* (2018) and is writing a novel based on her own family's tales of migration. She works at the University of London, teaching contemporary literature online to students across the globe. She is the author of *Magical Realism and Deleuze: The Indiscernibility of Difference in Postcolonial Literature* (2010).

Reza Aslan is a renowned writer, commentator, professor, Emmy-nominated producer, and scholar of religions. A recipient of the prestigious James Joyce Award, Aslan is the author of three internationally best-selling books, including the number 1 *New York Times* bestseller *Zealot: The Life and Times of Jesus of Nazareth*.

Alessandra Bassey is a researcher whose interests sit at the intersection of Shakespeare, Race, and African Studies. She has a Ph.D. from King's College London, which focuses on the representation of Shakespeare's characters on the Nazi stage, with a special focus on racialized "Others" such as Othello and Shylock. She has presented her work in multiple conferences worldwide, and has been published in journals like *European Judaism* and *Modern Language Review*. She is part of projects that examine state-sanctioned violence in Nigeria and its effects on people. She is the founding editor of the literary platform and non-profit organization Literandra, which promotes literary traditions and other art forms that emanate from the African continent and its diaspora.

Shane Belvin was born and raised in the United States and received a B.S. from the United States Military Academy at West Point and an M.B.A. from Northwestern University's Kellogg School of Management. While serving as a Captain in the Army, he was awarded the Bronze Star for direct fire engagements during Operation Iraqi Freedom and took part in the capture of Saddam Hussein in December 2003. Upon leaving the Army, he served as an engineer in the aerospace industry, focusing primarily on human space exploration. More recently, he worked as an investment banker, corporate strategy manager, and an entrepreneur developing a platform to trade weather derivatives.

Robert Brazeau, Ph.D., is Associate Professor of Irish Studies at the University of Alberta in Edmonton, Alberta, Canada. He is the co-editor, with Derek Gladwin, of the volume *Eco-Joyce: The Environmental Imagination of James Joyce* and has guest edited special issues of the *Journal of Urban History* and *Studies in the Literary Imagination*.

He has published a number of articles on figures in contemporary and modernist Irish literature, including Medbh McGuckian, James Joyce, J.M. Synge, and Sean O'Casey. His current project is a book-length study of J.M. Synge, the Abbey Theatre, and Irish Modernism.

Nicholas J. Cull is Professor of Public Diplomacy at the Annenberg School for Communication and Journalism at the University of Southern California in Los Angeles. He has written widely on the subject of public and cultural diplomacy, and the political side of media history. His works include *The Cold War and the United States Information Agency: American Propaganda and Public Diplomacy, 1945–1989* (2008), and *Selling War: The British Propaganda Campaign against American "Neutrality" in World War II* (1994). He was president of the International Association for Media History (IAMHIST) and is a fellow of the Royal Historical Society. He is originally from the United Kingdom.

Begoña Echeverria is the daughter of Basque immigrants to southern California. A native Basque speaker with a Ph.D. in sociology, she is a Professor at University of California-Riverside's Graduate School of Education. Her ethnographic work on Basque language schooling has appeared in academic journals in education, sociolinguistics, and anthropology. She has published work examining gender, identity, and language use in Basque songs, biblical texts, and folk tales. Her creative works include the historical novel *The Hammer of Witches*, loosely based on the 1610 burnings of Basque "witches" from the Baztan Valley from which her family hails. Published by the University of Nevada's Center for Basque Studies, the novel was the Historical Novel Society's Editor's Choice for May 2015. Her play, *Picasso Presents Gernika*, won third prize in the 2015 Basque Literary Writing Contest. She is a singer-songwriter with the Basque-American trio, NOKA (www.ilovenoka.com).

Alani Hicks-Bartlett is an Assistant Professor in Comparative Literature and French Studies at Brown University, to affiliations with the Department of Hispanic Studies, the Program in Medieval Studies, and the Center for the Early Modern World. Her research interests include gender and violence in Medieval and Early Modern texts, notions of power and empire in *chansons de geste* and Early Modern epic poetry, Petrarchism and the development of the love lyric, classical exemplarity, and Digital Humanities. Her current projects focus on gender and race in Medieval French literature, representations of disability in Medieval and Early Modern prose compositions, and Medieval and Early Modern women's writing and the (proto)feminist complaint tradition. Her research has recently been supported by the Mellon Foundation, New York University's Center for the Humanities, the Consortium for History of Science, Technology and Medicine, the Ford Foundation, the American Association of University Women, and the Electronic Cultures Lab and Digital Humanities Institute at the University of Victoria.

Bahar Jalali is an Afghan-American scholar who holds a Ph.D. from the University of California, Berkeley. From 2009 to 2017, she served on the faculty of the American

University of Afghanistan where she taught the History of Afghanistan, Gender, and World History. She is also the founder of the first Gender Studies program in Afghanistan. She has served as a consultant for a number of organizations in the United States, Afghanistan, and Germany in the field of higher education, cultural exchange, and international development. She is currently an Adjunct Professor of History at Wagner College. She is also affiliated with the University of Texas, Austin.

Shawn Renee Lent is Arts Integration Program Specialist at Columbia College Chicago, a dance teacher for Performing Arts Limited, and has been selected as a member of the British Council's Transatlantic Network 2020, the United Nations Alliance of Civilizations International Fellowship Program, the American Express Nonprofit Leadership Academy, and the YNPN Chicago Leadership Institute. Presently a member of the Open House Dance Collective, she serves on the Young Associates Board of Children's Memorial Hospital, the Founding Board for Donna's Good Things, the Advisory Board for the Chicago Arts Educator Forum, and is Founding Chair of the Associates Board for Links Hall. She holds an M.A. degree in Arts Management with a focus in Arts in Youth and Community Development from Columbia College Chicago, a B.F.A. in theatre and dance from Millikin University, and Post-Graduate Certificate in Youth Arts Development from Goldsmiths College—University of London.

Lindsey Mantoan is an Assistant Professor of Theatre at Linfield College. Her primary research addresses the intersections among war, militarization, and performance, and she is the author of *War as Performance: Conflict in Iraq and Political Theatricality* (2018) and co-editor with Sara Brady of *Vying for the Iron Throne: Essays on Power, Gender, Death, and Performance in HBO's Game of Thrones* (2018) and *Performance in a Militarized Culture* (2017).

Nancy Martin is a Teaching Instructor in Writing in the Department of English at Rutgers University. Her research interests focus on First World War British literature and life-writing, the languages of trauma and testimony, and theories of gender, sexuality, and identity. Her work has been published in several edited collections and journals, including *Textual Practice* and the *Journal of International Women's Studies*.

Kate McLoughlin is a Professor of English Literature at the University of Oxford, and a Fellow of Harris Manchester College. She is the author of *Martha Gellhorn: The War Writer in the Field and in the Text* (2007), *Authoring War: The Literary Representation of War from the Iliad to Iraq* (2011), and *Veteran Poetics: British Literature in the Age of Mass Warfare, 1790–2015* (2018), and editor of *The Cambridge Companion to War Writing* (2009). She is currently writing a literary history of silence, funded by the Leverhulme Trust.

Christopher Merrill has published seven collections of poetry, including *Watch Fire*, for which he received the Lavan Younger Poets Award from the Academy of American Poets; many edited volumes and translations; and six books of nonfiction, among them, *Only the Nails Remain: Scenes from the Balkan Wars, Things of the Hidden God: Journey to the Holy Mountain,* and *Self-Portrait with Dogwood.* His writings have been translated into nearly forty languages; his journalism appears widely; his honors include a Chevalier des Arts et des Lettres from the French government, numerous translation awards, and fellowships from the John Simon Guggenheim Memorial and Ingram Merrill Foundations. As director of the University of Iowa's International Writing Program since 2000, Merrill has conducted cultural diplomacy missions to more than fifty countries. He served on the US National Commission for UNESCO from 2011 to 2018; in April 2012 President Barack Obama appointed him to the National Council on the Humanities.

Daniel O'Gorman is Vice Chancellor Research Fellow in English Literature at Oxford Brookes University, specializing in contemporary literature, with a particular focus on transnational literary responses to the war on terror and its aftermaths. He is the author of *Fictions of the War on Terror: Difference and the Transnational 9/11 Novel* (2015), and co-editor of *The Routledge Companion to Twenty-First Century Literary Fiction* (2019). He has published articles on literature and the war on terror in journals such as *Textual Practice, Critique: Studies in Contemporary Fiction, The Journal of Commonwealth Literature,* and *The European Journal of English Studies.* He is also an Associate Editor at *The Journal of Postcolonial Writing.*

Emer O'Toole is Associate Professor of Irish Performance Studies at the School of Irish Studies, Concordia University. She is also a fellow of Concordia's Simone de Beauvoir Institute, and an Affiliate Associate Professor of the Mel Hoppenheim School of Film. Her current research, funded by the Fonds de Recherche de Quebec, examines the relationship between aesthetics and activism in contemporary Irish theatre. She is the author of the book *Girls Will Be Girls* (2015) and co-editor of the collection *Ethical Exchanges in Translation, Adaptation and Dramaturgy* (2017). Her academic work has appeared in international journals including *LIT: Literature, Interpretation, Theory, Sexualities, Éire-Ireland, Contemporary Theatre Review,* and *Target.* She is also a contributor to publications including *The Guardian, The Irish Times,* and *The Independent.*

Márta Pellérdi is Associate Professor at the Institute of English and American Studies, Pázmány Péter Catholic University, Budapest. She holds a Ph.D. in American Literature from Eötvös Loránd University, Budapest, and teaches courses in nineteenth-century and twentieth-century British and American fiction. She is the author of a study on Vladimir Nabokov's work published in English, *Nabokov's Palace: The American Novels* (2010). She has also published on Austen, Washington Irving, George Moore, and Robert Louis Stevenson in various journals and edited volumes.

Oana Popescu-Sandu holds a Ph.D. in Comparative Literature from the University of Illinois, Urbana. She is Associate Professor of World Literature at the University of Southern Indiana where she teaches classes in world literature, women's literature, literary theory, and international studies. Her recent publications include

"Translingualism as Dialogism in American–Romanian Poetry" in *Journal of World Literature*, Vol. 3, No. 1 (2018); "From Minimalist Representation to Excessive Interpretation: Contextualizing 4 Months, 3 Weeks and 2 Days," in *Journal of European Studies*, Vol. 44, No. 3 (2014), pp. 225–48 (co-authored with Oana Godeanu-Kenworthy); and "Haunted Transitions: Memory, Theatre, and Gender Discourse" in Florentina C. Andreescu and Michael J. Shapiro, eds., *Genre and the (Post) Communist Woman: Analyzing Transformations of the Central and Eastern European Female Ideal* (2015). Her research has focused recently on translingual authors from Eastern Europe and on issues of cultural translation.

Lynn Ramert earned her Ph.D. in English from Indiana University with a dissertation titled *Performing Scottish Identity: From the Rise of the Stage Scot to the National Theatre of Scotland*. She has also published work on Irish drama. Her areas of research include postcolonial literature and drama, and modern and contemporary British literature, with additional teaching interests in composition, professional writing, and second language learners. She currently teaches at the University of Nebraska and Metropolitan Community College in Omaha, Nebraska.

Tyler D. Reeb is a Canadian-born writer, researcher, and educator based in Los Angeles. He writes about international business, politics, technology, and culture with a focus on transnationalism and transdisciplinary studies. He serves as the Director of Research and Workforce Development at the Center for International Trade & Transportation. He is a member of two National Academies of Sciences, Engineering, and Medicine standing committees and is the editor and principal author of the forthcoming book, *Empowering the New Mobility Workforce* (2019).

Anna Rindfleisch is a Ph.D. candidate in English Research at King's College London, UK. Her research interests focus on interwar period mourning literature, gender studies, and the transmission of war trauma into the performing arts. She has published on interwar period bereavement and gendered mourning rites.

Kevin Riordan is Assistant Professor in the School of Humanities at Nanyang Technological University in Singapore. His research interests include modernism, theatre, and world literature, and his recent articles have appeared in *Modern Drama*, *Performance Research*, and *American Studies*. He is currently at work on his first book, a performance history of the around-the-world tour. Riordan is also a 2018 Writing Fellow at the Johannesburg Institute of Advanced Study, a co-founder of the Modernist Studies in Asia Network, and a Resident Artist in the New York–based company Theater Mitu.

Lauri Scheyer holds a Ph.D. in English from the University of Chicago. She is Xiaoxiang Distinguished Professor, British and American Poetry Research Center Director, and co-editor of *Journal of Foreign Languages and Cultures* at Hunan Normal University, China. She directed the British Council International Videoconference on *The Great Game: Afghanistan*, and co-directed (with Robert

Eaglestone, Royal Holloway, and Kate McLoughlin, Oxford) the British Council International Videoconferences on *Black Watch* and the 200th Anniversary of the Abolition of the British Slave Trade. Her books include *Slave Songs and the Birth of African American Poetry* (2008), *The Heritage Series of Black Poetry* (2008), and *A History of African American Poetry* (2019). Her next book is *The Selected Poetry of Calvin C. Hernton* (co-edited with David Grundy, forthcoming).

Mamata Sengupta teaches English at Islampur College, West Bengal, India. She worked on the plays of Arnold Wesker during her M.Phil. and did her doctoral research on the plays of Caryl Churchill. Sengupta has completed a national level research project on the works of Sarah Daniels and is presently working on the intersectionality between religion and performance. Her articles have appeared in different national and international journals and anthologies of critical essays. Sengupta's research interests include postwar British drama, performance studies, orality and audience reception studies, folkloristics, and gender studies.

Annika C. Speer is a Professor of Teaching at University of California-Riverside. She completed her Ph.D. in Theater Studies at University of California-Santa Barbara and Postdoctoral Research Fellowship in Communication at University of Connecticut. Her research interests include gender and communication, and documentary/interview-based activist theatre. She has publications in *Frontiers: A Journal of Women Studies, Stanislavski Studies, Communication Quarterly*, and *Contemporary Studies of Sexuality & Communication: Theoretical and Applied Approaches*. She also works as a dramaturgical researcher for films, including *The Girl on the Train* (produced by DreamWorks Studios and Marc Platt Productions, 2016), *Men, Women & Children* (produced by Right of Way Films, 2014), *Walking Stories* (produced by Out There/Frenesy Film, 2013), and *Call Me Crazy: A Five Film* (produced by Sony Pictures Television, 2013).

Jon Woodson is a creative writer and Howard University Emeritus Professor of English. He recently published essays in *Where Is All My Relation? The Poetics of Dave the Potter* (2018) and *Esotericism in African American Religious Experience: "There is a Mystery"* (2014). He published *Notes on Ralph Ellison's Three Days Before the Shooting* (2017) and *Summer Games: A Novel* and *The Esoteric Mission of Zora Neale Hurston* (2016). He is the author of *Endowed*, a comic novel (2012), and *Oragean Modernism: A Lost Literary Movement, 1924–1953* (2013); *Anthems, Sonnets, and Chants: Recovering the African American Poetry of the 1930s* (2011); *A Study of Catch-22: Going Around Twice* (2001); and *To Make a New Race: Gurdjieff, Toomer, and the Harlem Renaissance* (1999). As a Fulbright lecturer in American Studies he taught at two Hungarian universities, ELTE and the University of Pecs.

Farid Younos, Ed.D., is a professor of Middle East cultural anthropology and well-known women's rights and television activist in the Afghan-American community. He has been interviewed by such media outlets as the *New York Times*, *Los Angeles Times*,

Washington Post, San Francisco Chronicle, Associated Press, Voice of America, CNN, and NPR concerning Afghanistan and the politics of the region. Some of his previous publications are *Gender Equality in Islam, Democratic Imperialism: Democratization vs. Islamization, Principles of Islamic Sociology, Islamic Culture: A Study of Cultural Anthropology,* and most recently, *Principles of Islamic Psychology*. In 2010, he submitted his peace plan for Afghanistan to the US Congress, and was called for a Congressional briefing to propose, for the first time in that institution, an Islamic democratic political system for Afghanistan.

www.ingramcontent.com/pod-product-compliance
Lightning Source LLC
Chambersburg PA
CBHW061827300426
44115CB00013B/2279